Studies in Economics and Policy Making:
Central and Eastern European Perspectives

William T. Bagatelas
Getnet Tamene
David Reichardt
Bruno S. Sergi (eds.)

Studies in Economics and Policy Making:
Central and Eastern European Perspectives

Budrich UniPress Ltd.
Opladen & Farmington Hills, MI 2010

Reviewed by:
Doc. Ing. Juraj Šipko, M.B.A., Ph.D.
Professor Silvia Mihalikova, PhD

All rights reserved. No part of this publication may be reproduced, stored in or introduced into a retrieval system, or transmitted, in any form, or by any means (electronic, mechanical, photocopying, recording or otherwise) without the prior written permission of Barbara Budrich Publishers. Any person who does any unauthorized act in relation to this publication may be liable to criminal prosecution and civil claims for damages.

You must not circulate this book in any other binding or cover and you must impose this same condition on any acquirer.

A CIP catalogue record for this book is available from
Die Deutsche Bibliothek (The German Library)

© William T. Bagatelas, Getnet Tamene, David Reichardt
and Bruno S. Sergi, 2010
© 2010 for this edition by
Budrich UniPress Ltd. Opladen & Farmington Hills
www.budrich-unipress.eu

ISBN   978-3-940755-66-7

Budrich UniPress Ltd.
Stauffenbergstr. 7. D-51379 Leverkusen Opladen, Germany

28347 Ridgebrook. Farmington Hills, MI 48334. USA
www.budrich-unipress.eu

Jacket illustration by disegno, Wuppertal, Germany – www.disenjo.de
Editor: Máiréad Collins
Printed in Europe on acid-free paper by paper & tinta, Warszaw, Poland.

To those concerned with promoting economic justice.

Editors:

William T. Bagatelas City University of Seattle/Vysoká škola manažmentu Bratislava
Getnet Tamene City University of Seattle/Vysoká škola manažmentu Bratislava
David Reichardt Comenius University Bratislava
Bruno S. Sergi University of Messina

Table of contents

Foreword..12
Introduction..13

1. Supply-side Economics: Primary Cause of the Global
   Economic Downturn **(Bill Bagatelas)**. 17
2. Knowledge Management in the Context of Contemporary
   International Relations, Global Politics and Economics
   (Getnet Tamene)...39
3. Ethics and Experimental Economics
   (Paweł Kuśmierczyk)..77
4. Is New Research More Qualitative? (Treatment on
   Forecasting Methods) **(Jana Gašparíková)**...............................91
5. Trying Something New: the Role of Civil Society in the US
   Millennium Challenge Corporation's development
   assistance to Ukraine **(Juhani Grossmann)**............................102
6. A Values-Based Approach to Development: Principles of
   Content of Development, the Right to Development, and
   Sustainable (Human) Development **(Qerim Qerimi)**...............117
7. The Introduction to the Public Company Accounting
   Reform and Investor Protection Act of 2002
   (Branislav Bernadic)...145
8. Free Trade but not yet a Two-Way Street
   (Zoltan Boka)...156
9. How People Break the Law and Get Rich
   (Jana Straňáková)..164
10. Increasing democratization in local governance to improve
    regional competitiveness using the constructed regional a
    dvantage (CRA) concept **(Danes Brzica)** 177
11. Supply-Side Economics: Why Keynes and Batra Criticism
    Appear Stronger With Time **(Bill Bagatelas)** 196

Conclusion...215
Index...217

CONTRIBUTORS' AFFILIATIONS

William T. Bagatelas is a senior researcher with City University of Seattle/Vysoká škola manažmentu in Bratislava. He is an Adjunct Professor with Comenius University Bratislava, The Bratislava School of Law, The University of New York in Prague, and Tiffin College, Prague. He has coedited six previous books on economics and politics. His lecturing specialties in economics include International Economic Relationships and Great Economic Depressions.

Getnet Tamene is senior lecturer in international relations/political science at City University of Seattle/Vysoká škola manažmentu in Bratislava. He lectured with Slovak/Czech/US universities including Comenius University, University of Matej Bel, University of Trnava, University of Alexander Dubcek, University of Sts. Cyril and Metodus /Anglo-American College, Prague /Webster University, Vienna. Lecturing focus: International Relations, International Public Law, Political Science, African Studies and Development.

Paweł Kuśmierczyk is a senior lecturer and researcher with the Center for Innovation, Technology Transfer, and University Development with Rozwoju University in Poland, and the Polytechnic Institute in Krakow, Poland. He has done extensive research and publishing.

Jana Gašparíková is a senior researcher with the Institute for Forecasting at the Slovak Academy of Science, Bratislava. She has an extensive research and publishing background.

Juhani Grossmann is the Deputy Chief of Party for IFES in the Philippines, where he oversees the program directions focused on campaign finance monitoring and assistance to vulnerable population sectors, as well as the office's administration and finance operations. IFES Philippines assists electoral modernization and reform programs in light of the upcoming 2010 nationwide election automation.

Qerim Qerimi is Assoc. Professor at the University of Prishtina Faculty of Law and Co-Professor of Prishtina International Summer University; and Chief Political Adviser to the Foreign Minister of Kosovo.

Branislav Bernadic is a lecturer at City University of Seattle/Vysoká škola manažmentu in Bratislava. He has published on the Sarbanes/Oxley Act.

Zoltan Boka is a Ph.D candidate in Anthropology with NYU in New York City. He was a lecturer with City University of Seattle and Vysoká škola manažmentu in Trencin.

Jana Straňáková is a researcher with the Economics University in Bratislava, and is an analyst in the office of the Prime Minister of the Slovak Republic.

Daneš Brzica is a senior researcher at the Institute of Economic Research, Slovak Academy of Sciences in Bratislava, Slovakia. His research concentrates on urban and corporate competitiveness, networks, regional, and institutional and technological development.

David Reichardt is a senior lecturer in international relations at the Institute of International Relations, Comenius University in Bratislava, Slovakia. He also lectures at the Institute of European Studies and international Relations at Comenius, and Webster University, Vienna. His research interests include democracy promotion, international organizations, and Vatican foreign policy.

Bruno S. Sergi teaches International Economics at the University of Messina. He has authored, co-authored and co-edited several books on transition economics and global business, including Economic Dynamics in Transitional Economies (Routledge 2003) and Global Business Management (Ashgate 2007); The Political Economy of Southeast Europe from the 1990 to the Present (Continuum 2008); and Misinterpreting Modern Russia: Western Views of Putin and His Presidency (Continuum 2009).

Foreword

This new book concerning global economics and economic policy making represents an excellent examination of growing transformations taking place world-wide. At European and global levels, current economic transformation in the context of the greatest economic downturn since The Great Depression, requires greater scientific understanding and support. The chapters throughout this book address a variety of issues: economic policy, economics, new factors impacting economics, corruption: realities and solutions, all of which weigh heavily throughout these pages.

The timing of this book is not accidental. It is intended to illustrate the importance of intensive discussion, analysis, and solutions, regarding current regional and global economic transformation. Clearly, the book's timing is intended to offer all levels of society, many areas for greater interpretation and understanding. This kind of new thinking will effectively alter current living standards and expectations. Whether or not we consciously know of change that will follow, change is in fact what must happen following greater public awareness of new economic paradigms and increased public knowledge. That is already occurring. This book however, moves that process forward much faster.

Being aware of such a transformation allows us to make better choices individually about our future. Families, individuals, businesses, institutions, organizations, etc. need better, more timely, and accurate information regarding society's ability to achieve healthier priorities. This book, extensively researched and prepared, should be used as a major source by students, journalists, government, businesses, corporations, NGOs, and all private sector interests.

Understanding the current global transformations in economic related matters means being fully aware at all times of all issues which concern us in the long-term in all areas of life. This means living standards locally, regionally, and globally. It means understanding the larger and more powerful forces that truly affect all of us, not just war and peace. It means full realization of larger and more powerful forces that can impact locally, regionally, or globally. Not realizing this potential will weaken us at these same levels. The book will help each and every human being understand the forces that are truly impacting us now.

Ján Čarnogursky
Slovak Freedom Fighter and Former Prime Minister
Bratislava, Slovakia
20/05/10

Introduction

Our book on economic policy making represents three years of consistent labor. Our goal is to achieve the following: To create an objective, comprehensive, and analytical framework regarding economic policymaking as a user friendly source of information. Our goal here has been nothing less then to allow the public, media, governments, corporations large and small, NGOs and other institutions/organizations, immediate access to objective and broader economic interpretation.

Each chapter in our book offers the reader unique, specialized, and, above all, timely information regarding global economics. The methodologies used here concern a variety of "user friendly" forms of research taking economic interpretation into broader areas of analysis. In the context of the on-going economic crisis globally, we sincerely hope the reader will take extreme advantage of the opportunity offered by our book to see economics in different ways. We strongly believe the current crisis is greatly the result of policymakers at all levels not having adequate and in-depth interpretive skills to assess long-term thinking.

In this context, we have no doubt the following chapters all serve a crucial purpose. They inform, enlighten, prepare, and strengthen the reader's ability to see who, how, and why poor economic policies are pursued and their consequences. Today, people realize the economic downturn globally is the worst downturn since the Great Depression eight decades ago. The media have given us countless hours of coverage and so-called "expert" analysis. In these chapters we carefully and precisely challenge the narrow coverage offered thus far. We allow the reader to see how economic forces actually operate and use their influence. In other words, we help show readers why poor economic choices are so-often made and repeated by government. In short, we offer a comprehensive approach to understanding why the field of economics must change or die.

In chapter one, William T. Bagatelas, analyzes how and why the global crisis came to be. Very specifically, he analyzes economic policy commonly known today as supply-side theory and practice. He carefully shows how today's downturn is very similar to the downturn beginning in the US in 1929, leading to The Great Depression. Lasting ten years, Bagatelas analyzes how only a few economists were able to predict the economic crisis of the 1930's and currently. Specifically, he states two economists overall deserve a strong place in history for their ability to forecast the depression then and today's downturn.

In chapter two, Getnet Tamene, offers new interpretations regarding the relationship between knowledge management, international relations, and economics. Few people have questioned the impact of knowledge management overall on every aspect of our lives. Tamene however, goes one large step forward beyond traditional boundaries, asserting how effective knowledge mobilization could bring achievements to companies, organizations or institutions in the 21st century. He assesses a co-relationship having differing but equal impact on each. He assesses mutually reinforcing characteristics of both knowledge management and international relations as imposing on each other variables requiring mutual understanding. Such an assessment necessarily forces an objective observer to reexamine their so-called independence in their current world. Knowledge management and international relations, as simultaneously reinforcing variables, force us to ask whether co-dependence in every strata of society is a greater ethical good than traditional independence models.

In chapter three, Paweł Kuśmierczyk, assesses an understanding of the greater economic good through ethical paradigms as mutually reinforcing. The central essence of his thinking is that traditional utility theory may in fact be flawed. In reality, he argues, utility theory's assumptions that all human beings act in their self-interest regarding all economic choice, is a far from perfect theory. With today's economic problems worldwide serving as a backdrop, Kusmierczyk's questioning of utility theory will find strong agreement among all readers. He stresses the importance of ethical considerations first before finally assuming utility theory or self-interest represents primary economic reality.

In chapter four, Jana Gašparíková offers very powerful reasons and supporting arguments concerning how scientific research should be organized and conducted. She states, while exploring the future it is necessary to find balance concerning how qualitative and quantitative methods are used. It is necessary she believes to explain what happens in terms of when and how we use qualitative and quantitative methods. As such, she assesses two broad categories of forecasting technique: both quantitative and qualitative methods. Qualitative methods are based on educated guessing, while quantitative methods are based on algorithms of varying complexity. They come in two types: time series and explanatory methods. She prefers to apply use of qualitative and quantitative methods concerning future assessment overall, on actual investigative examples in economics.

In chapter five, Juhani Grossmann, offers extremely unique and timely perspectives regarding US development approaches. As a senior practitioner directly involved in such planning, his experience directing one of Ukraine's most influential NGO's, offers the best view yet concerning their actual effectiveness. This paper focuses on a recently established new role of Civil Society in development assistance issued through the United States Millennium Challenge Corporation (MCC). It briefly discusses the MCC approach to development aid, especially its indicator-driven innovations in the general context of development assistance. Three types of civil society organization (CSO) engagement are reviewed: indicator creation, in-country project design and implementation, and board membership and ongoing consultation. Finally, a conclusion about the degree of interaction and its effectiveness to date is made.

In chapter six, Qerim Qerimi carefully assesses the following: He argues the magnitude of interdependency on a global scale and at all levels of society is the cause for human development becoming a key planetary concern. He argues that the fate of the environment is no less vulnerable, in this case based on the frequency of its growing presence in national and international affairs. He forcefully states, the quality of human life is nowadays seen —and rightly so— as organically related to the notion of environmental health. Such a correlation between human development and the environment has given rise to what has come to be known as "sustainable development". He analyzes in detail this key concept in the field of international environmental law with growing implications in arenas for international relations, international trade, and human rights. As the senior adviser to the foreign minister of his nation, his belief system has the urgency and awareness required for impacting public awareness.

In chapter seven, Brano Bernadec allows everyone to truly understand the importance and purpose of major, fundamental, accounting reform in the first decade of the 21st century. In a major historic, economic, and business analysis, he assesses the following issue: the true nature of the fundamental provisions of the Public Company Accounting Reform and Investor Protection Act of 2002; officially known as the Sarbanes-Oxley Act and its implications.

In chapter eight, Zoltan Boka takes an extremely critical look at globalization. He is concerned with the economics and politics of globalization and the effect it has on poor communities in its present form. He also offers certain pragmatic suggestions, which are directed towards establishing great ethical and moral paradigms for economic development. In order to help make free trade more compatible with raising living standards for all, his assessment necessarily assumes that free trade cannot raise living standards for the majority. Only the prospect of fairer forms of trade, he asserts, holds out the promise of rising living standards for all. His analysis and suggestions are extremely timely relative to the current global economic downturn.

In chapter nine, Jana Straňáková carefully analyzes how ethical standards in advertising and other related areas of society have diminished and weakened considerably. She offers a powerful critique of why people today have less faith in overall consumer advertising and what corporations say in general. Her analysis strongly supports the overall conclusion by many that unethical standards exist at all levels of business and related society. She offers strong supporting documentation confirming this greatly increased cynicism by the public towards promotional and related business promises. From her analysis, it is clear there is very strong evidence this growing lack of trust by the public at all levels represents larger and deeper problems for society as a whole. In other words, public cynicism at these levels represents a threat to civil society as a whole.

In chapter ten, Danes Brzica offers a very comprehensive analysis, assessment, and study regarding a specific, new policy design. Constructed Regional Advantage (CRA), represents a step to improve regional action, governance, regional policy and also, indirectly, political responsibility. The implications for larger economic realities and development in this case are enormous. As he successfully argues, a region's competitiveness depends on changes in actors and "learning spillover" generated in modern sectors. He then very carefully highlights the role played by CRA in regional development. As an economic imperative, he forcefully argues that governments should not view seeking higher regional competitiveness as a way to increase technical and knowledge capabilities only. They can increase social capital as well.

In chapter eleven, William T. Bagatelas, argues the following. The present economic downturn globally offers yet greater evidence that two economists in particular, John Maynard Keynes and Ravi Batra, deserve much greater public acclaim. Bagatelas analyzes why the historic and current economic record supports their economic thinking and forecasting as being correct. He carefully assesses why Ravi Batra has taken Keynes's overall logic to new levels regarding causes of economic depressions and downturns. Today's economic crisis globally and causes, was predicted over thirty years ago by Ravi Batra. By greatly improving on the legacy of Keynes in predicting the current crisis, Bagatelas stresses Batra takes Keynes and his conclusions a great step forward. In short, Bagatelas shows the legacy of Keynes and contemporary contributions of Batra, offer further support for the following conclusion. Supply-side theory and policy historically and currently, suffer yet greater discrediting as a primary or primary cause of The Great Depression of the 1930's, and the current global economic downturn.

William T. Bagatelas
Getnet Tamene
David Reichardt
Bruno Sergi

Chapter 1
Supply-Side Economics: Primary Cause of the Global Economic Downturn

William T. Bagatelas

Abstract

The following article is primarily concerned with assessing, analyzing, and understanding the primary current, historic, economic forces helping determine economic reality. In this specific context I have primarily offered the unique and highly accurate assessment ideas of economist Dr. Ravi Batra. I believe Professor Batra's assessment methods are superior to traditional economic assessment.

Keywords: supply-side economics, supply side policy, wealth gap, debt, economic policy, global debt, demand and supply, falling demand

Introduction

Supply-side economics, or classical economics, an economic theory with little supporting evidence, states the following: If government reduces taxes primarily on highest incomes while raising taxes on middle class incomes, economic performance and living standards will then be higher for all throughout society. This has been practiced historically at different times, but mainly in the United States, especially in the 20th century. The first major attempt by the US government during the 20th century to practice supply-side economic policy was during the 1920's. The results should be known by many or most but, sadly, this seems not to be the case.
 In other words, we may safely conclude when viewing the global business economy today, what economists and the public refer to as "Supply-Side" economics, is the dominant and vastly practiced economic force in our global business universe. As we speak, countries, markets, areas, regions, continents, basically the globe, have been racing since 1981 to dramatically lower specific tax rates as applied both to the very wealthiest incomes and highest corporate profits. This is happening in each and every corner of the

globe. The motive is basically a repeat of the "Supply-side" policies that overtook the global economy and business community eight decades ago during the 1920's. Like then, the current economic downturn is increasingly worsening. Today, as one reads this, the US and the world are witnessing the largest economic transformation (most would say downturn) since the Great Depression of the 1930's. Paul Krugman, the 2008 Nobel Prize winner in Economics, recently stated the US and world are now in their third long depression of the last two centuries (International Herald Tribune, 2010).

Ninety years ago during the 1920's, governments, especially the United States during that decade, but also European, systematically reduced those taxes applied to the very highest or wealthiest incomes in society. They simultaneously reduced those taxes applied to corporate profits as well. Never mind these policies as now understood to be the primary cause of The Great Depression. Beginning in the US in 1929, with an unparalleled economic collapse, it quickly spread around the world. Ultimately, this caused the most horrifying business and economic events in human history, known as The Great Depression. It also culminated in the most fearsome event in human history: World War II.

The purpose of this paper is to support the notion that unless global/regional business leaders understand the full implications of supply-side theory and practice over the long-term, then events of the 1920's will repeat themselves, as they currently appear to be.[1] Universal laws governing Demand and Supply cannot now or ever be violated without major consequences (Batra, 1988). Many factors contribute to the cause of a depression, including the much discussed and controversial financial area of derivatives policy (Tett, 2009). However, whether discussing derivatives, the debt crisis, cause of the debt crisis, or cause of any financial and economic depression, the primary cause or most important factor leading to economic depression is government tax policy.

Currently, this global economic transformation or downturn, beginning in 2007, resembles the first year following the stock market collapse in the US of 1929. It also resembles the cause of the Asian financial crisis of 1997 and 1998 (Batra, 1997), which then as now was primarily caused by too much debt at government, corporate, and regional levels[2]. In other words, the first three years of the current economic downturn, which I prefer to call transformation (because all change in life represents transformation), resemble slow but sure worsening of many economic fundamentals world-wide. In the US, this is so when one considers that since 2007, the economy under two presidents from different political parties, have failed thus far to reignite or restart the US economic engine, the primary economic engine on the planet. To be completely fair to US President Obama, he is only in his second year as leader of the US.

Already, he does have significant political victories achieved, which should help the US and world economy in a noticeable way at some point. His recent economic achievements in the areas of health care reform and increasing regulation on Wall Street interests have most likely helped prevent a global depression. His health care reform will, however, take time to translate into larger economic positives for the US and the world. But the impact of both health care economic reform and increased Wall Street regulation have helped stabilize the dollar somewhat.

Separately, by agreeing to the most comprehensive nuclear weapons reduction agreements in history with Russia, President Obama is signaling to the world as well his determination to improve the US economy by reducing military costs. This will help the world economy as well, but he must continue finding other ways as well to reduce total US government debt. Major military reductions in nuclear missiles offer the world support for the Obama view that preventing a complete global economic meltdown requires the following. The US, Russia, and all major military economies must greatly reduce military spending simultaneously. The historic agreement in Prague clearly supports this view held by Obama.

More to the point of this article's primary argument is the following. It is useful to stress the only time supply-side economic policy was actually practiced in full, before its current era and rebirth (1981 to the present), was during the 1920's in the US, and Europe. Supply-side realities have appeared in modern business and economic history before the 1920's, but they have never been as deliberate government/big business policies holding specific long-term promises that cannot realistically be realized. There was strong belief by government in the following during the 1920's and now, after being greatly influenced by huge corporations.

Large and basically all corporations, if given the very largest tax reductions in all society (on both business profits and income), will somehow naturally respond to this government stimulus and benefit both consumers and corporate executives. Doing this is supposed to create greater employment opportunities for more people, whether consumer, employee or employers. This, thus, enhances living standards for all, from bottom to top of economic scale. I should stress here as well that many famous economists historically have disagreed with this assumption regarding Supply-Side theory and practice (Heilbroner, 1999).

At this point, it is important to remember that such historically radical economic assumptions were destroyed, following the disastrous events of 1929, which supply-side economics led to. This was The Great Depression – the single, most devastating global economic collapse in human economic history. It created such misery that World War II was the outcome and result, horrifying indeed. Again, please remember this dear reader, as we peel back and analyze what has passed for "sound" business, economic, and wage logic over the last three decades. All of this reemerged in the US in 1981. It is interesting and important to know that three US Presidents officially endorsed and supported these official supply-side policies leading to the events of 1929 and World War II (Batra, 1996). Presidents Harding, Coolidge, and Hoover, have since permanently found themselves ignored by official history.

These US presidential names are directly connected to events and causes leading to The Great Global Depression and World War II. Few today probably still remember this. It would seem the field of history has failed to warn current generations regarding causes of The Great Depression. Current generations seemingly accept without question what has passed for global economic and business policy since 1981. This brings us to the primary point of our paper.

Who is Ravi Batra? The Accuracy of his Economic Predictions

I will refer to Ravi Batra as the most accurate forecaster of the economics profession worldwide. Please remember shortly before Einstein became famous the world over (more than a century ago), he offered a series of official observations in his field, revolutionizing the way physics and ultimately Quantum Mechanics were viewed. In other words, members of his profession recognized Einstein's greatness long before he won the Nobel Prize in 1921. This is what will happen I believe, in the field of economics as well. At some time in the future, Ravi Batra should receive greater recognition for his correct economic predictions and assumptions.

Many of you, perhaps none, have yet heard of Ravi Batra. Please accept this accolade as testimony to a man who is revolutionizing the field of economics. He is improving its legitimacy through deliberate and judicious use of other non-quantitative fields: history, politics, psychology, religion, sociology, etc. Why does he deserve this? Professor Batra is the only economist or person in all of history to successfully show supply-side economic theory, when put into practice, must lead to major economic downturn and depression. He supports his claims by using the fields of economic and social cycles as his basis for reaching this conclusion (Batra, 1978). He believes economic depression is always the result if immense growth in wealth disparities (greatly increasing gap between rich and poor), fueled by the rule of aquisitors, who perpetuate their rule through greed, avarice, and completely self-centered financial rule (Batra, 1978).

Put differently, Professor Batra is an economic forecaster regarding future events and trends in economics, business, and even politics. He is the only economist or person to successfully predict the collapse of communism in Eastern Europe and the former Soviet Union. He predicted precisely when and why it must occur at that moment in history. In 1978 he predicted the collapse of Soviet and East European communism would occur in 1990. No one else publicly made such near-perfect forecasts.

He is also the only economist to predict in 1978, the beginning of the end of capitalism beginning in 2000. This would ultimately lead to the end of the unethical side of capitalism as we know it now. He predicted the current major economic downturn and transformation also in 1978. He refers to this as the beginning of the end of monopoly capitalism or complete corporate domination of society. Not only monetarily, but also in terms of values, norms, expectations, laws and so-called corporate "ethical guidelines". He believes global corporations have been poor ethical examples for the public in many societies.

Let me emphasize the crucial distinction that surrounds Ravi Batra. He is the *only* economist or expert I have observed to successfully predict long-term events at least three decades in advance. These events concern economic, business and political outcomes regarding events, nations, continents, regions, or markets globally. I am aware of few others in any field who predicted anything even just a decade ahead of time.

Perhaps the most powerful example of Batra's success concerns the following example. The following quote was made in 1929, only a week before the infamous economic collapse on Wall Street leading to global economic depression and World War II. The most widely recognized global economic expert at that time, Irving Fischer of Yale University confidently stated the following: "Stock prices have reached what looks like a permanently high plateau." (Batra 2005 p. 141) Perhaps few reading this article remember the name of Irving Fischer.

He was in his time, however, referred to as the preeminent economist in the entire economics field globally. Why has the kindly Professor Fischer become obscure, seemingly lost to historical oblivion as far as the general public is concerned? For the same reason US Presidents' Harding, Coolidge, and Hoover of the 1920's have faced less recognition today. Fischer's advice to use supply-side policy throughout the 1920's was accepted by US Presidents' Harding, Coolidge, and Hoover. It appears this advice led to the Great Depression of 1929, which led to global misery and World War WII.

History, apparently with good reason, is not kind to those who prognosticate in the economics profession. This is why the rise of Ravi Batra as history's greatest and most accurate predictor of global business, economic and political outcomes is finding admiration inside the global economics community, though not so much yet in public. Unfortunately, global business leaders are having a harder time accepting Professor Batra's proven logic, because acceptance of it means global corporations must pay increasing taxes on their profits and CEO incomes, not decreasing taxes. Supply-side policy argues against this but never supports with strong evidence.

Batra often makes predictions by including the impact of large growing wealth disparity or growing wealth concentration in his analysis. This is otherwise known to most as the explosive and growing gap between rich and poor in all societies. Since 1981, this topic has been important to Batra's perception of issues he believes all societies much respect and deal with. He believes a vastly growing gap between rich and poor in many societies means the middle class is disappearing in many nations. The wealthiest 10-20 percent of any society, he believes, are getting wealthier very, very quickly. They thus own more of the entire wealth of any country.

Batra states such an occurrence if unchecked (since 1981), weakens the universal laws of Demand and Supply and its proper application. This then leads to growing poverty and growing numbers of unemployed and underemployed. This occurs as falling numbers of the middle class enter the ranks of the poor, underpaid, underemployed, and unemployed. In other words, business profits and rising living standards for all societies depend on a growing middle class, where 80% of global demand comes from (Batra, 2005). Stiglitz also confirms this (Stiglitz, 2003). This includes rising business profit, rising wages for employees and creating higher wage jobs for all. The following graphs indicate increasing wealth gaps between rich and poor, especially in the US. I deliberately use graphs from before 2000, because the trends indicated continue currently. This is more realistic then only relying on current graphs, tables and statistics. In other words, over the last three decades, the exploding wealth gap in the US is a documented fact. The trend continues. All graphs and supporting evidence have been prepared by Ravi Batra. The following graphs tell this story:

TABLE 10.4 Concentration of wealth in America: Share of wealth held by one percent of U.S. adults or families: 1810–1995 (selected years).

Year	Share of Wealth Held by the Richest Americans
1810	21.0%
1860	24.0
1870	27.0
1929	36.3
1939	30.6
1949	20.8
1958	26.9
1969	24.9
1983	34.3
1987	36.0
1995	40.0+

Source: Ravi Batra, *The Great Depression of 1990*, 1987, New York, Simon & Schuster, p. 118, and Steven Sass, "Passing the Buck," Regional Review, Boston Federal Reserve Bank, Summer 1995, p. 16.

In this first graph above, we see the history of wealth concentration in the US going back two centuries. Clearly, wealth concentration is much higher now then at any time in US history. This is significant because the 1995 indication of wealth concentration is now fifteen years old. The percent of such concentration is much higher then 1995. I emphasize using Batra's graphs from the 1990's, so the reader can see he is clearly identifying this key problem for the US economy. It would seem this historically high wealth concentration level for the mid-1990 contributed in some way to today's economic problems in the US and globally as well.

The graph above clearly shows wealth concentration peaking in 1929 when The Great Depression began. It also peaks in 1987, when the US stock markets collapse again in the biggest one day fall since 1929. Wealth concentration in the US continued to increase after 1987, which was at all-time record levels when former president George W. Bush left office in January 2009. The current economic difficulties began during former President. George W. Bush's last two years in office. There does appear to

23

be a strong connection between wealth concentration at record levels and serious economic downturn. These graphs show that Batra was talking about growing wealth concentration as a primary cause of major economic downturn long before it became observable by others.

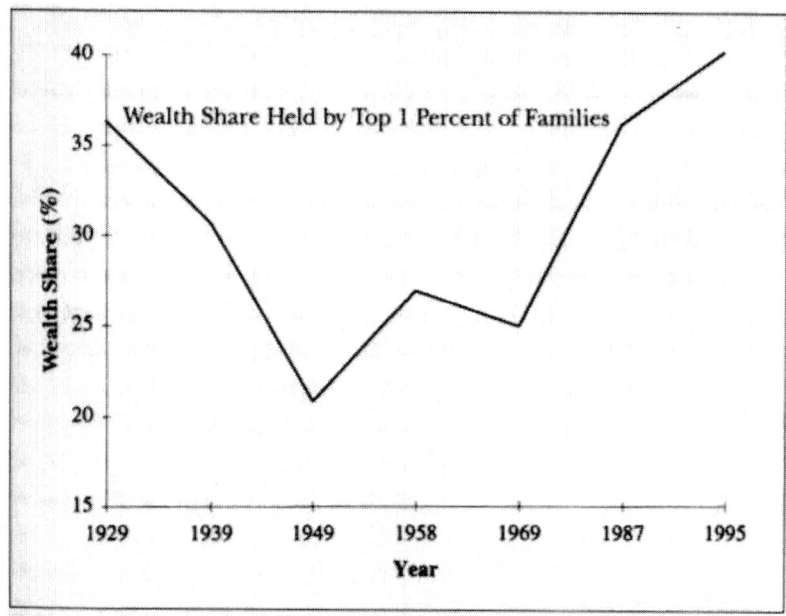

FIGURE 10.4 Concentration of wealth in America: 1929–1995 (selected years). U.S. concentration of wealth was the highest in 1995, higher than even in 1929, when the Great Depression began. (*Source:* Table 10.4.)

The next graph above begins by clearly indicating wealth concentration for the richest one percent in the US peaking in 1929. I mentioned a moment ago this was the beginning of The Great Depression of the 1930's. The graph clearly shows total wealth concentration reaching its lowest point for this same one percent twenty years later in 1949. This finding is consistent with the US economy showing strong growth after World War II. Wealth concentration for this same very small group of people was very low at the end of the 1940's. It rises somewhat during the 1950's, but not nearly enough to cause major problems. During the 1960's the wealth concentration level drops again then begins its long-term, relentless drive towards ever-higher levels of concentration.

TABLE 11.1 Income share of the poorest 20 percent and the richest 20 percent of population in G-7 countries and Australia: 1988 or 1989.

G-7 Countries	Lowest 20 Percent	Highest 20 Percent
Canada	5.7%	40%
France	5.6	42
Germany	7.0	40
Italy	6.8	41
Japan	8.7	38
United Kingdom	4.6	44
United States	4.6	44
Australia	4.4	42

Source: World Development Report, World Bank, Washington, DC, 1995, p. 221.

This next graph above indicates correlation between lower levels of total wealth for the poorest 20% in societies, with higher wealth concentration for the wealthiest 20 percent of societies. One can see in nations such as Germany, Italy, and Japan, when the poorest 20 percent have higher concentration of wealth, the wealthiest 20% also have lower such concentration. The trends identified in these graphs occurred long before it became popular today to analyze. Though not perfect evidence, there seems to be connection and correlation between growing wealth concentration for the wealthiest in society, with growing poverty for the poorest 20 percent. For the analysis offered throughout this article, my use of Batra's graphs offer support for Batra's conclusion: growing wealth concentration in any society leads to serious economic downturn.

The wealth gap in the US has been rising for decades. Batra has performed a strong service in making this a reality. All three graphs use precise methodology to make this point. More importantly, the scale of the problem is magnified when we realize his statistics give us even greater historical context. Graph one for example, goes back two centuries regarding the state of overall wealth gaps in the US. Few economists, if any, have tried to study this to the extent Batra has. The evidence does seem interesting though not perfect. In this context, no evidence can ever be perfect. What is most important is that no economist has effectively refuted Batra's claims and studies thus far.

Batra, as I have already mentioned, believes rapidly falling demand is the primary cause of the current crisis/transformation. *The Financial Times* of London, *The New York Times*, and *International Herald Tribune* officially endorsed the concept of falling demand as the important cause of current economic realities. In other words, falling demand globally, especially after global oil prices reached very high levels before 2007, were a primary culprit leading to today's problems. Only Batra made these predictions three decades prior to 2007. In the case of rapidly rising oil prices, he predicted this based on another prediction as well. The US president and administration of the twenty first century's first decade would be heavily deregulation (Batra, 1996). The US administration of President George W. Bush was just that. Batra was able to foresee this kind of administration back in the late 1970's.

Another way to appreciate Batra is to understand one of today's most influential economists, Robert Shiller. Like Batra, he's a macroeconomist and best-selling author. Unlike Batra, he is not a future forecaster of huge macro events. He officially stated the following on many occasions: "A great embarrassment for modern macroeconomic theory is that it has never achieved any [public] consensus on the basic questions of what makes the stock market rise or fall." (Batra 2005, p. 141) The statement rings with the credibility of truth. Shiller is using the word consensus in this context to mean agreement among the vast majority of economists to do the following. They should publicly endorse official evidence concerning a stock market's dramatic rise and fall. When markets go up and down very quickly, this must represent painful economic truth for global business and economy. Not admitting these fundamental economic realities keeps the profession in a state of non-improvement on crucial issues.

No perfect consensus then or now publicly exists in economic theory. Like Einstein, however, before his official 1905 relativity offerings, whose methodology was privately accepted by some, the same is happening in economic thinking since 1929 and WW II. A truly great economist, such as John Maynard Keynes, whose great contribution to economic theory was elevation of Demand side economy to equality with Supply, directly supports Batra. As is now known by some, Batra takes Keynes a step forward with his current thinking. This makes Batra the only economist/observer currently comprehending what happens to society when vastly growing wealth concentration goes unchanged. The only possible result according to Batra, and Keynes before, is much weakening of the Demand – Supply equilibrium domestically and externally.

Another method Batra uses to establish the reality of falling Demand caused by supply-side/classical economic policies is to analyze the following. What happens to overall Demand when tax structures change from being very progressive to regressive or ultra-regressive? Batra allows for this in the following graphs comparing different nations, whose tax policy shifted from progressive too regressive. Stated differently, when progressive tax policies are in place (higher tax per higher wage, salary, or income), overall Demand rises in societies following such tax policy.

When regressive tax policies are in place over time (tax rates fall with each increase in wage, salary, or income), Demand falls in societies. The following regressive country tax policies all bring about the same result: falling Demand. The following graphs/tables/statistics are all produced by Ravi Batra. As stated in the earlier graphs/tables/statistics, I make deliberate use of Batra's observations during the 1990's. In other words, long before current economic problems occurred globally, Batra identified key issues at least fifteen years ago. He predicted their trends would lead to today's challenges. Certainly fifteen year old data predicting current economic challenges globally is more impressive then current or recent data when assessing current problems.

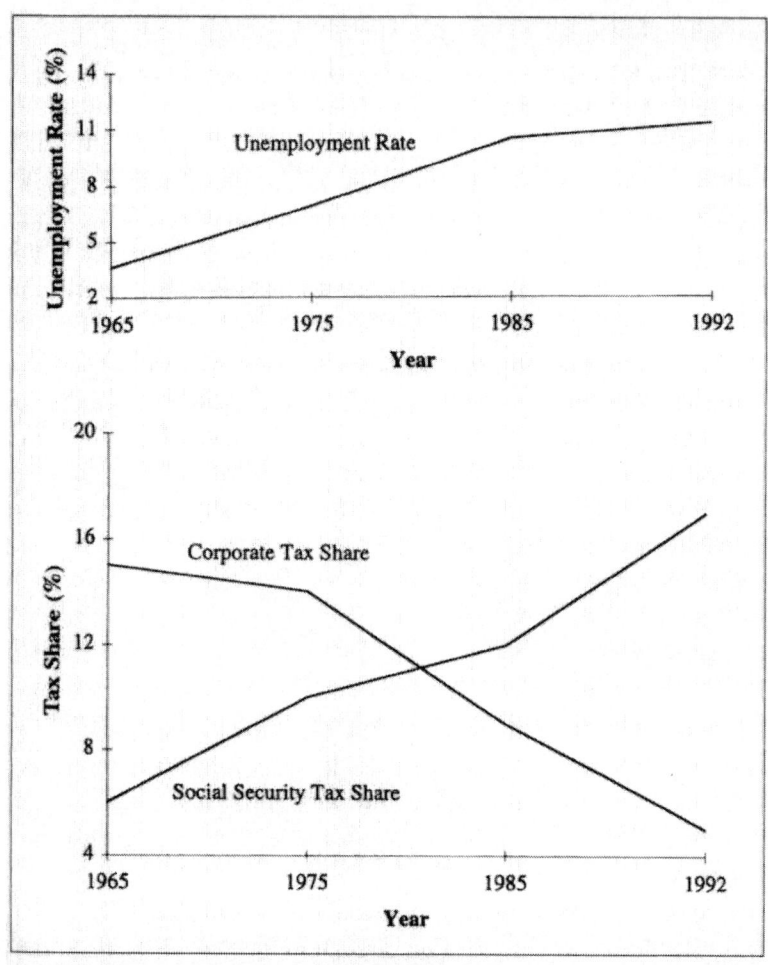

FIGURE 11.1 The unemployment rate and the corporate and social security tax shares in Canada: 1965–1992. As the Social Security tax rose and corporate taxes fell, the unemployment rate soared in Canada. Regressive taxation causes misery in society in the form of high joblessness. (*Source:* Appendix Table A.15.)

In this first graph regarding Canada, we can see what occurs, when the overall share or percentage of tax receipts paid by corporations, drops strongly over time. Starting in 1965, the average tax on corporate profits dropped over nearly three decades. By 1992, the average corporate tax in

Canada fell to about 5 percent. We can see as well Canada's overall unemployment rate rises consistently with a major increase to 1992. Equally important, the graph/table above indicates social security taxes on Canadian citizens rose dramatically during the same period corporate tax rates fell. It would seem from Batra's graphing, a relationship exists between falling taxes on corporate profits and increasing taxes on non-wealthy Canadians. Even if wealthy Canadians pay the social security tax also, this does not change the fact all non-wealthy Canadians saw their direct tax burden increase. When this kind of regressive tax policy occurs, Batra's conclusion is overall demand must fall.

Those who criticize this conclusion often state Canada's income tax did not rise on middle-class and poorer Canadians. This misses the key finding above. Direct taxes on income are only one form of direct taxation on citizens in industrial countries. Canada is no different. A rise in any payroll tax on Canadians like social security represents an increase in direct taxation as well. Since salaries did not increase as tax increases were applied, Batra concludes overall demand of the non-wealthy middle class and poorer groups fall in Canada. I agree with this conclusion.

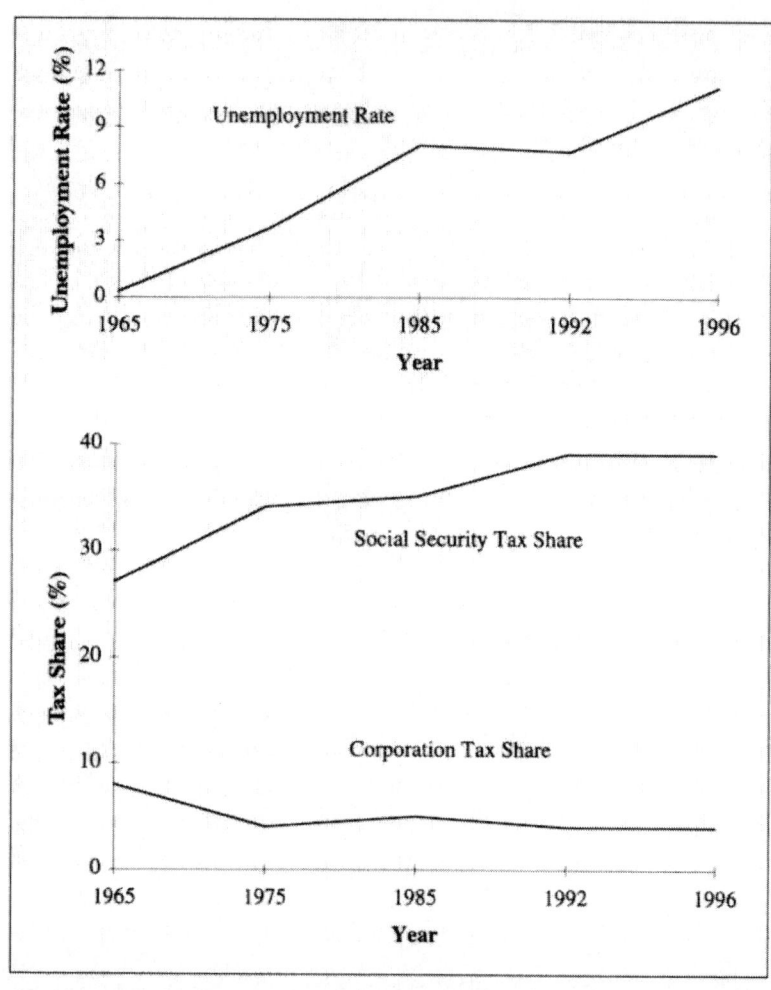

FIGURE 11.2 The unemployment rate and the corporate and social security tax shares in Germany: 1965–1996. Rising Social Security taxes and extremely low corporate taxes among others caused a huge jump in the unemployment rate in Germany. Regressive taxation hurts the economy. (*Source:* Appendix Table A.17.)

The graph above (Batra, 1993) indicates corporate and social security taxes for Germany, correlating with rising unemployment over the same time period (and a bit longer). Here we see the graph beginning in 1965. However, unlike Canada, Germany's social security taxes were already higher than corporate tax rates when Batra's graph begins in 1965. Nevertheless, we see regressive patterns apply as in the Canada finding. With Germany, as social security taxes rise from 1965-1996, there is a corresponding fall in corporate tax rates over the same period. The result indicates the following: as Germany's regressive tax structure increased starting in 1965, unemployment grew nationwide. Again, this finding is consistent with previous results in Canada.

Germany's unemployment rate begins and maintains a dramatic rise from 0% in 1965 to 8% over twenty years. Unemployment growth then levels for seven years before increasing again in 1992. It should be stressed the major oil price shocks of the 1970's (not graphed here) also play a role in rising German unemployment. We can deduce or assume this because increases in Germany's social security tax slowed considerably in the mid-late 1970's. Yet increasing unemployment rates slightly increase their momentum in the graph during the same period until 1985. We can also assume this same trend for Canada. Rising Canadian social security taxes slow their increase after 1975 for ten years, nevertheless, rising unemployment continued. In other words, rapidly rising oil prices also generate unemployment in Germany and Canada. They do not however, appear to weaken the relationship between falling corporate taxes, rising social security taxes and increasing unemployment.

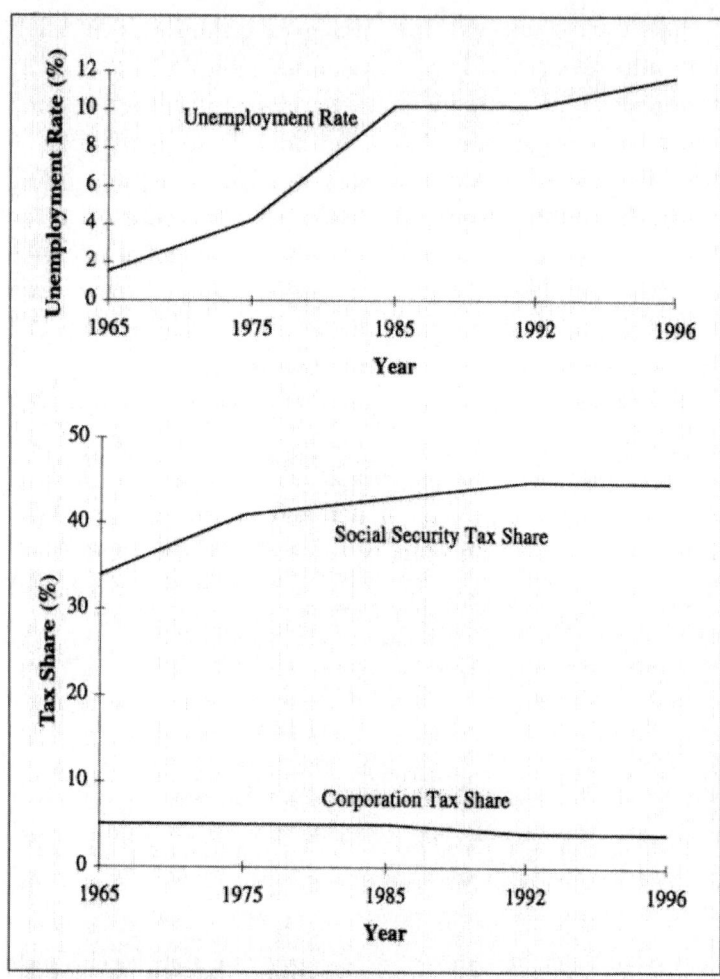

FIGURE 11.3 The unemployment rate and the corporate and social security tax shares in France: 1965-1996. Rising Social Security taxes and extremely low corporate taxes caused a huge jump in the unemployment rate in France. Regressive taxation hurts the economy. (*Source:* Appendix Table A.21.)

The graph above (Batra, 1993), shows social security taxes for France over three decades starting higher then even Germany's social security tax rate. Batra begins graphing in 1965 as well. If we also assume for high global oil prices after 1975, it appears France in this case breaks the connection between rapidly rising social security taxes, simultaneous lowering of corporate tax rates, and rising unemployment. A closer look at the graph above, however, clearly shows the following.

Batra's contention that rising social security taxes cause rising unemployment is maintained precisely by the French ten year period from 1965, to 1975. After 1975, rising global oil prices start impacting French demand. During the roughly ten year period 1965 to 1975, before high oil prices, one can see both French social security and unemployment rates rising simultaneously. The Batra link is clearly maintained for that ten year period.

I would stress the Batra link appears broken after 1975 between 1985-1992, as both corporate tax rates slowly drop and social security taxes rise as moderately. Unemployment should therefore rise moderately as well. Instead, growing unemployment stops for seven years until 1992. This can be explained by the slowing increase in French social security tax rates beginning back in 1975. Over ten years, this would slow overall falling demand. By 1985, the conditions for non-increasing unemployment are established since moderate long-term social security increases combine with rapidly falling global oil price increases during the mid-1980. This allows unemployment to completely stop growing from 1985 to 1992. Such is the power of rising demand. Batra's overall link between rapidly rising social security taxes over the long-term, and falling or very low corporate tax rates (over long-term), lower long-term demand leading to rising unemployment.

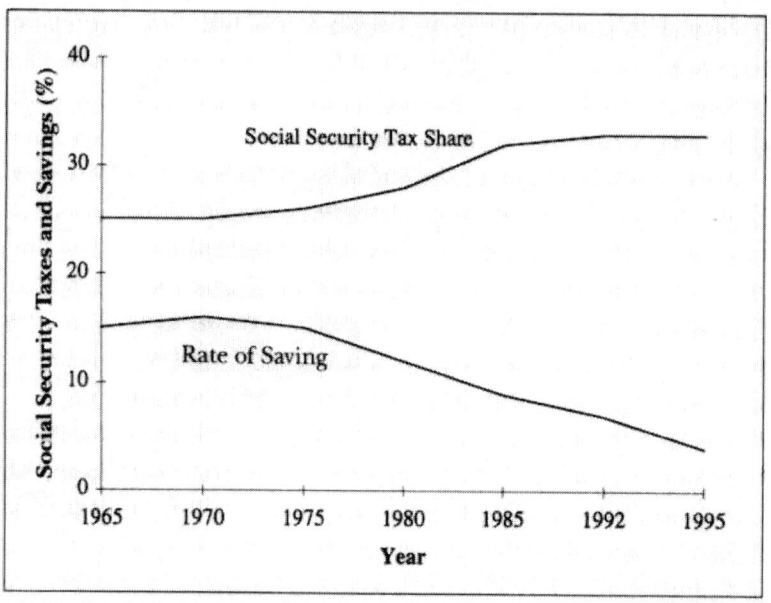

FIGURE 11.4 Social security tax share and the rate of saving in Australia: 1965–1995. Soaring Social Security taxes have crushed the rate of saving in Australia. (*Source:* Appendix Tables A.26 and A.27.)

The final graph (Batra, 1993) above regarding Australia, over the same time frame, shows interesting similarity for rising social security taxes and falling rates of saving. We may assume the steeper decline in Australia's rate of saving after 1975 is also caused by major global oil price increases of the mid-1970. As with Canada, Germany, and France, global oil price increases affected all nations[2] in the mid-late 1970's. However, as with Batra's primary findings for the previous three nations, the graph for Australia from 1965-1975 again clearly maintains Batra's link between falling social security taxes and falling demand. This is a safe assumption since all nations displaying reduced savings over time also experience reduced demand. This has been a consistent theme in modern industrial nations over the last two centuries at least.

We can therefore infer from the just-analyzed four graphs the following. Falling demand and rising unemployment is a serious problem for industrial economies when taxation on the middle-class grows without corresponding increases in middle-class salaries. Over time, a psychology sets in as middle class families realize their overall tax burden increases. It is not a realistic assumption for overall demand to increase long-term if increasing tax burdens without increasing salaries are carried by middle class and poor wage earners.

One can easily perceive significant reduction in economic performance per the four countries just graphed. Very simply, growing unemployment occurs when the burden of middle class social security tax increases over time. The same would apply if income taxes rose directly on the middle-class. The middle class clearly cannot benefit from this. The natural result is falling demand as the overall tax burden must reduce non-wealthy demand. Increasing unemployment is the result as increasing unemployment and falling demand always increase together.

Conclusion

Keynes proved the importance of equality between Demand and Supply. Batra has now gone beyond this to prove that Demand and Supply can only remain equal as long as government policy deliberately strengthens the middle class, which is where 80% of all business Demand is. The middle class can only be strengthened by a combination of progressive policies, especially creation of a progressive tax structure. As all of my students and elsewhere in my career can attest, the name John Maynard Keynes is the only economist's name recognized by any one of my students. Whether in the US or anywhere by the general public, in my experience between the period 1900-1946, the name Keynes is the only economist consistently aware of by most.

Keynes was the only economist or person in any field before 1929 to predict The Great Depression and its causes. He predicted it would happen in his famous book of 1919, "The Economic Consequences of the Peace", ten years before its occurrence. He deserves an enduring greatness for achieving this. Widespread acceptance of Keynes's greatness in predicting the crash, and how to prevent a future one after Keynes, created the most successful global economic system in history after World War II. This "Bretton Woods" system led to a consensus of sorts (for a time) as Shiller would have it, making Keynes widely accepted as the second most influential economist in history after Adam Smith. Though currently this perception may seem weakened, the larger belief system supporting Keynes's primary conclusions has stood the test of time. Will Batra eventually be so extolled?

Let me state this same acceptance of Keynes' greatness using a somewhat different paradigm. This difference concerned how Keynes achieved such elevation and stature. He was literally the only economist and person who not only predicted The Great Depression, but he offered his warning in a very public way. This occurred not only through his just-mentioned book. He publicly and angrily warned the British, French, Italian, American delegations, and global media present at Versailles. He also unofficially met with other delegations present in Paris at that crucial moment in history. Following the death, destruction, and carnage of WW I in 1919, in this case as senior British economic advisor to the British government at Versailles, his very verbal and written public warnings supported the confidence in his assertions. Not a single other person raised such warnings. He was the only senior official from any government to repeatedly warn the world. By repeatedly stating their would be a coming Great Depression followed by an even more horrific second World War, he earned the following stature. Victorious World War II countries asked him to be the lead designer and creator of the new post-WWII economic world following the war.

Keynes' primary conclusion regarding causes of the Great Depression of 1929 to 1939, and thus WW II, was this. He believed near total collapse of domestic and global Demand relative to global Supply was the main cause. His basic conclusions and lessons learned regarding this disaster still stand the test of time (Stiglitz, 2002; Tamene, 2007). In other words, too much wealth was in too few hands worldwide, a phenomenon repeating itself now. Keynes understood as no one else did, should the world's wealthiest 20% eventually have most of the world's money, the following happens. The 80% of non-wealth worldwide, or what's left of the middle-class, cannot possibly have enough demand to purchase as before. Global supply in this context would continue increasing ahead of global demand until economic/business collapse results. Too much unsold supply sitting in world markets creates long-term unemployment.

Finally, I wish to suggest I agree with those who believe economics as a field of study is primarily useful for telling us how the world works at a given time (Levitt, Dubner, 2006). This is different however, from saying the world should work only in one specific manner. For Ravi Batra, his primary conclusion regarding the actual practice of Supply-Side theory and practice is that a financial train wreck or economic disaster always eventually occurs.

The current global economic transformation (many call it downturn while some call it depression) seems to offer further support for Batra'a view. Why such a train wreck must always occur during supply-side eras is the great contribution of Ravi Batra. As I stated before, I conclude this is the equal of Einstein's tremendous contributions before he became universally recognized. The economics field today with Ravi Batra is, I believe, about where the field of physics was shortly before Einstein's revelations in 1905 became publicly accepted.

Notes

1 See Tamene, G. 2004, while confirming the author's line of argument, he asserts how wishful behaviors, selfishness, unfairness and unethical practices lead to harmful ends.
2 In this ongoing discussion, with regard to 3rd World countries, Tamene, G., 2007 seems to think that lack of strict norms which may regulate market and the behavior of impious actors at global level remains part of the legal, political and ethical deficit of the conditions in which the process of globalization has been running today.

References

Batra, Ravi. *Greenspan's Fraud: How Two Decades of His Policies Have Undermined the Global Economy*, Palgrave/MacMillan, New York, NY, 2005.
Batra Ravi. *Stock Market Crashes of 1998 & 1999: The Asian Crisis and your Future.* Liberty Press. Richardson, TX, 1997.
Batra, Ravi *The Great American Deception: What Politicians Won't Tell You About Our Economy and Your Future*, John Wiley & Sons, New York, NY, 1996.
Batra, Ravi. *The Great Depression of 1990: Has it already started coming true?* Dell Publishing. New York, 1988.
Batra, Ravi. *The Myth of Free Trade: A Plan for America's Economic Revival.* Macmillan Publishing Company. New York. NY, 1993.
Heilbroner, Robert. *The Worldly Philosophers: The Lives, Times and Ideas of the Great Economic Thinkers*. Penguin Books. London, 1995.
Levitt, Steven D., et al. *Freakonomics: A Rogue Economist Explores the Hidden Side of Everything*. Penguin Books. England, 2006.
Tett, Gillian. *FOOL'S GOLD: How Unrestrained Greed Corrupted a Dream, Shattered Global Markets and Unlished a Catastrophe.* Little, Brown Book Groop,. London, 2009.
Stiglitz, Joseph. *Globalization and Its Discontents,* W.W. Norton & Company, Inc. New York, NY, 2002.
Stiglitz, Joseph *The Roaring Nineties: Why We're Paying The Price For The Greediest Decade in History,*Penguin Books Ltd., London, England, 2003.
Tamene, G. 'Globalization and Progress. The Impact on Central European Regions' In: B.S.Sergi and W.Bagatelas (Eds.): *Ethical Implications of Post-Communist Transition Economics and Politics in Europe,* Iura Edition, Bratislava, 2004. Pp. 381-396. ISBN 80-8078-045-5.
Tamene, G. 'Some Problems of International Relations that Affect Sub-Saharan Africa: Factors that Affect Development in the Continent' in: *Rozvojova Pomoc A Spolupraca* , Tomáš Dudáš et al. (Eds.): University of Economics

in Bratislava, Faculty of International relations, Ekonóm Publishers, Bratislavava, 2007. Pp. 178-195.

Tament, G. (2007). *Contemporary International Politics: The Transatlantic Relations – Deepening Rifts and Ambition of Domination*, Habilitation Work (unpublished), University of Matej Bel, Faculty of Political Science and International Relations, Banyská Bystrica. Pp. 1-241.

Chapter 2
Knowledge Management in the Context of Contemporary International Relations, Global Politics and Economics

GETNET TAMENE

City University of Seattle/Vysoká škola manažmentu Bratislava

Abstract

As the pace of globalization intensifies, managing various human activities at present demands complex abilities including leadership skills, effective communication, capacity of knowledge mobilization and ethical requirements. These aspects are among the ones that determine the ability of managers to achieve success in the highly competitive, globalized, and turbulent international environment. At present, various state and non state actors including companies and institutions[1] interact in the international environment. Their success, however, depends on the aspects mentioned above, as well as on the quality of professional equipment and psychical strength and behavior of managers, which is a component part of overall prerequisites. Managers' personalities and performance are one of the determining preconditions of institutional success. Along with this goes the capacity of institutional knowledge management, which plays a key role in achieving strategic goals. Currently, knowledge management is a significant subject and consists of practices used by various institutions in the process of identifying, creating, and transferring knowledge. Several large institutions have separate resources dedicated to knowledge management, often as a part of 'information technology', 'human resource management', or the like. The article elaborates part of the broad problems of management in contemporary times.

Keywords: Leadership, managerial requirements, knowledge management, knowledge mobilization, artificial intelligence, international environment, managerial behavior, international actors, international relations, institutions, globalization.

1. Introduction

Since the 1990s "The discipline of knowledge management" is rapidly becoming established as an essential course or module in both information systems and management programs around the world. Many knowledge management texts pitch theoretical issues at too high a technical level, or present only a theoretical prescriptive treatment of knowledge or knowledge management modeling problems."[2]

It is easy to name contemporary international political and economic processes with one word – globalization. But what is difficult to say is whether globalization has more advantages or disadvantages. Now, it is obvious that most people worldwide are in a bad situation because of the economic crises. This marks the actual economic situation. As to the current political situation the majority of states feel pressure from international organizations like NATO, the European Union and the like, in the face of their slipping sovereignty. In fact, globalization appears to be an immutable phenomenon. Whether states should cooperate with each other within the context of globalization or whether they should insist on sovereignty to achieve their goals independently remains an open issue. Grappling with this issue and making appropriate decisions involves knowledge management and its indispensable role. Indeed, globalization continues to have an increasingly negative impact on the sovereign rights of individual nation states, even though it has many advantages.

Globalization may help to increase awareness of environmental protection in developed nations and also reduce wars in poorer countries, and may spread democratic ideas globally. Eventually, globalization must result in a loss of sovereignty to some degree if unity is to be achieved. For many members of society it may seem very important, for example that Nike organizes the global manufacture and marketing of shoes to achieve corporate objectives. Governments deregulate markets, float exchange rates and otherwise yield control to global markets to achieve their economic objectives.

The Hollywood entertainment industry - the largest export industry in the United States - attacks the defenses of cultural protectionism wherever it encounters them, generally with the supporting arm of US government trade authorities. On the other hand globalization is not working fairly for all who are forced to participate in the process. As there are advantages there are plenty of disadvantages that have emerged as a result of globalization. Making globalization work for most global citizens requires competent and fair management. Management may also refer to cost effective decision making behaviors (see Štefančik, 2007) at domestic and international levels.

This paper addresses some of the factors connected with management challenges at the outset of the 21st century and it tries to contribute ideas that strengthen achievement. The analysis is based on the performances of managers from institutions, which are considered to be successful within their scope or industrial segments. For the purpose of this analysis, results of a sample that relate to middle and top managers within each selected institution/company has been used, since the success of these institutions/ companies is not solely the work result of a single group of managers. The research is based on the presumption that managers of various positions as mentioned above within an institutional or company hierarchy, and their performances, have the largest share on actual institutional/company results. A manager's personality, his professionalism and dynamism are among the prerequisites needed for successful performance at work. However, the relationship between a manager's personality and his/her management style refers to the collection of personality attributes, which is most visible in the manager's management style in his/her, everyday work.

As the world moves through the 21st Century, business is becoming even more dependent upon professional managers, who can bring success to an organization. Issues such as globalization and decentralization add to the need for organizations to hire flexible managers capable of leading. A 21st century manager should possess three traits and utilize them to lead organizations: the ability to stimulate change, excellent planning capabilities, and ethics.

At the dawn of the 20th century, Henri Fayol,[3] for example, saw four functions of management: Planning, Organizing (Coordinating), Leading, (Commanding) and Controlling. (Fayol, 1949), (see appendix 1). According to Fayol, PLANNING refers to plans of actions, ORGANIZING refers to provision of such resources as capital, personnel and raw materials for the day-to-day running of the business. COMMANDING is related to optimizing return from all employees in the interest of the entire enterprise, COORDINATING, unifying, and harmonizing activities and efforts to maintain balance between activities of the organization. CONTROLLING refers to identifying weaknesses and errors by controlling feedback, and conforming activities with plans, policies, and instructions are four functions devoted to promoting an institution/company/organization.

These were probably necessary preconditions to cause success during Fayol's time, but obviously more complex traits are required, in a contemporary international environment, where the process of interaction is taking place between multiple actors, states and non-states alike.

At present this process of interaction assumes Knowledge Management more than ever before, as a key tool to achieve strategies. Knowledge management is an emerging discipline with many ideas yet to be tested, many issues yet to be resolved, and much learning yet to be discovered. This article surveys the existing literature and presents an overview of management in general, as well as the current state of progress in knowledge management in particular, by examining it from a variety of perspectives including: Conceptual, Organizational, Technological, and Managerial.

2. Forms of globalization

Major forms of globalization include economic and political globalization, and they take many intertwined or separate models.

2.1. Economic globalization:

This may involve trade between individuals or businesses in one country with those of another. "Ancient coastal tribes traded with those in the mountains and deserts, each gaining prized goods they could not otherwise have enjoyed. Today, we take for granted the fact that much of what we consume or use originated elsewhere, often in a strange foreign land."[4] Businesses may decide to produce their products not only at home but also in other countries, either to evade the tariffs or quotas of countries where they wish to sell their products, or to cut their costs of production by, say, hiring cheaper labor. "Then globalization involves the bundling together of financial capital, technology, and other strategic inputs in order to transfer them as direct foreign investment (hereafter, direct investment) in another country. Direct investment implies control over the assets transferred abroad."[5]

Foreign investments that don't involve control are called foreign portfolio equity investments. They are more likely to be made by financial institutions or investors like pension funds, insurance companies, or investment trusts, which are interested only in a return on their investments commensurate with risks they are taking. "If returns fall or risks rise, portfolio investment is much less dependable than direct investment as a source of longer-term finance for a country's development. The activities of transnational corporations are deeper forms of globalization. They coordinate their activities with many entities throughout the world, producing in many places with complex networks of production and finance.

This form of globalization has recently been named "alliance capitalism," in order to stress the growing importance of strategic alliances between business entities, as businesses search for ways to protect their competitive advantages and global market positions."[6] Governments also compete for economic advantage globally. They often support private research and development activities, finance worker retraining, and help to protect the environment. When governments decide it is in their interest to cooperate rather than compete, they may form supranational organizations like the International Monetary Fund and the World Trade Organization, or less formal regional bodies, in order to achieve shared objectives, for example more growth through trade, or "market-friendly" economies.

2.2. Political globalization:

This sees the classical doctrine of sovereignty widely as totalitarian, as producing external aggression and internal repression. Political leaders and opinion-makers throughout the world claim that the sovereign state is a barrier to efficient global governance and the protection of human rights.

"First, that the sovereign state is being undermined not by the pressures of globalization but by a diminished sense of political possibility. Second, it demonstrates that those who deny the relevance of sovereignty have failed to offer superior alternatives to the sovereign state. Sovereignty remains the best institution to establish clear lines of political authority and accountability, preserving the idea that people shape collectively their own destiny."[7] The authors claim that this positive idea of sovereignty as self-determination remains integral to politics both at the domestic and international levels. Politics without Sovereignty will be of great interest to students and scholars of political science, international relations, security studies, international law, development and European studies.

Still an increased global push for liberal democracy by the major western powers and international organizations - including the UN, the EU and the international financial institutions such as the World Bank and the IMF continues. "Contributors are leading international relations theorists who draw from current international relations theory, democratic theory, discourse ethics, cultural anthropology and development studies traditions to argue that contemporary international relations theories fail in their understanding of these important global trends; the contributors suggest ways forward so as to provide a fruitful and dynamic research program for the future."[8]

There are many specific geographical areas worldwide with different kinds of politics, economy, standard of living and conditions for life. The push for liberal democracy means imposing liberal democratic policies for those at the receiving end of global democratization policies – in regions including Asia, Latin and Central America, southern Africa, Russia, and the Middle East. Globalization in all its forms seems to punish specificities of the nation states, in the faith the whole world will start to look very similar.

"Globalization has carried with it a remarkably uneven distribution of costs and benefits. The result for the most part, has been exacerbating inequalities of wealth, consumption, and power within and between countries. It may be a truism that globalization entails interdependence, in the sense that what happens in one country is influenced by what happens in another. But the interdependence is dramatically asymmetrical: some are more vulnerable than others."[9] Some prosper by globalization, but many suffer from it. The prosperous embrace globalization and speed it along. But among the losers and those who fear to lose, globalization generates opposition and despair.

"More than 80 countries have per-capita incomes lower now than a decade or more ago; the gap between the rich countries and the poor grows worse. The income ratio between the fifth of the world's people in the richest countries and the fifth in the poorest was 30 to 1 in 1960, and 60 to 1 in 1990; by 1997, it had grown to 74 to 1."[10] Far from financing a convergence of fortunes between rich and poor people, globalization has coincided with a decade of increasing concentration of income, wealth, and control over resources.

The OECD countries, with 19 percent of the global population, account for 71 percent of world trade, 58 percent of foreign direct investment, and (another index of present and future wealth) 91 percent of all Internet users. Such growing disparities with the social upheavals and discontents they represent impose real demands on governance -- demands that more and more governments are unable to answer in the traditional methods that governments use. Inequalities have always been with us. What confounds the traditional methods of government is that the disparities now afflict far more people.[11] Thanks to the proliferation of the media, the disparities are more visible and more popularly understood; thanks to democracy, they are more effectively complained about.

Globalization has lots of fans and also many critics, for example the book *Politics without sovereignty* (Bickerton, C. J., 2007*)* shows both, the good and bad sides of sovereignty. Written by leading scholars, this volume challenges the recent trend in international relations scholarship – the common antipathy to sovereignty.

The most important thing that helps to increase globalization is internet use. It connects people all over the world and crosses borders, with the number of Internet users becoming bigger and bigger. It is unbelievable that in five seconds you can be connected with somebody who is a thousand miles away and you can find everything you need. The internet is something which has completely changed our life and its impact is huge.

3. Knowledge Management and Globalization Nexus

Increased globalization has brought with it increased competition, a multitude of international competitors, dramatic and frequent changes in customer tastes, shorter product life cycles, and frequent and rapid technological/product upgrading. Resultant competitive pressures have led to the emergence of two trends among some firms and industries. Firstly, there is an increased premium placed on the role of continuous learning and knowledge accumulation as the most dependable base for sustainable competitive advantage in today's dynamic global markets. Secondly, there is an increased trend towards organizing more economic activities as distinct projects. The above two trends provide both opportunities and challenges for any firm, especially project-based firms. A number of previous researchers have emphasized the importance of investment in inter project learning as a means to foster continuous upgrading of project competencies. This is equally applicable to more knowledge intensive, project-based firms in the consultancy services sector

Such an example explores, describes, and analyzes the various characteristics of inter project learning mechanisms and project competencies found in a sample of consulting firms in Sweden. The study focuses on the perceived importance of different inter project learning mechanisms and their perceived impact in developing project competencies in consulting firms. The study interrogates the 'perceptions' of 'key' informed project management practitioners, who have experience managing consulting projects. Their perceptions about project activities in their respective firms helped capture a 'managerial' view, as well as provide 'expert' opinion.[12]

The study finds the most highly ranked and value learning mechanisms involve some degree of face-to-face interaction. Learning mechanisms that enable the capture, storage, and transfer of explicit knowledge, though important, were not ranked highly in importance as person-to-person communication. The difference arises probably due to the efficient way the latter mechanisms have progressed in transferring socially embedded and context-dependant tacit knowledge, which comprise a large part of knowledge applied in projects. Most of the respondents in the above study seem to indicate that their respective firms emphasized development of project competencies that were underpinned by 'product knowledge', which emphasize capabilities to deliver short-term project goals."[13] Respective firms didn't seem to invest more in project competencies that are underpinned by 'process knowledge'.

The development of knowledge management in theory and practice continues to involve a wide range of disciplines and contributors, each bringing their respective experiences, beliefs, and practices. Two of the main disciplines that contribute to the knowledge management discourse are information systems and management. Approaches and models based on each perspective have emerged, but there is little evidence of synergy and convergence. Furthermore, it is proposed that knowledge management is currently in a state of "pre-science," wherein proponents of different paradigms have their own beliefs and values and often disagree with others about fundamentals within the field.

I think that the first point to note is that we are living for the first time in human history during a time when in principle we have the possibility of over-supply of all goods and services. Economics, business, society, legal systems, politics and government are based on a rather different and outdated assumption of what kind of world we live in. This business of living on outdated assumptions is true especially of the world of banking. Management arrived rather late in the world of banking, and of course knowledge management has not yet arrived. The reason is that our attitudes and structures are still mired in the past world of scarcity of opportunity for customers to put their money into a safe haven.

The theoretical benefits of knowledge management are clear: in order to maximize internal efficiency, internal co-ordination, service to clients, and overall profitability. One needs to make as explicit as possible the tacit knowledge of an organization.

3.1. Vehicles of Globalization and Knowledge Management

Obviously, the most important tools, which have significantly contributed to increase the intensity of globalization, include New Information and Communication Technology (NICT), in which the internet holds the most justifiable contribution. As knowledge management also feeds on the NICT, its role of responding to the impact of change and its role of bringing success to all citizens of the earth becomes a major expectation of this century. As indicated above, mainly the internet connects people everywhere while eroding borders, and the number of Internet users is still growing ever larger (see appendix 2).

3.2. The Scope of Knowledge Management in various institutions

What is this subject of knowledge management inside organizations? Many books, for example, (Miller, Paul, 1998), *Mobilizing the Power of What You Know*. London: Random House; and/or Terret, Andrew (2000); *The Internet: Business strategies for law firms, Law Society*, London.), present the key debates and a wide range of perspectives in knowledge management. What do we mean by knowledge? How is knowledge processed within the organization, and how is this linked to human motivation. Others discuss the social and cultural issues that surround the managing and sharing of knowledge. The dynamics of knowledge sharing and knowledge generation are examined, illustrating the different aspects of the collective and shared nature of organizational knowledge.

This section also looks at how knowledge processes are shaped by the conflict and politics within the organization and demonstrates how and why knowledge and power are inextricably linked. Moreover, the roles of information technology in the process of knowledge management and the human element of knowledge hold a significant place. In some sources we can find how we learn and acquire knowledge and examine the debates surrounding the learning organization. The character and dynamics of knowledge sharing in three contemporary organizational forms: the networked/virtual organization, global multinationals and, knowledge intensive firms and knowledge workers.

Actually, knowledge management is an effective current need, as it provides tools that help respond to changes globalization is continuously generating at present. It works in the sense of managing these changes rather than stopping them. It is a very important tool in today's highly competitive domestic and international environment, and the main working motto should be to know more than the competitors. Nevertheless, knowledge management needs to be accepted as a key tool for success, and institutions need to take formal as well as informal measures that put this major tool in place, if knowledge management is to have any chance of contributing to corporate success. (See Roos, J. Roos, G., Dragonetti, N.C. and Edvinsson, L. 1997).

As we live in the 21st century, we often talk more about knowledge institutions/companies and knowledge management. There is a definable vision of the 21st century. In the first place it is useful to touch on the meaning of knowledge management itself. Several authors for instance (Collins, James C., & Porrar, Jerry R. 2009), think that knowledge management is not about generating certain encyclopaedical knowledge, but first of all about generating institutional/company culture and technology that motivate knowledgeable so everyone can share in its achievements. The main meaning refers to the fact that knowledge should be transferred from those who know and possess it, to those who desperately need it. It is for this reason that knowledge management focuses on three general approaches:

- the first is *capture and creation*, which aims at capturing and creating knowledge – its purpose is to make sure that knowledge is saved and it is available to be easily found when needed;

- the second is *sharing and dissemination;* it targets the processes of transferring knowledge and related technology. The purpose of the latter approach is to establish connections between people, working communities and networks, as well as formation of directories of knowledge;

- The third is *acquisition and application;* this concerns how we gain knowledge and apply it.

The nexus of knowledge and management thus becomes a major trait of management for the 21st century, apart from the ones pointed out above. It appears to be a significant tool needed to cause a wider enduring change and achievement. This newest tool of change needs to be properly captured by managers of all levels (highest, terminal, and primary) to support efficiency. Supporting efficiency goes even further to relay artificial intelligence. Nowadays, as we also frequently talk of the knowledge society, more than ever before the knowledge and management nexus makes a lot of sense.

The field of knowledge management, unfortunately, contains such an abstract and cerebral term as 'knowledge'. Managers to the contrary, like things they can get their hands on and 'knowledge' doesn't sound like one of them. Many have tried to introduce a better term to name this concept, but failed. Such alternatives like 'intellectual assets' or 'intellectual capital', are even deepening the problem of understanding further rather than resolving it. In the knowledge management discourse, people are said to be the greatest assets. Senior management has been saying this for years without really meaning it. Of course, people are the key to the traditional areas where people matter, such as customer service, quality and relationships. Most importantly, they are also the 'containers' of everything that any organization – large or small – knows. It is starting to dawn on senior management that knowledge really can be power, and that managing and mobilizing what one knows as an organization, can produce a new level of organizational strength and competitive edge.

If one can link people together by using telephones, e-mail, intranets/internets, faxes, video conferencing, shared networks, global meetings and conferences, job rotation and easy air travel, then mobilizing the power of what one knows (knowledge) becomes achievable. When the technology for space exploration became attainable, talk of putting a man on the moon moved from science fiction to science forecasting.

Neither Drucker nor other mangers of the past knew clearly what a 'knowledge-based business's looked like, but the arrival of knowledge management in the nineties comes from the views and debate initiated by

Drucker. This helped to answer some of the questions with which countless managers have grappled.

One of the purposes of this paper is showing the effectiveness of using knowledge management and perspectives for its further use in small and big institutions or enterprises. It is known that knowledge management is a new management style in today's world, which makes the work more effective. Because of these facts, it is very important to point to these positive aspects and implement this new style as part of everyday working life. Making strategies real very much depends on knowledge management otherwise called knowledge mobilization. Statistics of sales before and after implementation of knowledge management show differences in favor of the latter. Customers of various institutions/companies have shown that the system of work needs to be improved. This work attempts to bring about new ideas, which could make the final profit of institutions/companies higher and the work of employees more effective, including better relationships in the workplace. Knowledge mobilization focused improved organizational behavior is vital for institutional survival in the highly competitive environment of this century. That is what organizational behavior is all about. *"Organizational behavior is the study and application of knowledge about how people, individuals, and groups act in organization,"* (Clerk, 2008).

An important system component of a certain institution or organization includes *task, people, technology and structure*. Basically, we must ask what is knowledge management and what does it do? At an institutional/organizational level:

> *"Knowledge management is a systematic process of connecting people to each other and to the information they need to effectively act. KM initiatives are intended to enhance performance through the identification, capture, validation, and transfer of knowledge".*

(American Productivity & Quality Center, 2003)

In fact, at a larger level we may anticipate a knowledge society, whose future success and perspective should base on knowledge including the enhancement of an artificial knowledge. Knowledge management usually refers to three major parts: information models, machines, and management of knowledge. This paper will focus mainly on the management of knowledge part.

Several institutions, in particular the multinational companies have a knowledge department (or knowledge office), for organizational learning and informational management to provide for there employees or labor force. However, many other institutions/organizations see human resources and information factors as the most important parts of knowledge management.

Many of these institutions/companies invest more in intellectual capital and maintain very close relationships with human capital.

However, the major problem in knowledge management is in the organizational culture. In any organization, there are two major aspects or concepts such as developed organizational structure and organizational culture. The organizational structure is formed by members of the organization, whereas the organizational culture is made of values, assumptions, attitudes and beliefs.

Employees come to institutions, organizations, companies or/and corporations every day, with all they know. They come with an inalienable expectation of appropriate management. This includes appreciations and compensation, however employees deserve them; adapting non-discrimination policies of various types; avoiding threatening and intimidating behaviors at several levels and the like. Moreover, in the context of knowledge management, managing refers to an effective mobilization of institutional/organizational knowledge, which is treasured by its employees (see appendix 3).

3.3. Knowledge Management and the Future

Until the past few year, most of knowledge, experience, and learning about Knowledge management have been accessible to only a few practitioners. However, during the past three years an explosion of interest, writing, research and applications in Knowledge management have occurred. Inevitably, some of the work in Knowledge Management and related fields is unknown to this writer. Every month new knowledge is created and older knowledge is uncovered, and old knowledge is made obsolete by better ideas.

There is some concern among practitioners, that Knowledge Management might suffer a fate similar to business reengineering, artificial intelligence, and total quality management. That is, interest in a discipline must last long enough to iron out the bugs while simultaneously delivering significant business value. Future work should focus on building practical experience through extensive experimenting, prototyping, and testing – especially in process, technology, organization, and implementation perspectives. In addition, the conceptual frameworks and integration across Knowledge Management perspectives need more investigation and development.

Although considerable progress has been achieved in Knowledge Management across a broad front, much work remains to fully deliver the business value that Knowledge Management promises. Ultimately, in order to realize the enormous potential value from Knowledge Management, organizations must motivate and enable the creating, organizing, and sharing of knowledge.

3.4. Artificial Intelligence as an Auxiliary Tool to Knowledge Management

Since it was born six centuries ago,[14] the discipline of artificial intelligence (AI) too, has turned into an important field, whose influence on our daily lives has become tremendous. The original view of intelligence as a computer program – a set of algorithms to process symbols – has led to many useful applications now found in internet search engines, voice recognition software, cars, home appliances, and consumer electronics, but it has not yet contributed significantly to our understanding of natural forms of intelligence. Since the 1980s, AI has expanded into a broader study of the interaction between body, brain, and environment, and how intelligence emerges from such interaction. This advent of embodiment has provided an entirely new way of thinking that goes well beyond artificial intelligence proper, to include the study of intelligent action in agents other than organisms or robots. For example, it supplies powerful metaphors for viewing corporations, groups of agents, and networked embedded devices as intelligent and adaptive systems acting in highly uncertain and unpredictable environments. In addition to giving us a novel outlook on information technology in general, this broader view of AI also offers unexpected perspectives into how to think about ourselves and the world around us. In the 21st century AI seems to be serving more as an additional capacity of knowledge management in favor of enhancing achievement.

Artificial Intelligence[15] is understood as the intelligence of machines and the branch of computer science, which aims to create it. The recognized Encyclopedia Britannica (EB), defines artificial intelligence as "the ability of a digital computer or computer-controlled robot to perform tasks commonly associated with intelligent beings. The term is frequently applied to the project of developing systems endowed with the intellectual processes characteristic of humans, such as the ability to reason, discover meaning, generalize, or learn from past experience."

Artificial intelligence would have to perform tasks such as learning (ability to adapt to new circumstances), reasoning (drawing deductive and inductive inferences), problem solving (search through a range of possible actions in order to reach some predefined goal or solution), perception (recognition), and using language (communication). As Marvin Minsky argues, the understanding of the use of intelligence shifts with the advance of technology. The more we know about ourselves the further the lower boundary of intelligence is. This would imply that creating a strong AI is not possible. According to Minsky, this is so simply because the term intelligence always means for us those characteristics we still cannot scientifically describe.[16] An example could be found with computers playing chess. A hundred years ago, nearly anyone would agree that a machine playing chess is intelligent.

The modern definition of artificial intelligence refers to "the study and design of intelligent agents" where an intelligent agent is a system that perceives its environment and takes actions, which maximizes its chances of success. John McCarthy, who coined the term in 1956, defines it as "the science and engineering of making intelligent machines." Other names for the field have been proposed, such as computational intelligence, synthetic intelligence or computational rationality. The term artificial intelligence is also used to describe a property of machines or programs: the intelligence that the system demonstrates.

In the 21st century, the occurrences of series of change are producing rapid progress in the realm of knowledge as well. The reconsideration of brain and body as a fundamental unit, physical and information ally, as well as the emergence of a new quantitative framework that links natural and artificial domains, produces new insights into the nature of intelligent systems. While much additional work is surely needed to arrive at or even approach a general theory of intelligence, the beginnings of a new synthesis are on the horizon. Perhaps, finally, we will come closer to understanding and building human-like intelligence. The superior adaptability of embodied, distributed systems has been acknowledged for a long time, but there is now theoretical evidence from artificial intelligence research and corroboration from computer simulations supporting this point. In summary, the ideas emerging from the modern, embodied view of artificial intelligence provide novel ways of approaching technological, social, and economic problems in the rapidly changing world of the 21st century.[17]

4. Inducing and Promoting an Enduring Change

An organization's environment has both specific and general components, and micro and macro environments. The organization also has its own personality or culture. This environment and culture can be the generator of forces for change. Needs from within the organization can stimulate change, which are internal forces for change. "Of course, the distinction between external and internal forces is blurred because an internally induced change may be prompted by the perception of an external event." (Barney, 1992, p.755) Today's organizations are characterized by frequent disruptions to its environment. New strategy, new technology and change in employee mix or attitudes are all internal factors that can create force for change.

The introduction of new equipment or technology can create the need for change within the workplace. The staff will need to learn how to use the new equipment and it may affect the duties required of them. Their jobs may have to be redesigned. New company strategies, which may involve the change in management practices, enterprise agreements and industrial relations, will create a vast variety of needs for change. So will the attitudes of the workers. In fact employee attitudes can create the need for new institution/company strategies in the case of job dissatisfaction, poor team spirit, lack of commitment and job insecurity. This is necessary to cause change and not deform it.

External forces affecting an organization demand change by creating threats and opportunities. The organization is forced to respond to these threats and opportunities. These external forces are apparent in many of the segments of the organizations external environment. These include political-legal, technological, economic, marketplace and socio-cultural dimensions.

The political-legal environment is that which consists of government bodies, pressure groups and laws. It is pertinent for companies to keep abreast of and change in the political environment because these changes can have dramatic effects. Change in the political environment can see legislation introduced that will not make selling or providing a product feasible or somewhat difficult. There are many political factors and laws that can affect business.

Pricing, competition, fair trade packaging, labeling, advertising, product safety and minimum wages can all affect business. The marketplace is a major contributor to forces for change. These forces are created by changes in customer buying needs, expectations and buying habits. The lifting of import tariffs or market deregulation are other factors. The technical environment is created by developments of new products or processes that affect an organizations opportunities and operations. These advancements in technology purvey benefits and impel organizations to change.

The first factor to consider for motivating change deals with whether the organization is facing some obvious need for change, such as increasing competition, pressure on prices, changing customer needs/expectations, advances in technology, reductions in external funding or regulatory changes (Cummings, 1997, p. 81). The actual change does not occur until the force for change exceeds that of the force resisting the change. People who may not necessarily lose from the change still contribute to the force resisting change. People inherently resist change because change causes uncertainty and ambiguity. Through good management these uncertainties and ambiguities will be removed and the resistance to change will not be as great.

Planning is, "A process that involves defining the organization's objectives or goals, establishing an overall strategy for achieving those goals, and developing a comprehensive hierarchy of plans to integrate and coordinate activities." (Robbins et al., 2000, p.247) One of the reasons for planning is to reduce the impact of change. It does this by creating an environment that is accepting of change and by predicting change. "Planning reduces uncertainty by forcing managers to look ahead, anticipate change, consider the impact of change and develop appropriate responses." (Robbins et al., 2000, p.247) No amount of planning or anticipation can get rid of change all together. "Planning cannot eliminate change. Changes will happen regardless of what management does."(Robbins et al., 2000, p.437) Planning just enables us to best cope with and manage change.

Change can be modeled by two different metaphors: calm-waters and white-water rapids. The calm waters model involves unfreezing, changing, and refreezing; this is also the same as Lewin's model of change. We have seen that planning is a tool that can be used to predict change. In this environment of predictability the calm waters metaphor is an apt model. The organization is in a stable environment and can anticipate change so it goes through a process of unfreezing, then performs changes implemented to overcome differences and meet new goals, and then refreezes to keep changes in effect and return to stable environment. Total quality management uses this model. "Total quality management is essentially a continuous, incremental change program. It is compatible with the calm waters metaphor..." (Robbins et al., 2000, p.454) Total quality management continually seeks out problems and implements changes as they strive to ever improve their organization's efficiency and effectiveness.

Plans are difficult to develop for a dynamic environment. "This calm waters metaphor has become increasingly obsolete as a way of describing the kind of seas that managers in today's organizations have to navigate." (Robbins et al., 2000, p.441) This calm waters metaphor "... is not very helpful to people faced with the detailed task of bringing change about." Today the white water-rapids metaphor is more prevalent in organizations and is a more comprehensive model. The white water-rapids metaphor depicts change as an ever-present perpetual event. An organization in white-water rapids is in an uncertain dynamic environment (Barney, 1992, p.757). Disruptions to the status quo may never stop and managers in this chaotic world need to respond quickly to every changing condition.

Organizing is defined as, "The process of creating an organization's structure." (Robbins et al., 2000, p.351) By comparing the definition of organizing to the definition of change we can come to the conclusion that organizing, as a function of management, can be a major contributor to the change of an organization through change in structure. Changing technology may be a contributor to an environment full of uncertainty, although this technology has enabled managers to organize much greater efficiency and effectiveness.

Work specialization is necessary as jobs become more complex and also increases efficiency, although job specialization does not create an environment capable of accepting change. Managers could adopt a structure of multi-skilling, which will provide the organization with an adaptable workforce.

Decentralization is, "The handing down of decision-making authority to lower levels in an organization" (Robbins et al., 2000, p.359) Decentralization is prevalent in organizations that exist in complex uncertain environments. An increase in decentralization would create an organization capable of making faster decisions. This faster decision making ability is far more capable of reacting to change. This ability to react quickly to change is hence conducive to change.

An organization that is well structured for change is one that is organic. An organic organization has the structural characteristics mentioned above and others prefer wider spans of control, cross-functional teams, free flow of information and low formalization. Organic organizations have "organizational structure that is highly adaptive and flexible with little work specialization, minimal formalization and little direct supervision of employees." (Robbins et al., 2000, p.362) Organic structures incorporate the use of teams, which use a much flatter design of management.

The learning organization is the best-structured organization for change. This is quite apparent in the definition, "An organization that has developed the continuous capacity to adapt and change because all members take an active role in identifying and resolving work related issues." (Robbins et al., 2000, p.376) To achieve this, the organization has a structure that is without boundaries.

Leadership "is the ability to influence and direct a group towards the achievement of goals." (Robbins et al., 2000, p.593) Transformational leaders are the style or type of leader best suited to change. They are a style of leaders that entail certain qualities that are conducive to change. These are "... individualized consideration, intellectual stimulation and charisma." (Robbins et al., 2000, p.617) Leadership is crucial to facilitate the vision required for an organization to become a learning organization. Leadership can be used to reduce the resistance to change by altering people's attitudes, expectations, perceptions and behavior through motivation, communication, participation, facilitation, negotiation manipulation and coercion. Some may use extreme methods of intimidation such as hidden phone calling, and many others to frighten some of their employees and control them. This is more likely in institutions where leaders or owners themselves are inferior in capacity than their subordinates, and have no significant value or contribution in ethical terms or by any standard contribute towards endurable change.

Control is "The process of monitoring activities to ensure they are being accomplished as planned, and of correcting any significant deviations." (Robbins *et al.*, 2000, p.683) The control of the organization needs to be flexible enough to absorb and deal with change. Managers need to move away from bureaucratic styles of control to encourage change. Bureaucratic organizations strain the use of rules, regulations, procedures, policies and hierarchal authority. For an improved environment of change organizations should use clan or market approaches to control.

How do we put the functions of management and possible changes of organizations into a process of change? Managers can use the process of reengineering, which is "A radical redesign of all or part of a company's work processes to improve productivity and financial performance." (Robbins et al., 2000, p.64) Rather than creating an environment for change this method just goes right on in and changes it. Reengineering is extremely stressful on the organization. "Yet, for all the enormously stressful uncertainty placed on employees, the payoffs from reengineering can be powerful." (Robbins et al., 2000, p.717) An organization that has gone through the reengineering process has experienced and adapted to change and therefore are better experienced to accept and embrace change in the future.

The environment that we create through change and trying to encourage change is one that is conducive to stimulating innovation. We need to have flexible structures, good communication, and a culture that is relaxed towards and supportive of new ideas. An organization's culture can be a prevailing force for innovation or seriously threaten the innovative endeavor. Crucial to the implementation of cultural change is management's ability to use leadership and provide a shared vision of the future. In a chaotic, dynamic world of change we must be able to come up with new ideas and inventions in order to compete in the global market. Those who are good innovators are the ones who can gain competitive advantages.

Change and survival are synonymous. Survival demands change. Managers must be intuitive and read the current and changing situation surrounding them and make the best decision to coordinate work and apply resources (Graham, 1997, p174). We have discussed what change is, how we depict it and what forces create change. Change implemented correctly can unleash employee creativity and potential, reduce bureaucracy and costs, and provide ongoing improvement for an organization. Given these benefits it would seem a good idea to encourage change.

Ethics can be defined as a process of evaluating actions according to moral principals of values (Griffin, 2000, p289). Throughout the centuries people were trying to choose between profit and moral values. Perhaps some of them obtained both, but in each time period it could and would have aroused ethical debates and issues. Those issues concern fairness, justice, rightness or wrongness; as a result it can only be resolved according to ethical standards.

Setting the ethical standards for ways of doing business in corporations is primarily a task of management. Corporations have to maintain the same standards as an individual person and, in addition, corporations as organizational units, have their own social responsibilities toward customers, employees and society. However, any business should keep its original purpose of functioning - making profit. Balancing the traditional standards of profitability and burden of social responsibilities is not an easy task. In recent years there has been a trend of setting standards of corporate ethics according to high degrees of morality.

Unfortunately, cooperation of some forms of unethical behavior, like for instance a manager cooperating with a journalist or judge may lead to undesirable results when the journalist fails to disclose his source or a judge fails to pass a just judgment ethically. This leads to a situation where neither management nor the editors or judge have in any way cared about conducting ethical behavior, which is discernible in several cases. The result has often been that innocent people were hurt.

On the other hand, being ethical can be clever marketing strategy. Increasingly, consumers are swayed by "non-commercial" factors, such as whether the product harms the environment. As mentioned in ("The Economist", December 1996, p.21), firms such as Ben & Jerry's, an ice cream maker and Body Shop international, a cosmetics retailer, have enforced their brands by publicizing their ethical standards. Calmins Engine, a maker of diesel engines, made the product greener while lobbying for stricter pollution laws. Du Pont, a leading producer of ozone damaging CFCs,[18] became an early member of anti-CFCs lobby, partly because it knew it was well ahead of its rivals in developing alternatives. But ethical self-promotion can backfire. As in the case of the Body Shop company publicly forced to rephrase a statement that its products were not tested on animals (some other companies did this in the past as well). This made many consumers question Body Shop ethical standards. Another interesting issue in corporate management is social responsibilities. Responsibilities can be defined as a set of obligations an organization has to protect and enhance society in which it functions (Griffin, 2000, p. 168). There are a few main components of social responsibilities.

Any business has responsibilities to its customers. The paramount duty in this respect is to provide customers with quality and safe products. Unfortunately, not all businesses follow this rule. The example of such deception is the tobacco industry, which deliberately manipulated the level of nicotine in cigarettes. Despite declarations of managers, scrutinizing research has made it clear the industry in the US tried to maintain the addictive levels of nicotine.[19] The purpose of it was far from humanistic - addicted smokers kept buying cigarettes, making the industry prosperous and profitable. There have been a number of other different customer abuses such as sale of fruits with overdoses of chemicals, breast implants for women etc. Though the responsibilities to its customers are a crucial point of management, the way managers treat employees is another parameter of evaluation of a companies' ethical well-being. Unfortunately, the biggest concern of managers has become their own jobs rather than that of their employees.

Another problem is equal employment opportunities for everyone. Although a lot was done to destroy the system that kept women and minorities away from top management positions, many corporations still rely on white male stereotypes and prejudice. Women are primarily considered solely as accessories for men and are not treated on equal bases. In fact, a firm's attitude towards employees often determines the way employees feel about the company. As a rule, corporate codes of ethics contain patterns of behavior an employer expect from employee.

Another responsibility of company management is to stockholders. This usually arises as a so-called "agent problem" (Dyckman, 1998, p.67). Managers are in control of the property of stockholders; however, the interests of these two groups may not be the same. As a manager is looking for more power and prestige, his company can tend to have less profitable operations. Also corporate officials may vote for high salaries and bonuses for themselves, decreasing the dividends of stockholders by such action.

There is no particular solution for all of these issues. There is only hope that ethical standards and social responsibilities would guide every manager throughout his/her career. Professional conduct should be governed by a code of ethics that reflects positively on the practitioner and managerial profession. Simply stated, nothing should prevent a manager from maintaining high ethical standards and social responsibility in the quest for high performance and quality. With regard to this, Juza (2008) tries to question tendencies of international business management in areas of energy security, from Central European region perspectives, whether they are simply in geopolitical vogues or actual geopolitical necessities. In addition to this, Hrivík (2009) expresses a critical view in light of international political relations about the issues, while Bočáková (2009) examines the issues in terms of an urgent need for a model that will provide an improved quality of services.

5. Managers' behavior studies and findings

This study has taken into consideration a sample of top and terminal (middle) managers within a selected group of institutions including automobile companies, mobile phones, educational institutions, information technology, shops, machinery, textile, and electro technical segments.[20] The assessment has utilized the DELF [21] method where two types of questions (open and close in the ratio of 1:3) are involved. The respondents designated their best choices using the closed questions' form.

This part encompassed questions that seek to find out dominant personality traits, current styles of managing, motivating factors as well as value priority. Open questions give a wider chance to respondents and they were thus able to convey themselves freely. The advantage is that such questions do not restrict the respondents' choices. Such questions are usually sources of new and unexpected responses, which are difficult to explore using closed questions. Open questions offer respondents the chance of thinking and expressing their opinion. Such questions present highly predicable values. The questionnaire included 32 questions (24 open and 8 close questions). In fact, the questionnaire was undisclosed. In some cases face- to- face interviews were conducted to balance questions that lack responses in the questionnaire. For the purpose of this contribution, only a relevant part of the findings have been included. Posed questions include:

1. Name three characteristics which match you best in the list below: Perseverant, ambitious, resolute, self-confident, courageous, modest, well-disciplined, optimist, independent, consistent, initiative, responsible, creative.

This question is aimed at identifying the personality characteristics of managers, top and terminal (middle) alike. After counting the responses, the results have shown a clear profile of identical traits for both groups of managers. These are: *resolute, responsible,* and *self-confident.* They seem to have under-estimated such traits like *consistency,* which is very important with regard to achieving goals at an interpersonal level. Regarding self-confidence, the ratio of the responses has been 6:4.

2. Identify the three best capabilities that accompany you while performing activities at work, from the list below:

Listening to others, dispute resolution, understanding others and being understood, motivating, delegating power, flexibility, self-criticism, and recuperation.

This question is directed towards defining abilities that highly accompany the performance of managers' profession. Whatever genius a manager may be, he should not decide himself on behalf of his team. Motivating coworkers in connection with short and long-term strategies, sharing power substantially is essential to causing favorable results and perspectives. The flexibility and ability of conflict resolution, too, are significantly useful. Self-criticism induces a state of being able to recuperate in terms of physical and spiritual strength. Unfortunately, this vital trait from which management should draw its strength has received a minimum response. Experiences show this is the cause in every level of management, mainly; top management has impiously denied applying this mechanism.

3. Indicate three strong traits that describe your personal behavior, in a sequence of importance, from the list below:
Professionalism, consistency, communication, empathy, enthusiasm, joy from work, seriousness in approach and own life, rationality, loyalty, honesty, friendliness, openness, straightness, candor, tolerance, and fairness.

It has been obvious from the open questions that managers did not escape their professional preferences. Also, from a personality point of view they indicated communication and empathy as their dominant, self-motivated attitude. Self-discipline and rationality are important traits that often separate successful managers from unsuccessful ones. An ethical dimension of managers' personality is discernible from the last usually subjective and strongest traits (honesty, tolerance, fairness).

4. Indicate at least one trait that describes your weak side in the list below:
Pigheaded, inconsistent, irresolute, emotional decision making, impulsive, delay unpleasant decisions, and excessive perfectionism.

Basically, this question is designed to balance so far positively tuned questions. The results show that many of the managers are aware of their down sides to a lesser extent. However, the fact they are aware of some of the attitudes, which describe their weak side is an incredible finding, because the improvement of these weaknesses will help enhance effectiveness in their work place.

Nevertheless, in spite of all their strong sides such as capabilities of communication and empathy, stubbornness also presents the weakest side of most managers. This implies to the fact that managers probably try to listen to their subordinates (employees), nevertheless, in most cases managers rigidly defend their own stance or decisions, whatever the decision may be. This finding thus confirms the result in question two, where self-criticism, understood as the most significant attitude of managers at all levels, has plunged downward very much as a strength. Regarding decisions as mentioned in question one, in most cases top and terminal managers make decisions quickly, even rationally in some cases, quite easily. The down side of decision making, however, refers to serious strategic and personnel related cases.

5. Indicate the choice that best suits how you usually spend leisure time, with the list below:
I spend leisure time with colleagues from work, with family, while taking passive rest, while actively relaxing, and with no leisure time.

This question tries to find out how adequately managers regenerate themselves. Adequate physical and psychological energy is believed to be very helpful to managers, because they enhance effective performance in the work place. As much as quality of rest is important for managerial performance, so to social backgrounds are equally important, since they too motivate managers' performances. The results confirm most respondents spent their leisure time with their families. Only a quarter of respondents have confirmed they use their leisure time actively.

The behavior of managers and their decisions are, in fact, key for the success of an institution, organization, or company. All bring success to the institution, people, approaches, and strategies, which usually start at the leadership level. This is closely connected with the behavior of managers. On the other hand, there is no such thing as very easy or general instructions concerning how to manage institutions correctly. Thus, environments in which managers act and situations in which they find themselves largely remain unique.

6. Why the Term Knowledge Mobilization Gives Better Meaning?

There are endless conceptual discussions regarding *intellectual capital*, *knowledge assets*, and *knowledge-based business*es, nevertheless, the term *knowledge management* itself needs further qualification to address the concept it explains. As it stands now it sounds vague and senseless. Talking of ‚management' in such vagueness has led towards creating the illusion this huge and nebulous thing called knowledge can somehow be managed in the same way that a company's pay and benefits systems can be managed (Miller, P., 4-8). This indicates a contradiction in terms. Knowledge cannot be managed in any strict sense – particularly in an internet world – rather what business wants to do with knowledge is to use it, share it, develop it – and mobilize it rather than manage it.

In fact, the term *knowledge management* sounds dry, but is actually saturated with energy and vigor. People who run an organization want to get hold of its collective knowledge, wisdom and understanding so they can really use it during every customer interaction, new product meeting, process improvement, brand development and the like. They want the passion, energy and dynamism that comes from mobilizing the power of what their organization knows.

'Knowledge management', conveys a static, inert and uninspiring message and this image might have contributed to damaging the field in several ways. It has allowed the process to be taken hostage by management theorists, academics, and technology firms.

What organizations/companies want to do is mobilize the power of what they know – they want to mobilize everything their people know. Thus, according to Miller (above), knowledge mobilization sounds like an appropriate term to tell day-to-day experiences of people in companies that share with each other; on other words, stories of knowledge being successfully managed. The reassuring news is the best approaches and most effective solutions are those that are simple and practical. There are numerous theories, models and concepts of knowledge management, which run parallel to the stories of progress that organizations/companies have made in achieving a degree of knowledge mobilization, however, knowledge mobilization is, in the end, a practical activity.

As we can observe from the foregoing management and knowledge discourses, the behavior of most managers is not adequately tuned towards enhancement of knowledge mobilization or knowledge management. They rather solely target profit making.

In fact, one of the major expectations of the 21st century is producing managers and institutions that perceive their employees as valuable human capital and not as a liability. This would help treat employees differently, because employees are those whose knowledge they eventually mobilize and transfer to any destination, whether home or in the environment of complex interdependence between actors abroad (see appendix 4).

Most probably, these ones would also do better in the process of complex interaction taking place today between actors of various types in the international environment. This cooperative approach would utilize the capacity of institutions and organizations to survive, then gradually crumble. Improvement of an institution/organization is not dependent solely of the men on the top but also of those at the bottom. An institution/organization seems to function effectively, when there is honest cooperation between its élites (positional, ideological, and social). If a reasonable balance is missing between these elites, then something is going very wrong inside the organization, as well as in the whole system of society.

6.1. Models of Various Managerial Orientations

One such model may be 'the pretending elite model'. This ordinary model is one among several models of managerial orientations (see appendix 5). The positional elite are those who occupy the highest position in the hierarchical structures of an institution/organization in this type of model. This may include owners and/or top managers, as they are the ones who make major decisions that affect institutions in the affirmative or negative sense. There is a wide gap between them and the social élite, who occupy the bottom place on the hierarchy. It is the social élite that form the cultural and traditional base of the institution/organization, which is understood as the demos of the institution.

The ideological élite refers to a group of people between the positional and the social élite, who are less active in decision making but proactive in advising and implementing decisions that are made. They do all, in order to secure their statues. In institutions/organizations, where the use of knowledge mobilization or management is not applied, or where the balance between these elites is not maintained, the rule of the game becomes uncertainty, fear, cheating, corruption and intrigue, impunity and the like. These result with ethical behavioral[22] bankruptcy to endanger, mainly, the condition of employees at the bottom. Improving such down-sides like the ones mentioned above is among concerns of managers during the early phases of this century.

6.2. Four Major Models and Challenges to Management of All Ranges

Various studies, which were conducted towards exploring personalities, [23] indicate several types of managers and models of managerial orientations. One such study presents four managerial orientations as listed below:

    a) Autocratic – the basis of this model is power with a managerial orientation of authority. The performance result is minimal.

    b) Custodial – economic resources with a managerial orientation of money. The employee need that is met is security. The performance result is passive cooperation.

    c) Supportive – leadership with a managerial orientation of support. The performance result is awakened drives.

    d) Collegial – partnership with a managerial orientation of teamwork. The employee need that is met is self-actualization. The performance result is moderate enthusiasm. (Clerk, 2008)

In relation to these studies of organizational behavior, some authors have gone as far as using metaphors that describe major organizational and managerial orientations. These metaphors are connected with the ancient Greek gods and goddesses.

6.3. Handy's Managerial Models

The idea of each employee having their own workplace Gods is a metaphor that reflects the prevailing organizational cultures of varying firms/institutions in relation to knowledge management. According to Handy, we each have our gods as individuals within the workplace. Handy's Gods of Management are defined as follows: **Zeus, Apollo, Athena,** and **Dionysus**. (Handy, 1976) As shown below, he goes on to describe Gods of the Greek mythology to illustrate how each institution's organizational culture looks like.[24.]

Zeus – the supreme God in Greek mythology. 'He was feared, respected and occasionally loved. He represented the patriarchal tradition, irrational but often benevolent power, impulsiveness, and charisma'. This is used to describe an organization usually based around a single leader with a one man vision. This culture is often the norm in smaller professional services firms, demonstrated by high levels of trust, personal commitment, quick decision making, an absence of bureaucracy and office politics. A Zeus culture is also symbolized by a power structure with one or more charismatic leaders, a club culture. Individuals are inclined to think, 'now what would the boss do in this situation?'

Apollo – the God of order and rules. This represents a role culture, where everyone in the organization understands their own purpose and mission. Good examples of role cultures are the Civil Service, monopolies and state industries, although such cultures can also be found in larger financial and insurance organizations. In terms of running the actual intranet project, everything must be done by the rules and corners cannot be cut. This type of organizational culture is not usually found in professional services firms where the focus is upon getting results for clients no matter what the internal structure of the firm.

Athena – a young warrior goddess. This represents a task-oriented and problem solving culture. Such organizations are non-hierarchical, encourage creativity, imagination, and a team-based approach to problems. Many law firms aspire to be Athena-like in their approach to problems and the intranet can play a key role in facilitating this. In terms of actually running the intranet project, it is probably the easiest culture in which to develop an intranet.

Dionysus – in Greek mythology strictly, the God of wine but also the God of wine and song. This model is used to refer to individuals who are unorthodox, individualistic, and even anarchic in their approach to work. In an organizational context, it is used to describe companies or firms that are characterized by informality, a decentralized power structure, and in some cases, incompetence. In a law firm context, it will be illustrated by lawyers who use the vocabulary of 'their own practice' without reference to the firm's practice or to its development. Dionysian individuals are very difficult to mange, usually highly self-motivated (rarely motivated by others). They are the very antithesis of the team player. Dionysians proliferate in research institutions and universities, and unfortunately, in law firms as well. From an IT perspective, it is the most challenging of all environments.

7. Assessment of Current Knowledge Management Practice

This part attempts to show the summary of assessment results with regard to implementation of knowledge management in practice. The result is based on the Global Law Firm Knowledge Management Survey, which was conducted in 2006. Requested institutions had an average 611 employees including 193 partners and 787 members of assisting personnel, with an average income of between 200 and 300 million USD. (See the chart in appendix 6)

Law institutions were the ones who spread usage of knowledge even though their emphasis was on knowledge of juridical practices more than business law. Law institutions/firms have incorporated in their fields the usage of knowledge in its explicit as well as implicit forms. They have projected a considerable strength of managing knowledge with regard to legal institutions. While disregarding other areas, they simply focused on knowledge management in the sense of legal practices. Most frequent performances of knowledge management appear in the form of legal research tools and systems, and practical group meetings. Almost half of the law firms have accordingly implemented files, crafts of clause libraries, professional developing programs, CRM systems and contact databases of third parties. The graph below presents a summary of the findings.

8. Conclusion

Globalization has placed businesses everywhere in new and different competitive situations where knowledgeable, effective behavior has come to provide the competitive edge. Enterprises have turned to explicit and systematic knowledge management (KM) to develop the intellectual capital needed to succeed. Further developments are expected to provide considerable benefits resulting from changes in the workplace and in management and operational practices. Changes will partly come from information technology and artificial intelligence developments.

However, more important changes are expected in people-centric practices to build, apply, and deploy knowledge and understanding for support of innovative and effective knowledge-intensive work. Much remains to be done. Next generation KM methods will still be crude. Our understanding of knowledge and how people use it to work has a long way to go. We need a "theory of knowledge" and perhaps a new theory of the firm to create a solid foundation for future KM. Still, users can expect significant benefits from KM as it develops over the next decades.

In conclusion, it is obvious the ability to stimulate change, excellent planning capabilities, and ethics are essential traits a manger should possess and utilize in leading an organization in the 21st Century. On top of these, the ability of mobilizing knowledge or as it is usually called knowledge management holds a significant place. These traits help managers' focus on success for their organization, and these traits are subordinate when defining such traits in their leaders. By using these traits, a manager can place him/herself on a path that can lead to success.

Many institutions/organizations reshape themselves because they aim to be global leaders and a provider of services all over the planet. They however, face enormous difficulties with issues of knowledge management because management spends much time exploring and adopting something new in the institution. This requires more time as well to adopt themselves to a different country. Almost all institutions, mainly multinational companies, usually find themselves starting businesses in regions where conditions are not assessed adequately, and includes whether or not it is appropriate to start business there automatically (for example, Nokia in Finland, Yamaha in Japan and many others).

They apparently achieved success only after listening to people and identifying what they want. They scored more success in other parts of the world compared to home. Nevertheless, several institutions have failed shortly after entering the globalization's highly driven complex competition. They failed largely because they were not able to determine what had gone wrong, or they had unworkable strategy, inefficient human resource and other value added factors. These factors, which may not seem important when everything works well, are very important. Also, management might have chosen bad strategy, or they were not able to calculate their approximate chances to success in the new markets. Human resources are one of the most important components in any institution showing concern to interact in the global market place. It thus deserves careful treatment.

Knowledge mobilizing, or as it is usually called knowledge managing, has currently needed a valuable new tool, ever since it emerged in the 1990s. Business desperately needs to use this tool, share it, develop it, and mobilize it if it wants to bring success to an organization or to interact with other actors in the world out there. Many managers failed to embrace this tool adequately in their strategies, as they solely targeted profit while undermining other values. Others introduced resort kinds of Knowledge management or mobilization in their respective organizations, companies or institutions, and they were able to implement this tool in their structures and comparatively showed better results.

A surge to the international environment yields high returns with this tool being applied in various areas. For example, the proportion of GDP generated in Europe via using this tool was in 1990 – 10%, currently it is – 50%; by the year 2020 it is estimated to be 70%. Knowledge management or mobilization is a natural step, resulting in effective use of existing information technology in a way to help employees and managers obtain the kind of information they require. Moreover, knowledge management has become key to development of an information society, which is no longer a technical problem. It is already around us as part of today's economic, legislative, regulatory, social, political and ethical challenges to be addressed. It feeds on the New Information and communication technology, which removes geographic barriers and promote globalization of the economy and international cooperation between actors.

Notes

1 In this paper the term institution refers to multiple types of actors or organizations and or companies including corporations which are capable enough to interact in the international environment.
2 Seehttp://www.informaworld.com/smpp/title~content=t905451308~db= all accessed 10 May 2010.
3 Fayol's proposal, which include Planning, Organizing, Commanding, Coordinating and Controlling, has been useful since the dawn of 20th century.
4 See http://www.oup.com.au/titles/academic/business_and_economics/ business/9780199262069 accessed 12 May 2010.
5 See http://www.oup.com.au/titles/academic/business_and_economics/busi ness/9780199262069 accessed 2 May 2010.

6 See http://www.oup.com.au/titles/academic/business_and_economics/business/9780199262069 accessed 2 May 2010.
7 See http://www.routledge.com, accessed 2 May 2010.
8 See http://www.palgrave.com/products/title.aspx?is=0333682130 accessed 3 May 2010.
9 See http://www.idrc.ca/en/ev-34561-201-1-DO_TOPIC.html accessed 3 May 2010
10 See http://www.idrc.ca/en/ev-34561-201-1-DO_TOPIC.html accessed 3 May 2010..
11 See http://www.idrc.ca/en/ev-34561-201-1-DO_TOPIC.html accessed 4 May 2010.
12 See http://jmi.sagepub.com/cgi/content/abstract/14/1/31 accessed 5 May 2010.
13 See http://jmi.sagepub.com/cgi/content/abstract/14/1/31 accessed 5 May 2010.
14 Artificial Intelligence was born in the summer of 1956 at Dartmouth College in Hanover, New Hampshire.
15 See Woolf, A. *Artificial Intelligence (21st century Debates)*. Wayland. 2002.p.68.
16 See Lungarella, M., Iida. F., Bongard. J., Pfeifer. R. *AI in the 21st Century – With Historical Reflections*. University of Zurich.p.43.
17 See Waltz, E. *Knowledge management in the intelligence enterprise*. Artech House, 2003.p.73-76.
18 This refers to emissiosn of chlorofluorocarbons or CFCs that cause damage to the ozone hole. Nevertheless, the full extent of damage it has caused to the ozone layer is not quite clear yet.
19 See http://www.echeat.com/essay.php?t=26961 accessed 5 May 2010; see also http://www.tobacco.org/Documents/980126minnesota.htm accessed 5 May 2010
20 The study incorporates 20 Europe based top and terminal managers.
21 See http://www.french-paris.com/uk/adults/delf.phpDELF--Diplôme d'Etudes en Langue Française evaluates a candidate's language level, it also assesses the candidate's ability to communicate effectively in French.
22 The ethical tone or climate of organizations is set at the top. Organizations can also enhance an ethically-oriented culture by paying particular attention to principled organizational dissent. Principled organizational dissent is an important concept linking organizational culture to ethical behavior. Organizations committed to promoting an ethical climate should encourage principled organizational dissent instead of punishing such behavior. Also, Sims elaborates this issue in his article, 'The Challenge of Ethical Behavior in Organizations'.

23 A Personality is defined as totality of an individual's behavioral and emotional characteristics. Personality embraces a person's moods, attitudes, opinions, motivations, and style of thinking, perceiving, speaking, and acting. See http://www.infed.org/biblio/learning-organization.htm

24 Handy, however, had no preference for any of the four archetypes since they co-exit in most organizations. To reflect his point of view, he named the four cultures after ancient Greek gods who were worshipped simultaneously. The Handy model helps consultants and managers become aware of the different cultures within the client organization. Effective interventions must aim at striking a balance between the four cultures while remaining faithful to an organization's dominant culture.

References

Ackoff, R. L., "From Data to Wisdom", *Journal of Applies Systems Analysis*, Volume 16, 1989 p 3-9.

American Productivity & Quality Center. (2003). The *World Bank Profile: Best Practices in Knowledge Management*. Retrieved February 21, 2010, from http://www.researchandmarkets.co.uk/reportinfo.asp?report_id=42692

Barney, J. (1986). 'Types of Competition and the Theory of Strategy: Toward an Integrative Framework'. In: *Academy of Management Review*. Vol. II, no. 4. University of California.

Bellinger, G., (2004). *Data, Information, Knowledge and Wisdom*. Retrieved February 27, 2010 from Systems Thinking Web site: http://www.systems- think in-g.org/dikw/dikw.htm

Bergman, R. at al. (2000). *Management* 5th Ed. Coulter for sale. New Zealand

Bickerton, C.J. et al. (2007). *Politics without Sovereignty: A critique of Contemporary International Relations*. London: UCL Press

Bočakova, O. and Jakušová, V. (2009). Manažerstvo kvality v službách. In: *Siločiary: Odborný mesačník o ekonomike a politike,* VII. ročnik, č. 5. Bratislava: máj, 2009. s. 3-5.

Clerk, D., (2008, May 21). Maslow´s Hierarchy of Needs. Retrieved February 27, 2010 from Leadership & Human Behavior Web site: http://www.n wlink.com/~donclark/leader/leadhb.html

Clerk, D., (2009, September 3). 'Organizational Behavior'. Retrieved February 27, 2010 from http://www.nwlink.com/~donclark/leader/leadob.html

Collins, James C., & Porrar, Jerry R. (2009). 'Building Your Company's Vision' in : *HBR Onpoint Article,* accessable at: http://bookfiesta4u.com/?p=1302

Cummings, T. G., Worley, C.G. (2008). *Organization Development and Change*. Cengage Learning Publishers. Cambridge.

Davenport, T. „ Some Principles of Knowledge Managment": *Strategy Managment, Competiton*. Winter. 1996.

Fayol, Henri. (1949). *General and Industrial Management*. Pitman. UK.

Griffin, James. (2000). Value Judgment: Improving Our Ethical Beliefs. Oxford. OUP.
Handy, Charles B. (1976). Penguin. United Kingdom.
Hrivík, Pavol. (2009). Kľúčové factory a krutá realita v medzinárodných vzťahovh – prípad USA (Prípadová štúdia). In: *Siločiary: Odborný mesačník o ekonomike a politike,* VII. ročnik, č. 5. Bratislava: máj, 2009. s. 6-7.
Juza, P. Energetická bezpečnosť – geopolitická móda, alebo geopolitická nutnosť? In: *Slovgas: Odborný plynársky časopis*, XVII. ročník. Bratislava: december, 2008. s. 7-9.
Knowledge. (n.d.). Retrieved January 28, 2010, from http://www.nwlink.com/~Donclark/knowledge/knowledge.html
Liebowitz, J. *Knowledge Management (Handbook).* CRC Press. 1999.
Lungarella, M., Iida. F., Bongard. J., Pfeifer. R. *AI in the 21st Century – With Historical Reflections.* University of Zurich
Miller, Paul. (1998). *Mobilizing the Power of What You Know.* London: Random House.
Personality, (2007). Retrieved February 27, 2010 from Answers.com: http://www.infed.org/biblio/learning-organization.htm
Roos, J. Roos, G., Dragonetti, N.C. and Edvinsson, L. (1997). *Intellectual Capital: Navigating the New Business Landscape.* Macmillan Business Press, Basingstoke, pp.17-25.
RUSANOW, G.: Global Law Firm Knowledge Management Survey 2006. [elektronická verzia][cit. 5. 2.2008]. Dostupné na internete: http://www.llrx.com/node/1705/print
Sims, R. R., (1992 July). The Challenge of Ethical Behavior in Organizations. Retrieved February 27, 2010, from: http://construct.haifa.ac.il/~danielp/soc/sims.htm
Sechrest, Dale K. and Collins, W.C. (1989). Management and Liability issues. Springer Boston.
Sveiby, K. E. (1997, December 31). Tacit Knowledge. Retrieved February 2, 2010, from http://www.sveiby.com/articles/Polanyi.html
Štefančík, R. (2007). Ekonomická analýza volebného správania in: *Slovenská politologická revue.* Trnava: UCM. Pdf (1,2,2007), s.71-88
The Economist, December 1996.
Waltz, E. *Knowledge management in the intelligence enterprise.* Artech House, 2003.
Winch, G., McDonald, J. (1999). 'SMEs in an environment of change: computer-based tools to aid learning and change management'. In: *Journal of Industrial and Commercial Training.* Vol. 31. Issue 2. MCB UP Ltd.
Woolf, A. *Artificial Intelligence (21st century Debates).* Wayland. 2

APPENDIX

Appendix 1: **Fayol's four functions of management (Annex)**

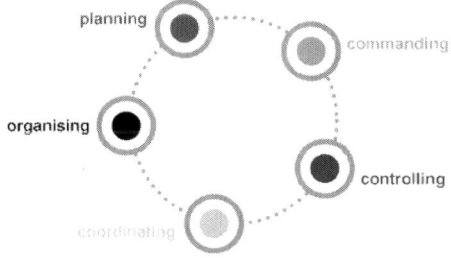

Source : http://www.rahulgladwin.com/henry-fayol-and-modern-management-theory

Appendix 2: **Distribution of world internet users (Annex)**

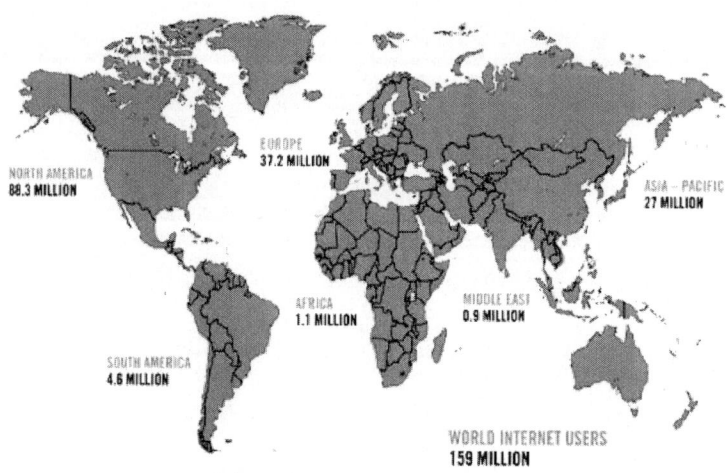

Source: http://www.idrc.ca/en/ev-34561-201-1-DO_TOPIC.htm

Appendix 3: **Mix of employees. The arrows indicate the direction of employee flow.**

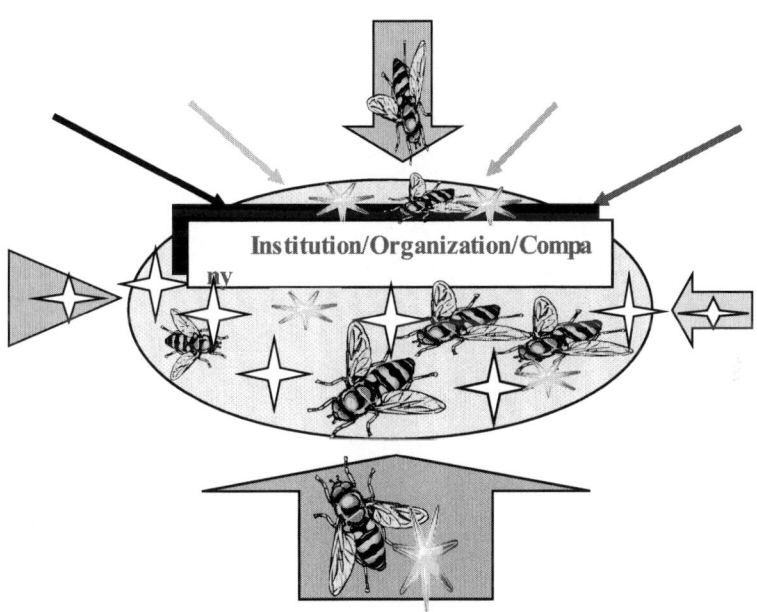

Source: Author's archive.

Appendix 4: **Actors' interaction and interdependence in contemporary international system**

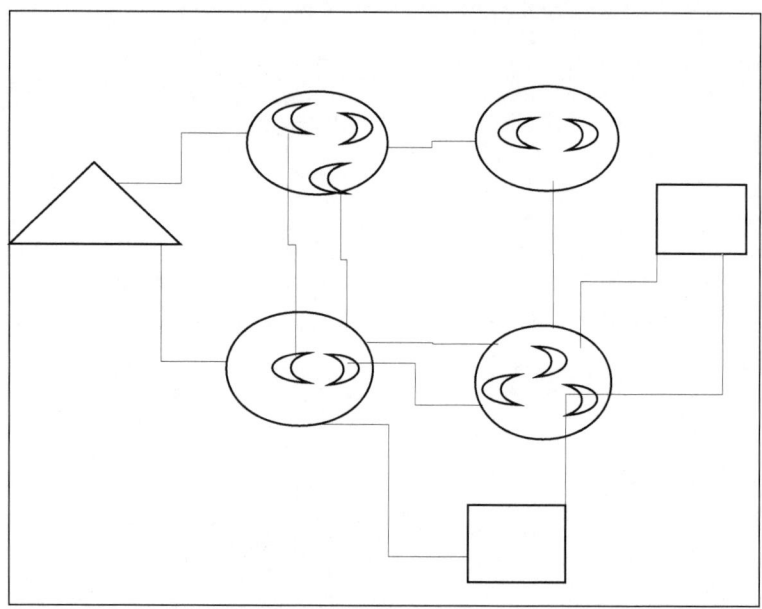

Source: Author's archive.

The figure in appendix 4 indicates the essence of complex interdependence, where interaction takes between states (ovals) and transnational corporation (squares) including international organization (triangle) such as United Nations Organization (UNO) and International monetary fund (IMF) but also between sub state organizations (crescents) such as towns and regions. In the picture, dotted double arrows indicate bilateral ties setting, that the actors involved influence the behavior of states, similarly like state influence them. Also, these actors mutually influence each other. They are autonomous actors and are not tools for states. They influence the authority of states differently than what the realists and neorealist have envisioned. The behavior of one state does not depend only on the behavior of other states. International organizations, transnational businesses and other aspects of international political economy appear to have significant influence, thus they need to be added in the international system of interaction.

Appendix 5: **The pretending elite model.** (an ordinary model with categories of élite)

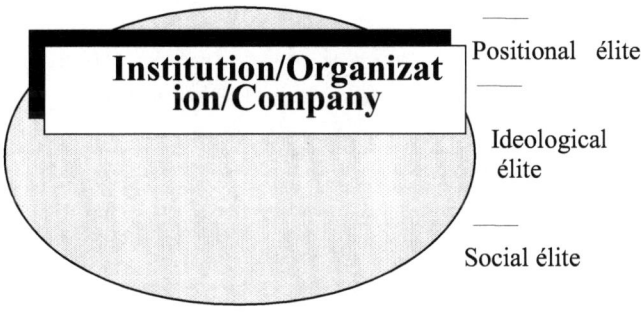

Source: Author's archive

75

Appendix 6: **Graph. The graph shows recent knowledge management practice** (the data is adapted from the source below)

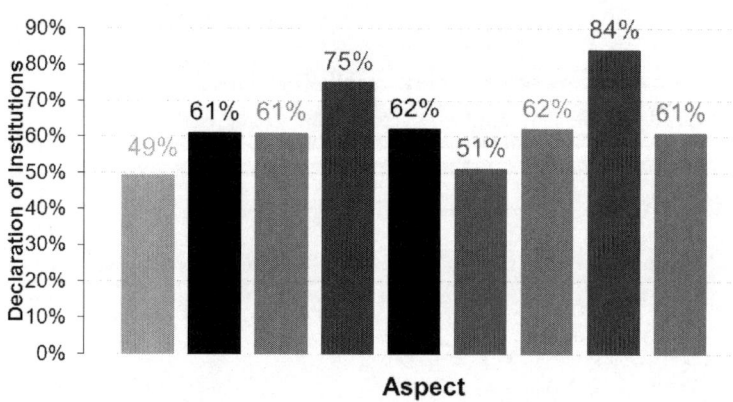

Source: http://casopisy.euke.sk/mtp/clanky/3-4-2008/4.mesaros-toma.pdf, 20.01.2010, 20:20

Explanation of the graph above:
- We use porofessional knowledge management (KM) development programs
- We apply hybrid approach of KM practice
- We prepare ahead a formally introduced strategy of KM
- We design a project earlier before application of KM
- We conduct business simulation prior application of KM
- Heads of department of KM are responsible for organizing KM
- Improving communication in other areas is important
- Institutional culture of the organization is supportive
- We are able to prove the aspects of our companies' KM to clients

Chapter 3
Ethics and Experimental Economics

Paweł Kuśmierczyk

Keywords: classic economics, utility theory, self-interest, economic models, ethics, free rider, fairness, economic agents

1. Introduction.

The classic economic theory describes an economic agent as a selfish, rational man whose all choices are aimed at maximization of his own preferences. The dominating model of human behavior is the expected utility theory according to which people choose goods and actions maximizing their (expected) utility function. By this definition no economic agent can take an action that would violate his system of preferences and bring him disutility. Theoretically even the altruistic acts can be explained by means of the expected utility theory if we assume the agent's utility function is also a function of goods consumed by other agents. Nevertheless in most applications of the theory a more self-interested version is being used.

The expected utility model has long been and still is the main model by which economists describe human behavior. But is it necessarily true? Can all human beings' acts be described according to this theory? And if there are violations, how often do they take place, and how much do they influence the economic reality? Is the *homo economicus* model the proper theory of human behavior or do some other motives influence human behavior? How big is the role of ethics on choices made by economic agents?

The theory of the rational, "unethical" man has its consequences in many economic models. But what has been realized was that the predictions of these models were often contradicted by behavior that by no means could be called self-interested. Let's look at some examples. First, it has been observed that people are far more willing to contribute money or time for the public good than the theory of selfish man would predict: public television successfully raises money from viewers to broadcast, charities receive enough contributions to carry on with their mission, people vote in elections, even though their vote has no chance of changing the elections' results. Also the voluntary reduction of water-use during droughts, the conservation of energy to help solve the energy crisis or many forms of voluntary labor show that people are motivated by more than just their own interest (Rabin, 1993).

The habit of tipping in restaurants is also difficult to explain within the rational man framework, especially when it is observed when dining in restaurants away from home, in a place never likely to be visited again (Dawes, Thaler, 1988). And what is most important, such "unexplainable" behavior can be observed not only in actions of individual consumers but also in actions taken by the companies; for example (Okun, 1981, p. 170) argues that ethics and fairness issues help explain why firms operate with backlogs in periods of shortages (e.g. automobiles), and why sport tickets are not priced to clear the market.

All the given examples are an important argument why issues of ethics became a matter of interest for the economists. In the sections that follow I will describe what economists mean by ethical behavior in economics, how do they experimentally study an importance of ethics for the actions taken, what are the results of this research, and how important are they for the theory of economics.

2. What does it mean to behave ethically and how can it be measured?

As has been argued ethics might influence the behavior of economic agents but what do we actually mean by ethical behavior? How to measure it? By definition ethics is a system of norms that influence human behavior, the system that is not necessarily fixed. Different societies, different cultures can have different ethical systems. In this sense to behave "ethically" means to behave in accordance with the norms of the given society. This definition doesn't unfortunately say anything about what are these norms. To measure if economic agents behave "ethically" using an experimental framework we need a more precise and simple definition that would let us discriminate between an "ethical" and "unethical" behavior.

One of the first definitions of this kind trying to establish a system of norms for the state's policy was proposed by (Rawls, 1971) who defined "the most just society" as the one which maximizes the welfare of its worst off members. This is a very demanding definition; according to Rawlsian understanding of justice, there actually exists no just society whatsoever and what's more the definition is useless if we wanted to valuate which of the two "unjust" systems is more "just". A bit more helpful definition is given by (Feldman, Kirman, 1974) who define a "fair state" as a one in which there is "no envy". They propose the following definitions: "A completely fair social state is one in which no citizen would prefer what another has to what he himself has; a relatively fair social state is one in which few citizens would prefer what others have to what they themselves have; a totally unfair state is one in which every citizen finds his position to be inferior to that of everyone else." (Feldman, Kirman, 1974, p. 995).

To describe a behavior of individuals which is taking into account some norms of social coexistence and doesn't only concentrate on self-interest different terms can be used: "ethical", "just", "fair". The first one is (as has already been mentioned) too vague and general, the second one is more appropriate in describing the state's policy. That's why when economists and psychologists try to depict individual behavior, which respects some social norms, they usually use the word "fairness". But what does it mean to behave "fairly"? How can we judge if a given behavior was "fair" or "unfair"?

In general, "fair" behavior is opposed to the selfish behavior of the *homo economicus* i.e. the behavior aiming at maximization of the agent's own interest. That's why for example (Fehr, Kirchsteiger, Riedl, 1993) simply associate "fairness" with deviations from self-interested behavior. But this still says rather little about what constitutes a "fair" behavior. If experimental economics is to find out how important the issues of "fairness" are in the process of decision making it needs more precise rules. Even though there is no unique definition of what is "fair", just as there is no unique definition of what is "ethical", there is a general agreement on some basic rules. For instance it is obvious for most people that if in some situation two parts of the deal have similar positions a "fair" trade will be an equal split of a potential surplus. That's why many studies test if people, when making economic decisions, really tend to divide the potential gains into equal parts.

In the paper by (Kahneman, Knetsch, Thaler, 1986) the authors used the form of questionnaire to find out what behavior is being named "fair" or "unfair" (the participants of the poll were to judge different real-life situations as "Completely Fair", "Acceptable", "Unfair", or "Completely Unfair"). As the authors put it: „The cardinal rule of fair behavior is surely that one person should not achieve a gain by simply imposing an equivalent loss on another." (Kahneman, Knetsch, Thaler, 1986, p. 731). The authors have presented examples of different economic situations to many groups, asking in every situation to give a judgment about a given decisions. The questions were mainly concerned with the situations of price or salaries setting and proved that people tend to judge "unfair" the actions of the agents making use of their stronger position to force their point of view. But the questionnaire also showed that whether an activity is called "fair" or "unfair" is strongly dependant on the reference point. For example decrease of the workers salaries by 7% in times of no inflation was called "Unfair" (by 62%), whereas increase of salaries by 5% in times of 12% inflation was called "Acceptable" (by 78%) (Kahneman, Knetsch, Thaler, 1986, p. 731). In terms of change of the real income this two situations are identical but human judgments about the "fairness" differ substantially.

It has to be underlined that "fair" behavior doesn't necessarily mean the same thing as "altruistic". The altruistic behavior is unconditional. To behave altruistically means to act as if to maximize the utility of the other person without any hope for reward or reciprocation. There is strong evidence that most people are not altruistic. But "fairness" doesn't necessarily mean that much. Most people declare themselves "fair". One of the aims of the experiments was to find out what people actually mean by that.

In order to find out how strongly the issues of "fairness" influence the decisions made by the economic agents, economists and psychologists carry out the laboratory experiments. Why is the laboratory setting used and why don't we just base our findings on the field results, i.e. real life observations? There are some good reasons. First of all, the observations from reality can be usually interpreted in many ways and not necessarily prove importance of "fairness" in human behavior. A good example of this kind of situation is given by (Clark, 1998, p. 709) who describes how in 1994 Greenpeace mobilized public support in European countries for a supplier boycott of paper products from clear-cut forests in Canada. The interpretation of the strong European reaction is not obvious. As (Clark, 1998, p. 709) puts it: "European indignation may have been caused by concerns over fairness: why should present consumers benefit from cheap paper while future generations lose access to old-growth forests? Alternatively, however, Europeans simply may have wished to preserve pristine travel destinations for themselves...". Of course the field observations are an important source of information but if we want to build precise economic models we need more unequivocal results. And that's the second good reason. The laboratory setting offers a possibility of a thorough examination of all potential explanations and aspects influencing the agent's decisions. Using laboratory experiments the researchers can control all the elements and repeat different variants of the task to check the real importance of every element.

Of course the environment of the laboratory classes is never the same as the real-life pressure but economists and psychologists do a lot to imitate the real-life conditions. The decisions to be made are thoroughly explained and the participants of the experiments are financially motivated to make decisions according to their real preferences. That's why the experimental economics became so popular in the recent years and why its findings have to be taken very seriously.

3. Results of the experiments

The experiments studying the importance of "fairness" for the economic theory went in many directions. Generally most laboratory experiments were concentrated on testing those economic models in which the assumption of selfishness plays an important role and leads to the strong and controversial conclusions.

Public goods experiments

The first group of these experiments was concerned with the provision of money for the public goods. Public goods are the special kind of goods in case of which no one can be excluded from beneficiating from them, even the individuals who haven't participated in financing them. The resulting phenomenon is known in economic literature as a *free rider problem*. A "free rider" is a person who achieves benefits thanks to the commitments of others, without providing any money or effort by himself. The classical economic theory claims that in case of public goods commitments every individual should behave as a "free rider", since this is always a winning strategy. Therefore no public good could ever be produced by free decision of individuals and the state is responsible for delivering it.

To test if people are really unwilling to participate in public projects economists and psychologists run tests in which participants have to decide about their engagement in some public project. The good (the project) they are financing is usually abstract, so as to exclude any possibility of subjectivity in participants' decisions. The experiment is normally constructed in such a way that it is in the best interest of the whole group to contribute all the money for the project but individually there is a strong temptation of acting as a "free rider". The decisions of each individual are taken independently and are unknown to any other participant. Compare also (Tamene-Matusovic, 2008), who confirm this finding, while stressing the innovative aspects necessary for further development that the whole process should reflect and incorporate.

In a paper by (Dawes, Thaler, 1988) there is an exhaustive summary of the results of many experiments of this kind. The authors also describe a standard procedure used in these experiments. Each subject is given a sum of money, that can be either kept or partially (or completely) invested in a "public good". The money invested from all participants is multiplied by a factor $k>1$ and divided into all participants. For example suppose all participants were given initially \$5 and $k=2$. Then if everybody contributes \$5 to the "public good" each ends up with \$10. This solution is the Pareto efficient allocation because no other allocation could make everyone better of. But each participant has a temptation of becoming a "free rider". For example if there were 4 participants and all but one contributed $5 and the last one kept all $5 for himself then the 3 participants would end up with $7,5 and the "free rider" would end up with $12,5 (the public good by it's definition is divided among all members of community and not only among the ones who participated in financing it) (Dawes, Thaler, 1988, p. 188). The classic theory of economics predicts that in this situation each participant will behave like a "free rider", which will lead to the not Pareto efficient allocation in which every participant ends up with an amount of $5.

One of the first results of the experiments of this kind was obtained by (Marwell, Ames, 1981) who found that about 40%-60% of potential money are contributed into the public good project. The 0% would mean that all participants behaved like "free riders" whereas 100% contribution would mean that everybody contributed all his money into the project. Definitely the results contradict the hypothesis that all agents act like "free riders" and cast a new light on the public good theory.

Even though (Marwell, Ames, 1981) obtained the similar results in many different groups, there was actually one laboratory group for which the results were different and whose behavior more resembled the "free rider" hypothesis. This group consisted of... economists for whom the contribution level was only 20%. That's why (Marwell, Ames, 1981) decided to name their paper: "Economists Free Ride, Does Anyone Else?" This leads to the hypothesis that economists are less likely to act "fair" which, if true, could have an important implications, as most of the companies are run by them. The hypothesis that economist are less likely to act "fair" has been actually studied by (Frank et al., 1993) who found proofs that studying economics really intensifies the willingness to selfishness. Nevertheless the results showing as little participation by economists as the ones obtained by (Marwell, Ames, 1981) haven't been obtained in other public good experiments.

The results proving that people are actually willing to contribute some amount of their money for the public good has been confirmed by many other researchers (compare for example (Dawes, Thaler, 1988) or (Clark, 1998)). But the paper by (Dawes, Thaler, 1988) also cites the results showing that the willingness to contribute money for the public goods drops quickly when the experiment consists of a several sessions. The participants of the experiments start with a "fair" behavior (contributing about 50% of their money into the public project) in the first sessions but in the final ones their contribution rate falls close to the "free rider" hypothesis level (only about 20% of all money is contributed in the last sessions). Does it contradict the "fairness" hypothesis? These results could lead to the conclusion (very convenient for the "old-school" economists) that observed "fairness" (contribution of money to the public projects) is only a matter of misunderstanding of some rules and that the economic agents under the real-life pressure quickly learn what their optimal strategy is. Unfortunately (for the "old-school" economists) this claim is not true. It has been observed that even well trained participants, who already had contact with these kind of public good experiments, always start with a "fair" behavior when enrolled in the experiment for the next time and then again start to contribute less and less money as the experiment unfolds. What is then the reason for such behavior?

The answer is given by (Andreoni, 1995) who ran a series of experiments to study in detail the motives responsible for the observed results. His experiments showed that the contribution to the public goods comes mainly from what he calls "kindness" and the observed decline in the rate of the contribution is due to "frustrated attempts at kindness" (Andreoni, 1995, p. 892). Other motives as "learning", "confusion" or "reputation building" have been contradicted by the experiments' results. This means that participants have a natural inclination to act "fairly" which weakens when observing "unfair" behavior of others. "Fairness" is not altruism and it has more to do with reciprocity. This point will be discussed more thoroughly later on.

Ultimatum game experiments

The second huge group of experiments concerned with "fairness" is so called *ultimatum game* experiments. An ultimatum game is a simple game in which two people are supposed to split a given amount according to the following rules: first a "proposer" offers some division and than the "decider" either accepts it or not. If the proposed split is accepted both people get the amounts according to the proposal. And if the proposal is being turned down by the "decider" there is no possibility of additional bargaining and they both get no money.

In standard laboratory procedure the game is anonymous, the participants don't know whom they're playing with, they are going to play with each other only once, and will never know who their partner was. They also normally keep the bargained amounts (or some part of it) so they should have a motivation to treat the experiment seriously. Suppose the participants of the game are given $10 to split among themselves. What should be the offer made by the "proposer"? The classical theory of self-interested man predicts that he should offer the "decider" as small as possible, let's say $9,5 for himself and $0,5 for the "decider". Because the "decider" can either accept it and gain $0,5 or turn it down in which case they both get $0, he will accept it (it's better to get $0,5 than nothing). This prediction of the classic economic theory differs from what is commonly accepted as "fair", i.e. an equal split of $5 for each participant.

The results of the experiments prove the classical economic assumptions wrong: people are much more willing to act "fair" than anybody would have expected. For example in the experiments carried out by (Kahneman, Knetsch, Thaler, 1987) as much as 76% of participating students decided to split money equally! As has been noted they had no chance of learning who their partner was so no possibility of, for instance, reputation building existed. Moreover, in cases when the "proposer" made an "unfair" offer, it was very often declined. People preferred to suffer a loss of getting no money at all than to agree for an "unfair" split in which they were for example offered only $1. These results also prove that people are not altruistic, as they didn't agree for the split in which their partners were to get most of the money (they preferred that they both got less!). Compare also (Thaler, 1988, Tamene, 2007) who summarize the results of many experiments confirming these findings.

Does this prove that people are simply so good that they sacrifice their own money in order to act "fairly"? Well, no, rules of "fairness" are more delicate. Equal split of money in the ultimatum game proves that people have a tendency to stick to a social rule of "fair" behavior, but more in a sense of reciprocity. As (Rabin, 1993, p. 1281) puts it: "Indeed, the same people who are altruistic to other altruistic people are also motivated to hurt those who hurt them. If somebody is being nice to you, fairness dictates that you be nice to him. If somebody is being mean to you, fairness allows – and vindictiveness dictates – that you be mean to him." People start with a "fair" behavior toward others because they believe it is the right thing and because they believe the others will behave in the same way. But if they happen to be treated "unfair" by others they react with the same. The "fair" behavior is not only the "right" thing to do but also the profitable one. If people understand the common rules of "fairness" they understand that if they make an "unfair" offer it might be turned down.

Thus rules of "fairness" resemble the "tit for tat" strategy in the repeated games of the Prisoner's Dilemma type. According to this strategy a player starts the game with a "fair" decision of "cooperation" and then repeats the last round move of his co-player. If his co-player "cooperates" all the time there is no need to renounce the "fair" moves of "cooperation" and both players use it till the end of the game. But if in any round the co-player chooses the "unfair" move of "fight" he'll be punished with the same in the next round. The "tit for tat" strategy is the strategy of reciprocity: I'll be good to you as long as you're good to me, but if you strike I'll strike back. As has been proved by (Axelrod, 1990), the "tit for tat" turns out to be the evolutionarily winning strategy in the repeated Prisoner's Dilemma game. This helps understand why rules of "fairness" became so widespread: evolution proved them right.

In this sense "fairness" has more to do with what people expect from each other than with altruism. As (Franciosi et al., 1995, p. 948) argues: "'fairness' in our context is best characterized as affecting agent expectations, not their utility functions". This explains why participants of repeated experiments often change their attitude throughout the experiments: it's not that they change their preferences; it's that they change their expectations of what others will do.

Other experiments

There are many other experiments testing the importance of "fairness" for the economic theory and functioning of markets. Most of them use the similar procedures and awesome variations of the described games. The paper by (Fehr, Kirchsteiger, Riedl, 1993) describes a labor market experiment that consisted of two phases. First, the group of "employers" offers the "wage" in the market, and then the "workers" who accept the "wage" are hired for a one period contract. After accepting the contract the "workers" set their "effort" level. The higher their "effort" levels the bigger the gains for the "employer" but the high "effort" level leads to a loss of the "worker's" welfare. The experiment consists of a series of repeated periods, in each of them the "workers" and the "employers" remain anonymous to each other and in every period the new offers can be posted and the new decisions taken.

Obviously in this setting the "employers" are interested in obtaining the maximum "effort" level for the minimum "wage" and the "workers" are interested in obtaining the maximum "wage" for the minimum "effort" level. Because of the way the experiment is constructed (first "employers" set the "wage" and then anonymous "workers" react with the "effort" level) the economic theory predicts that all "workers" choose the contracts with the maximum "wage" and then respond with the minimum "effort" level. The "employers" have no way of reacting with any "punishment" because they have no control over the "workers". In the end the "wage" and the "effort" should drop to the minimal levels.

But the results of the experiments were different. It turned out that "workers" who chose the high "wage" offers responded with high "effort" levels. Because the contracts were anonymous and one period long, this could not be explained by the reputation building (the "workers" could not gain by building a reputation of "high effort employee" because all the transactions were anonymous). The authors conclude that such behavior is a proof of significance of "fairness" in economic decisions making. The "workers" react with the high level of "effort" because they appreciate the high "wages" and find it proper to react with the same (the rule of reciprocity). The similar experiments carried out a couple of years earlier by

(Walker, Williams, 1988) didn't end with such strong evidence in favor of the "fairness" assumption.

An interesting group of experiments is the one consisted of the experiments which study if "fairness" is dependent on the scale of financial gains and losses that result from the decisions. A strong counterargument given by economists opposing the relevance of "fairness" assumption is that matters of "fairness" might influence agents' decisions but only when deciding about small amounts of money. In case of bigger amounts the "fairness" disappears and economic agents remind themselves of their true selfish nature. The results of many experiments studying the importance of the gains' level are described in (Rabin, 1993) who acknowledges that there is some evidence that "fairness" assumption plays the most important role in case of small financial incentives. Nevertheless Rabin, who is a strong protagonist of incorporating the "fairness" assumption into economic models, argues that even if this were true, "fairness" could still play an important role for the economic theories because many decentralized markets are the accumulation of minor economic interactions and so small individual changes can have a big aggregated effect (Rabin, 1993).

The importance of the level of potential gains or losses resulting from the "fair" behavior has been analyzed thoroughly by (Zwick, Chen, 1999). In the series of well-planned experiments they studied how "fairness" changes with the changes in the experiments settings. The results proved that the willingness to act "fairly" does depend on the level of potential gains resulting from the decisions. The authors conclude: „These findings indicate that „fairness" has a price, and the higher its price, the lower the "demand" for it. This suggests that demands for fairness are subject to cost-benefit evaluation, and are in this sense deliberate and well thought out." (Zwick, Chen, 1999, p. 822). There is often a trade-off between "fairness" and self-interest and "fair" behavior is chosen when it doesn't cost too much. As we can see again economic ethics is far from altruistic.

The described experiments are just a few from a long list, but they are good examples showing the way these kinds of studies are carried out and what their main results are. The next part discusses what the implications of these results for the economics are.

4. Importance of the results for the theory of economics

What conclusions can be drawn for the theory of economics from the results of the laboratory experiments? As has been shown even though people are not completely altruistic they do follow some ethic rules which have been named "fairness". The rules of "fairness" have been well summarized by (Rabin, 1993, p. 1282) in a form of three claims:

(A) People are willing to sacrifice their own material well-being to help those who are being kind
(B) People are willing to sacrifice their own material well-being to punish those who are being unkind
(C) Both motivations (A) and (B) have a greater effect on behavior as the material cost of sacrificing becomes smaller.

Such "fair" behavior can have a serious impact on some economic results and functioning of markets. As one of their conclusions (Kahneman, Knetsch, Thaler, 1986, p. 738) present the following proposition: "When excess demand in a customer market is unaccompanied by increases in suppliers' costs, the market will fail to clear in the short run." This result is a direct consequence of the studies on the importance of "fairness". In people's opinion increases in prices, which didn't result from the increase in costs, are "unfair", and because people are willing to punish "unfair" behavior some of them might not make a transaction in this case (even though it was beneficial for them in the light of classical economic theory). Such behavior has been observed in experiments by (Thaler, 1985). In the experiment participants had to assess the maximum price they would have paid for their favorite beer if it were to be bought in a luxury hotel (group A), or in a small grocery store (group B). Even though the beer was the same (the given favorite brand) the maximum accepted price of the beer from the hotel was substantially higher than the maximum accepted price of the beer from the grocery store ($2,65 compared to $1,50). This (in author's opinion) prove that the market might not reach the theoretical price because of matters of "fairness" (the price $2,65 won't clear the market because people won't buy for that much from the grocery store because they will find this price "unfairly" high).

One of the most often analyzed consequences of the "fairness" assumption is the situation of monopoly prices. As it is known from the microeconomics because of lack of competition monopolies can increase their price to a higher level, known as the monopoly price. But if we take into account the importance of "fairness" it turns out that monopolies cannot set their price as high as they wish because consumers might find it "unfair" and decide not to buy their product (see for example the discussion and examples in (Thaler, 1985), (Kahneman, Knetsch, Thaler, 1987) or compare (Rabin, 1993) who proves formally that incorporating "fairness" into economic theory leads to the results that monopolies should set the price below the theoretical monopolistic level).

Other market influences of the matters of "fairness" are suggested by (Kahneman, Knetsch, Thaler, 1986, p. 739) who claim that: "Price decreases will often take the form of discounts rather than reductions in the list or posted price". This is the consequence of their findings about the importance of the reference point. If the company lowered the price then after some time it would have problems with increasing it back, because such increase will be called "unfair" by the customers. Canceling out the discounts is on the other hand not considered "unfair", and so this form of temporary decrease is more convenient.

The issues of "fairness" have most applications in these fields which were analyzed throughout experiments, like labor economics (compare for example (Rabin, 1993)) or public and welfare economics. In this last field the economists are interested in assessing how issues of "fairness" should influence the state's policy. If, as it turns out, people pay attention not only to the final allocation of goods but also to the "fairness" of such allocation the state's policy cannot disregard it (compare for example (Zajac, 1995)).

Because scientific papers are presenting the results of more and more experiments and supporting observations from the real-life economy, the assumptions of "fairness" are slowly being incorporated into the economic models. This means that the level of "fairness" has started to be treated as one of the parameters of the mathematical models. A good example of such a work is a paper by (Rabin, 1993).

5. Conclusions and discussion

The theory of selfish rational man surely has its failures because human behavior is influenced by more subtle factors than the economists initially thought. Many observations and results of many experiments have shown that individuals in their decisions take into considerations some ethical values which can influence substantially the functioning of the markets. As it turns out this "ethical" system is well thought of and far from assumptions of altruism. The economic agents' "ethics" is the "ethics of fairness". And this "fairness" turns out to be quite profitable. Neither consumers nor companies stick to it without a reason. As (Franciosi et al., 1995, p. 947) puts it: "The long-term result (hidden form the average consumer) may actually build the market power of the large firms, reduce competition and decrease welfare: all in the good name of 'fairness'".

Not all economists are fond of incorporating "fairness" assumption into the economic theory. Some of them believe that the results of the experiments on "fairness" can be explained within the standard economic framework and that the observed "fair" behavior results either from some misunderstandings on the participants' part or from the long-run self-interest (e.g. building of the reputation). Of course this reasoning is right to some extent but on the other hand as long as the experiments on "fairness" assumption help us understand better some rules of human behavior they should be carried out.

To understand properly the way the "fairness" "works" more studies and theoretical analyzes are needed. So far, economists and psychologists have discovered some basic rules. We are still far from understanding all the nuances of human behavior but the results of the experiments on "fairness" have gotten us a bit closer to it. What seems to be unquestionable is that people are neither completely selfish nor completely altruistic. The truth about human nature lies somewhere in between. People do take into account the issues of "fairness" when making their decisions but at the same time they take into account its price. What is this price, i.e. when people are willing to act "fairly" and when will they behave more selfishly is the subject of further work of the experimental economics.

A good summary of how "fairness" "works" can be an example by (Dawes, Thaler, 1988, p. 195): „In the rural areas around Ithaca it is common for farmers to put some fresh produce on a table by the road. There is a cash box on the table, and customers are expected to put money in the box in return for vegetables they take. The box has just a small slit, so money can only be put in, not taken out. Also, the box is attached to the table, so no one can (easily) make off with the money. We think that the farmers who use this system have just about the right model of human nature. They feel that enough people will volunteer to pay for the fresh corn to make it worthwhile to put it out there. The farmers also know that if it were easy enough to take the money, someone would do so." Economists can still learn a lot by observing the human behavior.

References

Andreoni J. (1995). Cooperation in Public-Goods Experiments: Kindness or Confusion? *The American Economic Review*, Vol. 85, No. 4, pp. 891-904.
Axelrod R. (1990). *The Evolution of Co-operation* (Penguin Books).
Clark J. (1998). Fairness in Public Good Provision: An Investigation of Preferences for Equality and Proportionality. *Canadian Journal of Economics*, Vol. 31, No. 3, pp. 708-729.
Dawes R. M., Thaler R. H. (1988). Anomalies: Cooperation. *Journal of Economic Perspectives* Vol. 2, No. 3, pp. 187-197.
Fehr E., Kirchsteiger G., Riedl A. (1993). Does Fairness Prevent Market Clearing? An Experimental Investigation. *The Quarterly Journal of Economics*, Vol. 108, No. 2, pp. 437-459.
Feldman A., Kirman A. (1974). Fairness and Envy. *The American Economic Review*, Vol. 64, No. 6, pp. 995-1005.
Franciosi R., Kujal P., Michelitsch R., Smith V., Deng G. (1995). Fairness: Effect on Temporary and Equilibrium Prices in Posted-Offer Markets. *The Economic Journal*, Vol. 105, No. 431, pp. 938-950.

Frank R. H., Gilovich T. D., Regan D. T. (1993). Does Studying Economics Inhibit Cooperation? *Journal of Economic Perspectives*, Vol. 7, pp. 159-171.

Kahneman D., Knetsch J. L., Thaler R. H. (1986). Fairness as a Constraint on Profit Seeking: Entitlements in the Market. *The American Economic Review*, Vol. 76, No. 4, pp. 728-741.

Kahneman D., Knetsch J. L., Thaler R. H. (1987). Fairness and the Assumptions of Economics In Hogarth R. M., Reder M. W. (ed.), *Rational Choice. The Contrast between Economics and Psychology* (pp. 101-116) (Chicago: The University of Chicago Press).

Marwell G., Ames R. (1981). Economists Free Ride, Does Anyone Else? *Journal of Public Economics*, Vol. 15, No 3, pp. 295-311.

Okun A. (1981). *Prices and Quantities: A Macroeconomic Analysis* (The Brookings Institution).

Rabin M. (1993). Incorporating Fairness into Game Theory and Economics. *The American Economic Review*, Vol. 83, No. 5, pp. 1281-1302.

Rawls J. (1971). *A Theory of Justice* (Harvard University Press).

Thaler R. H. (1985). Mental Accounting and Consumer Choice. *Marketing Science* Vol. 4, pp. 199-214.

Thaler R. H. (1988). Anomalies: The Ultimatum Game. *Journal of Economic Perspectives*, Vol. 2, pp. 195-207.

Walker J. M., Williams A. W. (1988). Market Behavior in Bid, Offer, and Double Auctions: A Re-examination. *Journal of Economic Behavior and Organization* Vol. 9, pp. 301-314.

Zajac E. (1995). *Political Economy of Fairness* (MIT Press).

Zwick R., Chen X.-P. (1999). What Price Fairness? A Bargaining Study. *Management Science*, Vol. 45, No 6, pp. 804-823.

Chapter 4
The Need for Upgraded Forecasting Methods

Jana Gašparíková[1]

Abstract

This paper focuses on upgrading research methods in economics, and suggests the importance of using additional qualitative methods, not only in what is the subject of investigation, but also the field of forecasting. The major step in developing this idea is enumeration of different qualitative approaches, which are typical for forecasting including methods resulting from those approaches. In the process of compiling this paper, the grant from VEGA[2] has been very helpful.

Keywords: development strategy, globalization and regionalization, qualitative methods, quantitative methods, systematic approach, participative approach, scenarios

Introduction

If we want to deal with the future, we must think about research methods we can use, whether the research increases levels of certainty in the fields of investigation - or, to the contrary, whether it causes more uncertainty. The multidimensionality of overall reality, dictates we need to use special approaches concerning how to investigate reality, because we need to accept not only future forecasts of reality investigated, but also its multidimensionality. It is not possible to achieve this without oscillation between different diversities in thinking, and of course between qualitative and quantitative methods.

In the wake of exploring the future, it is also necessary to find a balance concerning the use of qualitative and quantitative methods. It is necessary to explain how and when we use qualitative and quantitative methods. There are two broad categories of forecasting techniques: quantitative methods and qualitative methods. Qualitative methods are based on educated guessing, while quantitative methods are based on algorithms of varying complexity. They come in two types: time series methods and explanatory methods. I wish to apply the use of qualitative and quantitative methods concerning the future overall, on real investigative cases concerning economic issues. Therefore, the paper will attempt to follow the logic of the author's investigation as the author will concentrate on the necessity of using qualitative methods in the area of economic investigation. On the other hand, it will use qualitative methods in the areas of forecasting.

This process starts with applying the view that use of qualitative methods in forecasting goes hand in hand with use of qualitative methods in the study of economics. This reality is consistent with the statement that economic research also changes, and these changes by themselves indicate a shift to more „qualitative issues". We will describe and depict some of these issues, which alter economic research significantly nowadays.

Application of Qualitative Approaches to Economic Research

In the 1980s, strategic focus on development shifted from microeconomic to macroeconomic policies and, in particular, to adjustment of fiscal imbalances and monetary policies. Given the existing macroeconomic imbalances, it was impossible for markets to function, or at least function well. (Stiglitz,J 2003).

Now, the critical feature of each of these development imbalances was that development itself was a technical problem requiring technical solutions: better planning, algorithms, better trade, FDI, and pricing policies, and better macroeconomic frameworks. There was no attempt to focus on the economic, social, developmental, or cultural substance of society, nor was there a belief in such a participatory approach (e.g. of civil society), as in the decision-making process itself not being considered necessary.

These scientific laws were not bound by space and time. Little attention was paid to institutional constraints or cross-cultural value differences. The situation is different in recent times, as the world economy is now inclined to more abrupt collisions and changes nowadays. Successful transformation of society depends also on **development strategy.** In this sense, it is necessary to concentrate not only on quantitative methods offering different comparisons of GDP in different countries, but to compare different tendencies and scenarios taking into account positive and negative impacts of globalization of the world economy.

These scenarios can be regarded as investigative qualitative methods offering us a multidimensional and more accurate picture of reality. They ought to reveal the real interests of people and the background of events, which influence development strategies, and resulting natural abrupt collision and change as such also.

The other reason for accepting the importance of qualitative methods concerning investigation of economic models is the reality indicating equivalence between market socialism and capitalistic economies, which were both fundamentally misguided. This is partly so because they did not properly acknowledge the larger role of institutions, and partly because they did not grasp the important interface between economic transactions narrowly defined, and the broader goals and values of society.

Development strategy goes hand in hand with institutional infrastructure, and that is why modern economics needs an investigation of **institutional infrastructure**. Institutional elements are necessary for effective participation in decision making and, as an essential part of successful development in transformation of society. It is very obvious that standard theorems of economics emphasize an economy, which needs private property, competition (Nemcová, 2006), and appropriate legal infrastructure within which markets function properly. All economic institutions can be influential as both sources of macro stability and excessive government deficits. Compare also (Tamene, G., 1999, p.5), who confirms the argument of this paper, while emphasizing mainly the case of Sub-Saharan Africa.

Globalization and Regionalization

We are entering an age of **global** alliance between different forms of capitalism (Šarmír, Eduard, 2005), where to better advance one's own economic objectives, individuals, enterprises, governments and other non-market institutions need to cooperate with each other in a wide variety of ways. We have therefore witnessed to date huge growth in all forms of inter-firm coalitions and inter-governmental agreements, etc.

New actors have emerged in the form of cross border businesses, led by organizations such as the International Business Leaders Forum and World Business Forum for Sustainable Development, as well as many at national levels to forge collaboration in good overall practice. Inter-governmental organizations, such as the OECD, the United Nations through its UN Global Compaq and the World Bank, have become a force to emphasize the value of corporate citizenship.

Regionalism in this sense does not mean lack of ability to achieve independently of others, but regionalism may equally undermine or enhance policy autonomy, depending on the context and policy priority at issue. For instance, a country suffering loss of policy independence and hence state capacity as a consequence of deepening global neoliberalism might be able to restore this capacity by forming a regional agreement. (Beran, V.-Dlask, P.-Frková, J.- Tománková, J.- Nivenová, R. 2004).

Comprehensive development strategies must identify the most important distortions in the economy-particularly regarding entrepreneurial experience, and in particular regarding full accounting of social cost and distributional impact of overall policies. Accordingly, the ingredients that make up economic management need to be both more comprehensive and more institutionally oriented than traditional plans, which focused largely on liberalization, privatization, and macro-stability. As far as regional and municipal problems are concerned, regional strategies must go hand in hand with community level orientation. At each level, the strategy must be consistent with capabilities and needs of institutions in the economic environment, which is embedded with societal norms and values (Tamene, G., 2006, p. 143).

It is important to build economic openness in a country, which is in tandem with development strategy. The evidence suggests that opening up to the outside world leads to many changes in different economic factors, as for instance an improvement in the technology of production. We understand that under technology there is a broad, special concept, with technology meaning anything affecting how inputs transform into outputs, including market and non market institutions and modes of organizing production, the so called soft ware and hard ware of technology. Trade is also one of the most important vehicles that reduce discrepancies in development.

In all cases, governments and international agencies should seek to construct not just good policies, but also a sense the process by which policies are devised is in itself fair and open. Economic development must be connected with political applications, and these applications go hand in hand with moral and ethical background, and qualitative methods (Tamene, 2004, p. 382).

Qualitative Methods in Forecasting

Qualitative research in forecasting insists on the integrity of its work and variety of its strategies. These strategies reflect the contested and eclectic nature of qualitative research as an interdisciplinary research, spanning a variety of methodological variations. The validity of such research is offered by witnesses through the researcher's credibility and satisfaction using normative standards.

To understand the main idea "between certainty and uncertainty" means to find a balance for objective investigation and more subjective policy making, along with strategic acting and shaping of the future. In this way we can understand the use of quantitative methods as tools for objective modeling, with qualitative methods used especially in forecasting as fundamental to shaping a future with specialized areas and understandings of the globalizing economy. Each offers its own particular challenges, especially regional ones. Equally important, the geographic radius of the market place, through such means as commerce, travel, and the internet, is now covering institutions from more diverse ideologies, social structures, and cultures than before. Secondly, the critical engine of wealth in today's economy is human capital, and not only as a primary source of innovation, entrepreneurship, and upgrading of managerial and organizational expertise, but also of ideals and moral values. (Stiglitz, J. 2003).

The Importance of Qualitative Methods for Forecasting

Qualitative methods must reconstruct not only tendencies in future development of a changing economic world or economic region, but also in the real status quo of problems being investigated. In a globalizing new world, it is necessary to investigate problems through use of qualitative methods - without which we will lose the larger dimensions of reality.

Qualitative methods are very hard to capture via simplified indicators, or where such data are not available. In addition, various forms of creative thinking are encouraged by such qualitative approaches as brainstorming, utopian writing, and science fiction. Methods for working systematically with qualitative data are becoming more widely available with the development of information technology - tools for mind mapping or conversation analysis etc.- which can also be helpful devices for facilitating new approaches.

For many years, the development of qualitative methodologies in social sciences as well as in forecasting lagged behind that of quantitative approaches. There has thus been an explicit and implicit reliance on a so-called expert figure to pull together the strands of qualitative analyses and come up with a synthesis by more or less intuitive means. In the last decade this situation improved considerably, and a great many tools, often computer based for capturing and analyzing qualitative data, and processing and representing results of such analyses, have become available.

Qualitative approaches also involve some quantitative elements

Equally important also is the reality surrounding factors that need to be taken into account, which may be captured and grouped according to their frequency. For example, this would be in different types of scenarios or via the use of computer conferencing techniques. Also, quantitative judgments will necessarily inform quantitative activities - the definition of parameter, the interpretation of quantitative activities, the interpretation of a questionnaire, etc. It is not possible to investigate the future without using quantitative methods, which means comparing certain sets of data. Without this we will lose fixed reality structures, which means investigation will then depend on collection of statistical data. If we want to understand for instance a regional economy, we must also rely on different types of data in regional sub-contexts.

Quantitative methods

Qualitative methods place heavy reliance on the numerical representation of development. They have considerable advantages, such as the ability to examine rates and scales of change, engagement in basic accountancy, certain types of testing, and consistency of different elements of the whole. They also have notable disadvantages: a limited grasp of many important social and political variables, dangers of spurious precision, etc.

Quantitative methods come in two main types: time-series methods and explanatory methods. Time-series methods make forecasts based purely on historical patterns in data. Perhaps the most important issue differentiating the approaches is that qualitative methods still remain less documented rather than the quantitative ones. This is particularly true of some newer computer based methods for group work. Expert based techniques are very important in this sense, as they seek to articulate views about the future, and of trends and contingencies that may arise, as well as alternative futures. The approach may involve large scale surveys of opinion (such as Delphi), or much smaller and more detailed elaboration of vision (such as cross-impact analysis, scenario workshops, etc.).

Recent research has clearly shown that projects with higher levels of participation are more successful, probably partly because those projects make assumptions about the needs and capabilities of beneficiaries. One of the reasons is that policymakers can have better understanding of which incentives are necessary. Equally important, institutions, incentives, participation and ownership, can be viewed as complementary development tools.

Validity of Forecasting Qualitative Methods

Forecasting methods are extremely important for making decisions in policy making, with innovative assumptions and outcomes, and for development strategies, etc. The main thematic areas of such foresight are still technology trends on one hand, and market trends on the other. We still very often as well forget to use broader social, political, or regional aspects, which are also necessary to forecast.

Special forms of classification concerning actual foresight activities are, in terms of broad coverage, the following: a) holistic foresight is concerned with the entire spectrum of science and society; b) macro-levels, such as foresight that covers a range of disciplines; c) meso-level, i.e. foresight relating to a single scientific field, technological area, or product range, and d) micro-level, i.e. foresight for a specific research project or product (Becker Patrick:, October 2002)

Reflections of Qualitative Approaches in Qualitative Dimensions and Forecasting

Qualitative methods offer a picture influenced by **development strategy**, because development strategies focus more on the broader vision, including entry into new technologies or industries. The process of constructing a development strategy may itself serve a useful function in helping to build a consensus. This would be not only regarding a broad vision of the country's future and key short and medium term objectives, but also about some of the essential ingredients for achieving those goals as well. Consensus building is not only an important part of achieving political and social stability (and avoiding the economic disruption that comes when claims on a societies resources exceed the amount available), but also leads to credibility of policies and institutions, which in turn enhances likelihood of their overall success. To be truly effective, any role for government in becoming a catalyst for overall development will need to embrace the much larger goal of encouraging society as a whole.

The participatory attitude is also very important for this approach (Gavigan, Scapolo, 2001). It means on one hand more objective validity and transparency, because it also reflects the interests of issues investigated and involvement of interested parties with problems being dealt with. Qualitative methods depend as well on discussion of interested parties, and are connected with the practical side of problems being investigated.

These include how such problems connect with their actual realization and decision making issues overall. Specifically, decision making problems are in line with the above-mentioned realities overall, which is why there is more positive inclination for qualitative methods, meaning a more participatory approach and objective validity. The participatory approach helps to guarantee integrity of the investigation to make certain we apply such methods, as we must be sure how many people take part in this presentation. The integrity of participatory methods can be understood from two points of view: first, there is long-term investigation based on understanding of different trends in development, and second, the follow-through of strategy concerning previous development. The output of this participatory approach is in conjunction with determination of different types of problems, as for instance in finding a strategy and working out official action statements. The other very important point helping to systematize knowledge resulting from the participatory approach, is sharing common values among all participants if such an approach is based on short-term investigation. If the participatory approach is used by an enormous number of people (using sin con methodology or charted methodology), (Potuček, 2006), the output of this participatory approach is also very interesting: the understanding of different values and interests shared by different participants. If we wish to understand the entire spectrum of economic development, it is especially important that there be a **holistic attitude**. This attitude influences the general view on problems being forecast. Different problems often look like they are identical from different aspects, but this is not so, because they are influenced by interests of different groups of people. In investigating such problems, we must take into account its multidimensionality, and the possibility of finding balance and truth in such multidimensionality. Globalization and regionalization are also in link with the systematic approach (Norberg, 2006). This approach helps by investigating problems in a new perspective. In this way, it is necessary to accept the phenomenon of time and space, as all such processes are realized in a certain time and space, and are influenced as well by time and space.

This type of investigation is not objective, but rather subjective. Among different time series and space regions are the creation of different types of relations, whereby this complexity is also connected with much variety. The substance of this approach reveals it is not possible to come to a universal or general assessment very quickly. It is necessary to use different types of generalization for comparison of different levels of investigations. Behind this complexity, it is also necessary to see goals and interests of people who are actors in these complex processes. Without knowing the hidden interests or purposes of these processes, it is difficult to reveal the real dimensions of complexity of such systems. All those hidden purposes and interests need to interact during their entire period of existence with this system. Due to their interactions, we can identify relations among them. In order to identify different relations and factors, which are the most substantial in a system, it is necessary to identify basic boundaries of such a system. One very important phenomenon helping to identify those boundaries and relations within these systems are different types of models.

The **Model of system dynamics** is one of the very widely used models, and the founder of this system, Jay W. Forrester, developed this method and gained popularity. It is necessary to take into account all relevant factors, and try to find different types of relations in these factors. Using this method, it is also very appropriate to use quantitative methods, because with such assistance, we can reduce very often, many false interactions. On the other hand it can also help us find more simple interactions inside a system, and the possibility of all reduced elements interacting among themselves, and creating a dynamic system.

The other very important approach is in link with **mind mapping** – which is in link with building alternative scenarios. The approach called mind mapping is the substance of the futures wheel: a very important procedure trying to distinguish primary, secondary, tertiary etc. impacts of different systemic changes regarding the future, such as concerns for instance different globalization trends.

Other very important procedural methods or approaches are **scenarios,** which are complex stories about possible and alternative futures. Those stories combine descriptions of a certain future status with descriptions of a real situation in a given investigated field, and concern different developmental and strategic relations, which illustrate political decisions and their results. Scenarios do not mean unambiguous future forecasts; instead they are more about ways to manage different alternatives about a future. Specifically, we use scenarios in that sense when past and present do not offer an unambiguous future. Scenarios help us systematically investigate, form, and control long-term strategies, policies, and plans.

The important thing is to develop more scenarios in a way to concentrate on different conditions for creating a new future. Behind such qualitative methods, there is always the possibility to use the outputs of these methods and approaches for working out strategies and decision making processes. This includes active participation of people in creating a new future - in this way also concerning and including the study of economic problems and problem solving.

Do upgraded research approaches intertwine with certainty?

The unique position and reputation of quantitative methods concerning scientific oriented studies as such, is a little uncertain at this time. This is because of the sense their unambiguous position in reaching objective certainty in science is now more modified, thus qualitative methodology has the same ambition to be more effective in depicting reality with great certainty.

The dilemma that concerns certainty and uncertainty is in tandem with understanding certainty as an approach based on participatory, dynamic, and systems qualification oriented study. We can also follow how objective certainty is more stable in this context with its so-called subjective, participatory approach. This approach is guaranteed by operating in a more ethical domain, as you can see and follow in many works of famous economists-as for instance Stiglitz. (Stiglitz, J., 2003). Also, Tamene in his article confirms the findings of this work (Tamene, G. 2007, p. 133; 2008, p. 111). These approaches are somehow linked with approaches in the field of forecasting, as qualitative methods are also being used there.

The ambition of this paper is not to enumerate on all forms of qualitative methods, but to elaborate on in a systematic manner their shared importance, which could be useful for depicting and analyzing the future in economic research.

Notes

1 Jana Gašparíková, is an employee of the Institute for Forecasting, AS, Šancová 56,811 05 Bratislava I., Slovak Republic, e-mail: progjari@savba.sk.
2 This paper was made possible through grant VEGA No. 2/6027/6, entitled: Globalization, Regionalization and Entrepreneurial Environment (perspectives and strategies for development), and COST A-22 Foresight Methodologies- Exploring New Ways to Explore the Future.

References

Becker, Patrick: Corporate Foresight in Europe.(2002): A First Overview. Institute for Science and Technology Studies, University of Bielefeld, Germany, October 2002. (Working paper)

Beran, Václav - Dlask, Peter- Frková, Jana -Tománková, Jarmila -, Nivenová Renáta (2004): The Evaluation of Regions and Structures in Relation to Sustainable Development: In: Proceedings of Workshop 2004, Prague, CTU, 2004, volume B.p.1068-1069.

Gavigan, James-Scapolo, Fabiana (Eds) (2001): A Practical Guide to Regional Foresight. For Regional Development Network. European Commission, Jopint Research Centre, Sevilla 2001.

Nemcová Edita (2006): Nové trendy vo vývoji priemyselnej politiky – hľadania nových stratégií v období globalizácie a zintenzívnenia konkurenčného boja.. Prognostický ústav SAV, Bratislava 2006,23.s.

Norberg, Johan: Globalizace.Praha, Alfa Publishing 2006.

Potuček, Martin (ed.). (2006): Manuál prognostických metod. Sociologické nakladatelství Slon, Praha 2006.

Stiglitz, J. (2003): Towards a New Paradigm of Development In:.Making Globalization Good. The Moral Challenges of Global Calitalism edited by John H.Dunnung, Oxford 2003.p.76

Šarmír, Eduard (2005): Súčasný globalizačný proces a premietnutie jeho implikácií v dlhodobom prognózovaní ekonomiky.Prognostický ústav SAV, Bratislava 2005, s.33.

Tamene, G. (1999). Demokratické zmeny súčasnej Afriky, in: *Politické Vedy II*. UMB Banska Bystrica and SAV Bratislava. Pp. 5-45.

Tamene, G. (2004). 'Globalization and Progress. The Impact on Central European Regions'. In: Sergi B.S.; Bagatelas, W. T. (Eds.). *Ethical Implications of Post-Communist Transition Economics and Politics in Europe*. Bratislava, Iura Edition, 2004, pp. 381-396. ISBN 80-8078-045-5.

Tamene, G.(2006). "Problems of Development Aid in Sub-Saharan Africa." In: *Development Aid – Rozvojová pomoc*. University of Economics, Faculty of International Relations in Bratislava. Bratislava, EKONÓM Publishers, pp. 136-152.

Tamene, G. (2007). "Political Ethics and the Human polity – The African Dimension". In: Sergi, B. S. and Bagatelas, T.W. (Eds.): *Economic and Political Development Ethics: Europe and Beyond*. Bratislava, Iura Edition, pp.103-134.

Tamene, G. & Matušovič, M. (2008). Globalna ekonomika ako zdroj pokroku a inovácií. In: *Nová teorie ekonomiky a management organiyací*, sborník z medzinárodní vědecké conference. Nakladatelství Oeconomica—2008, Praze. ISSN 978-80-2451403-1

Chapter 5
Trying Something New: The Role of Civil Society through the US Millennium Challenge Corporation's development assistance to Ukraine

Juhani Grossmann

1) Abstract

This paper focuses on the recently established new role of Civil Society concerning development assistance issued through the United States Millennium Challenge Corporation (MCC). It briefly discusses the MCC approach to development aid, especially its indicator-driven innovations in the general context of development assistance. Three types of civil society organization (CSO) engagement are reviewed: indicator creation, in-country project design and implementation, and board membership and ongoing consultation. Finally, a conclusion about the degree of interaction and its effectiveness to date is made.

Keywords: civil society, MCC, non-state actors, development assistance, modus operandi, legitimacy, eligibility, corruption control

2) Introduction and Background

"[G]overnance refers to the development of governing styles in which boundaries between and within public and private sectors have become blurred." (Stoker, 1998 p. 17) Traditionally, these have been a virtual monopoly of the state, but an increasing share of governing one's society has been implemented by non-state actors. On the domestic government side, this is an extremely common process. Even in the traditionally conservative field of international development assistance, however, this theme has taken foot. As Ann Florini (1999) points out, "states increasingly have to share authority in the international arena with a range of different non-state actors." (p.28)

The Millennium Challenge Corporation actively utilizes new forms of governance. Its aim is the decrease of poverty in low and middle-low income countries, in line with the Millennium Development Goals. It does so through an approach that is radically different from other development agencies: countries that show promise and perform well from a governance reform perspective receive substantial financial support to boost their initial successes. This sum is usually up to half a billion USD for the larger countries. The idea is that those countries who go through the necessary governance reforms will utilize funds more effectively. If funding is conditional upon performance, the obvious question becomes how objectively "performance" is defined.

This time, the definition is not chosen by the government itself, but by a group of research institutions and NGOs. Their annually published indicators have to reach a certain level for a specific country to become an eligible recipient of MCC assistance. Furthermore, NGOs are often engaged in measuring effectiveness of the aid, especially in so-called "threshold" programs. The paper surveys the novelty of the approach, compares it to similar previous efforts, with feedback from the first 4 years of MCC operation.[1]

3) The MCC – systems and approaches

Traditionally, development assistance is heavily dependent on political importance attached to a certain country. This has led to much cynicism about the US financing corrupt dictators around the world who receive tremendous cash inflows, while struggling countries seriously trying to reform themselves receive insufficient support.

While US government departments and agencies that conduct development work, first and foremost USAID, have long been operated with performance indicators, a large portion of development work is notoriously difficult to quantify. Funding decisions were often unclear to the principals and difficult to justify to the American public, which as a result "appear[s] to have an innate antipathy to transferring resources to foreigners" (Bacchus, 2004. p. 57).

The effectiveness of foreign aid is often criticized: "Fifty years of failure have demonstrated that foreign assistance more often harms than helps." (Bandow, 1999). Development assistance as a result, has been subject to much pressure to increase its effectiveness. Two opposing trends have been prominent in this process: closer ties to supporting political aims on one hand, and greater independence for development professionals concerning priorities to ensure sustainable growth, on the other. The MCC represents an interesting middle ground between these two concepts: while created during a time when development assistance was streamlined to be in line with political priorities (the so-called "F process"[2]) as reflected in its general structure, the individual assistance disbursements are explicitly separated from political decision-making, and can thus only indirectly assist political goals. Only the deep involvement of independent judges (CSOs) makes this possible. In some ways, civil society here charts a parallel course to the processes noted by Salamon and Anheier (1999): "...civil society organizations have become strategically important partners in the increasingly urgent search for a "middle course" between dominance of the market and dominance of the government" (Quoted in Schuppert, 2006)

Understanding that "foreign aid can't buy reform" (Bandow 1999), the US government in 2004, however, decided to try and find ways to encourage the reform process. The result is a progressive formula: a combination of nascent reforms and a sufficiently-sized "carrot" with clear and transparent conditionality. The Millennium Challenge Corporation was created to implement this vision. It is this formula that allows the Brookings Institution (2008) to refer to the MCC as the "outstanding innovation of the eight-year presidency of George W. Bush." (p.1)

The MCC is based in Washington, led by a CEO and overseen by a Board of Directors consisting of principals of the US government that deal with foreign policy: State, Treasury, USAID, and Trade Representatives, and four non-governmental members. The Board makes the funding decisions. (MCC, 2009a, p. 20)

The MCC is currently partnering with 39 countries at various stages of implementation, with financial outpourings of 6,7 billion USD (MCC, 2009a) having passed through the MCC system. These Compact funds are allocated according to two major forms of cooperation. The so-called "Compacts" are the primary *modus operandi* of the MCC. Countries become eligible if they meet certain indicators, which are provided by outside sources (see next section). However, there are a number of countries that are seen as reformers, but do not meet the indicators. If they meet a minimum level, they are eligible for smaller-level assistance: the so-called "threshold" programs. These programs "provide financial assistance to improve a low score" (MCC, 2009b), and are typically administered by USAID. MCC retains a staff of 300 that is small in comparison to its budget. Its presence in partner countries is also kept to a minimum (usually one or two persons).

The following tables give an overview of the Compact and threshold programs:

Compacts	
Cumulative	
Total Number of compacts approved through fiscal year 2008:	18
Total approximate value of compacts approved through fiscal year 2008:	$6.32 billion
FY 2008	
Total Number of compacts approved during fiscal year 2008:	4
Total approximate value of compacts approved during fiscal year 2008:	$1.77 billion

Threshold Programs (including Stage II)	
Cumulative	
Total Number of threshold programs (including Stage II) approved through fiscal year 2008:	19
Total approximate value of threshold programs approved through fiscal year 2008:	$440 million
FY 2008	
Total Number of threshold programs (including Stage II) approved during fiscal year 2008:	6
Total approximate value of threshold programs approved during fiscal year 2008:	$124 million

Compact Program overview (Source: MCC, 2009a, p.12) . Threshold Program overview (Source: MCC, 2009a, p.17)

The MCC maintains a very active public outreach policy, with a highly interactive website, numerous public events, and quick response mechanisms. These efforts have come into existence after a period of unfortunate relations with other players, notably Congress, during start-up. George

105

Guess notes: "that foreign aid lacks autonomy among American public policies is harmful..." (Guess, 1987). It is this challenge the MCC is apparently trying to tackle through its aggressive public relations policy. While certain concerns continue to exist and some voices suggest the dismantling of the MCC and integrating it into either USAID or a new all-encompassing developing agency, it was able to gain mention during Barack Obama's presidential campaign (Obama, 2008) and during Secretary of State Clinton's confirmation hearing (2009): "President-Elect Obama supports the MCC, and the principle of greater accountability in our foreign assistance programs. It represents a worthy new approach to poverty reduction and combating corruption..."

4) CSO Role #1: Indicators

Of note is the inherent belief in the quantifiability of development work. This is especially noticeable in the Threshold programs, where funded reform programs are aimed at increasing specific indicators. The MCC utilizes a system of 17 indicators that establish a country's eligibility. They break down into three categories: Ruling Justly (supplied by Freedom House, World Bank Institute), Investing in People (WHO, UNESCO, Yale University), and Economic Freedom (IFC, IMF, Heritage Foundation, World Bank Institute). Four of the indicators are provided by Civil Society organizations, and 13 by international organizations of which the US is a member (the US rejoined UNESCO in 2003 after having withdrawn in 1984). Of note, World Bank Institute indicators are so-called composite indicators that utilize data from various sources, including those of universities and civil society organizations.

Indicator	Category	Source
Civil Liberties	Ruling Justly	Freedom House
Political Rights	Ruling Justly	Freedom House
Voice and Accountability	Ruling Justly	World Bank Institute
Government Effectiveness	Ruling Justly	World Bank Institute
Rule of Law	Ruling Justly	World Bank Institute
Control of Corruption	Ruling Justly	World Bank Institute
Immunization Rates	Investing in People	World Health Organization
Public Expenditure on	Investing in People	World Health

Health		Organization
Girls' Primary Education Completion Rate	Investing in People	UNESCO
Public Expenditure on Primary Education	Investing in People	UNESCO and national sources
Business Start Up	Economic Freedom	IFC
Inflation	Economic Freedom	IMF WEO
Trade Policy	Economic Freedom	Heritage Foundation
Regulatory Quality	Economic Freedom	World Bank Institute
Fiscal Policy	Economic Freedom	national sources, cross-checked with IMF WEO
Natural Resource Management	Investing in People	CIESIN/Yale
Land Rights and Access	Economic Freedom	IFAD / IFC

(Millennium Challenge Corporation, 2009b)

Countries receive publicly available scorecards on an annual basis (see a sample score card for Ukraine 2009 in attachment 1). Countries need to "perform above the median in at least half of the indicators in each of the three policy categories" (MCC, 2009c, p. 2). If a country fulfills these criteria, it can prepare an official Compact request that the MCC board will review and approve if satisfactory.

As Schuppert (1996) notes: "specialist knowledge often allows NGOs to play the role of experts in the political process." (p.213). MCC utilizes the expertise of NGOs to produce some of its indicators. In addition to the three direct CSO-provided indicators and the composite indicators that include CSO data, the MCC Board also uses Transparency International's Corruption Perception and Global Integrity In-dices as supplemental information.

Adopting these indicators brought about a number of advantages:
- *Legitimacy*: as Stoker (1998) points out "the issue to consider is whether or how governance can obtain legitimacy" (p. 21). The MCC gained legitimacy by adopting standards that were generally accepted as truthful and impartial due to the expertise of their authors. Additional legitimacy was gained by making the selection process completely transparent;

- *Less criticism of subjectivity:* since the decisions are taken on the basis of outside indicators, the MCC can shield itself largely from attacks of subjectivity and political preference in decision-making;
- *Ability to quantify development goals:* partner countries are subject to the changing indicators that are not under the MCC's control. As such, they are much harder to influence to suit political preferences. The MCC legislation prescribes performance indicators that allow one to quantify development goals, a major challenge in previous work;
- *Support from NGO community*: the involvement of the NGO community gave the MCC several critical allies, despite their overwhelming criticism of other Bush policies;
- *Clearly understandable benchmarks*: the MCC has set the stage for a discussion among the expert community about its implementation, which takes place in earnest. While discussion focuses on improving efficiency (through better indicators, for example) the general framework has become widely accepted.

The Control of Corruption indicators warrants separate attention. It is "the only indicator that countries *must* pass in order to qualify for MCA eligibility is Control of Corruption..." (Herrline and Rose, 2007). The MCC points out that "corruption increases poverty" and "corruption slows growth", (MCC, 2008) thus seeing it as an efficiency-hampering concern, rather than an ethical or governance issue, in line with the overall trend of the organization. Of note, this requirement is not stipulated by law, but due to the tremendous damage corruption has on development assistance efficiency, this "soft law" has all but become the norm and it would not be surprising to see it transit into "hard law" under the new administration.

The importance of the control of corruption indicators causes many threshold programs to specifically focus on improving the anti-corruption indicator. Of the current Threshold Programs, 52,2 percent are focused on improving this indicator (MCC, 2009a, p. 17).

The utilization of NGO indicators has also affected these organizations. Freedom House provides the Civil Liberties and Political Freedoms indicators through its annual publication "Freedom in the World", as well as contributing the various composite indicators. While Freedom House's indicators have long been the standard in global comparative freedom and democracy studies, they were working with the hope that, as Heritier (2001) calls it "a reputation mechanism (naming and shaming) may induce a behavioral change accommodating a desired policy goal." (p. 188). Their inclusion into the selection indicators of MCC funding, however, has unleashed market forces and thus contributed to tremendous growth in the international reputation of the ratings. Freedom House finds itself the subject of increased attention from senior foreign government delegations who seek meetings with this NGO to better understand ratings and how to improve them (and argue for an "upgrade"). Furthermore, these ratings and their methodology, while based on generally accepted documents (The Universal Declaration of Human Rights), have long been the subject of controversy and accusations of bias and subjectivity, especially from the countries that receive "bad" ratings.

With their codification by the MCC, however, they have been elevated to a new level of importance to the countries seeking funding: it matters little whether they agree or not – they need to understand the ratings and improve their score if they seek access to MCC funds. While many (including the author) would argue in favor of the ratings, it is noteworthy this cooperation between a new government institution and an old NGO has elevated a freedom ranking system from a more or less obscure academic and civil society tool to a policy and finance tool of tremendous proportions (6,7 billion USD have been issued so far using these indicators). This is true both in the sense of tax expenses and the overall impact on recipient countries.

5) CSO role #2: Program Implementation and Progress Measurement

Both Compacts and Threshold programs have clearly-established programs that are developed by the applicant countries, in which they outline priorities and measures to be implemented. In the case of Threshold programs, they include extremely detailed performance indicators on the basis of which success of the program is to be judged. This has caused MCC to be substantially more willing to suspend some countries from financing (for example, Yemen and Mauretania), than other donor agencies. (Herrling, 2007)

In Ukraine, the indicators are to be reached over a two-year period and include, among others:
- 10% of the population is to be aware of anti-corruption research;
- 10% percent decrease in corruption perception;
- 20% percent decrease in corruption experience;
- 30% of NGO advocacy campaigns resulting in government reform

(Government of Ukraine, 2006).

In Ukraine, the MCC Threshold program is focused on assisting the government in decreasing corruption in education, regulatory policy, the court system and civil service. There was involvement of civil society in the drafting of the plan, largely through individual and town-hall meetings. It clearly played a secondary role to a relationship between the recipient and donor countries. Nonetheless, it resulted in the inclusion of a robust role in the Threshold Country Plan, the guiding document for the program. Of a total 45 Million USD allocated to the program, 10 million were assigned to a program to channel civil society anti-corruption efforts.[3] It should be noted that such a degree of CSO involvement is clearly larger than average threshold program. However, it is a growing trend and other MCC programs are considering the incorporation of similar approaches.

Zuercher (2006) states of developing countries, the following: "a rational behavior for states would be to try enjoying the full sovereignty rent without paying the price for good governance" (p. 13). NGOs provide a valuable service in assessing whether (and if so, to what degree) the state is succumbing to this temptation. Zuercher, however, seems to overestimate the ability of developing countries in purposefully creating "cunning states" that are weak by design to "prey on international support" (p.21). While preying does unfortunately take place, it is usually the result of a group of individuals in government. Chaos and lack of ability are far more defining reasons for weak statehood.

In Ukraine, civil society efforts under the threshold plan break down into the following responsibilities:

"1) support for civil society anti-corruption efforts; 2) support for investigative journalism and other media anti-corruption efforts; and 3) monitoring of corruption trends and the results of government and civil society-sponsored anti-corruption initiatives" (Management Systems International, 2007). In addition, the four consultative components of the Threshold program also relate to NGOs, engaging them in public outreach efforts and utilizing their expertise.

The author's project has support from over 120 Ukrainian CSOs in their anti-corruption efforts through funding, training, and networking. These NGOs were able to achieve over fifty anti-corruption reforms at the local level. While they are not overhauls of the entire state system, they nonetheless represent concrete important steps toward decreasing corruption (such as simplifying licensing procedures, introducing anti-corruption education in public schools, and introducing greater inclusion of citizen concerns in construction projects).

Arguably the largest impact from civil society efforts has been caused by the reports and surveys conducted to evaluate progress of the Ukrainian government toward results pledged in the Threshold program. A substantial challenge thus lies in the capacity and motive of the civil society organizations. In Ukraine, for example, it was a tremendous challenge to find absorption capacity among NGOs to utilize substantial funds issued by the MCC. This is a common mistake as policy-makers and program designers often see civil society as a panacea that can kick in when government reforms have stalled. While there is much truth to such potential, the limitations of CSOs need to be carefully assessed and kept in mind. When this is not done, much money needs to be shifted quickly to satisfy the financial and programmatic requirements. As a result, financing can become akin to "venture capitalism," with each grant being a rather high-risk investment. About a dozen contracts had to be terminated in Ukraine due to the NGO's non-fulfillment of their obligations.

The capacity problems are exacerbated by the fact that civil society is not immune from all-permeating corruption in Ukraine. The overall corrupt functioning of the economy influences civil society as well. This is apparent because of an insufficient understanding of the concept of conflict of interest, challenges with obtaining financial accuracy, and lack of focus on performance and results. This in turn, increases management and performance evaluation efforts and costs required from those managing the project to ensure transparency required of US-funded projects. This challenges the MCC's vision of being an action-oriented player with significantly less bureaucracy. It also leads to less money available to those NGO who are honest and trying to do good work.

Political danger also exists as the few NGOs that are corrupt themselves can undermine efforts of others, especially in high profile projects under tremendous scrutiny from the media, which the MCC programs invariably are. For a young organization like the MCC is, the capacity to absorb such scandals is rather limited.

Notwithstanding these challenges at a time when the political environment in Ukraine is characterized by tremendous infighting that has paralyzed most government reform efforts (EUBusiness, 2009), the modest progress by NGOs on the anti-corruption reform front stands out as a positive.

6) CSO role #3: Board membership and ongoing dialogue

As mentioned above, four members of MCC's board are representatives of the "public." While it is arguable whether they all represent civil society, some certainly are: Lorne Craner (International Republican Institute), Ken Hackett (Catholic Relief Services), Alan Patrikof (Greycroft investment company), and Bill Frist (former Senate Majority Leader).

Adding them to the decision-making body on Compacts and Threshold fund allocation further underlines importance paid to the civil society vision concerning programs. The appointment mechanism (members are suggested by the Senate and appointed by the President) is likely to encourage the selection of representatives of "political" NGOs, rather than those who are development focused. Nonetheless, there is evidence that non-government members of the Board yield considerable influence and their likely votes are being discussed in detail and anxiously anticipated ahead of

Board meetings. The influence, however, seems to function both ways. The "public" members of the Board were actively utilized in the campaign to raise the importance of the MCC's status ahead of the Obama administration coming into office. They stated in an open letter to the New York Times (2008): "As he [President Obama] seeks to adapt American foreign assistance to a transformed world, one decisive step he can take is to signal his strong support of the corporation's approach to global development."

There are also other direct and indirect ways in which the MCC is different from other government agencies in its openness to civil society. As discussed earlier, its transparent functioning invites scrutiny, which is readily provided. For example, the Center for Global Development runs a blog that discusses minute details of MCC operations and sometimes receives active feedback.

Also, MCC CEOs continuously invite CSOs to provide their feedback and to "...continue educating officials in the U.S. administration on development issues" (Applegarth, 2005). At least some of the feedback seems to be welcome and incorporated into future work. At the beginning of its functioning, the MCC was "holding monthly meetings with US-based NGO working group...the NGOs have shared expertise in monitoring and evaluation and have offered suggestions that contributed to the modification of 1 of MCC's 16 quantitative indicators" (Gootnick and Franzel, 2005. P. 26).

7) Conclusion

MCC is run with significantly less bureaucratic luggage than other development agencies carry comparatively. As a new organization, it benefits from the ability to introduce new rules and has chosen to select a combination of rules and processes for funding eligibility selection that are generally viewed as successful. This includes the incorporation of authoritative independent indicators into its decision-making process. Nonetheless, there are numerous organizational and political challenges to this emergent Corporation, first and foremost insufficient speed, which is a key determinant to make conditionality effective (Dugger, 2007). Internal US government (fiscal year 2007) evaluations conclude that "to a large extent, the performance of MCC compares favorably to other programs with similar purposes and goals," while noting that its performance was only "adequate" (US Office of Management and Budget, 2008). Rieffel and Fox (2008) note that, "no other aid agency- foreign or domestic – can match its [MCC's] purposeful mandate, its operational flexibility, and its potential muscle."

Also, the MCC engages with civil society at various levels. Several of its funding indicators are provided by NGOs, which significantly improved their status. This process provided legitimacy for the MCC and increased power with the NGOs. This cooperation has been most fruitful to date. At the design stage, Civil Society input is often limited. During in-country implementation, however, the CSO role is seen as significant, most prominently as advocates of anti-corruption reforms and independent in-country evaluators concerning effectiveness of national reform programs. However, capacity and integrity limitations of civil society in developing countries need to be taken into account during project design and implementation.

Finally, the MCC Board membership of non-government members has, despite the political nature of some members, provides an additional effective tool to increase the efficiency of funding decisions.

Notes

1 The author is the director of a MCC-funded NGO monitoring project in Ukraine, so practical experience and feedback is used in the discussion.
2 For more information on the F process, see
 http://www.allbusiness.com/government/government-bodies-offices-us-federal-government/11735250-1.html
3 The author is the director of this project.

References

Applegarth, Paul V. (2005) "NGOs: Indispensable or Unaccountable?" Presentation at conference in December 2005 at American Enterprise Institute for Public Policy Research. Retrieved January 30, 2009 from

http://www.aei.org/events/filter.all,eventID.1199/summary.

Bacchus, William I. (2004) "The Price of American Foreign Policy: Congress, the Executive, and International Affairs Funding" Philadelphia: Penn State Press. Retrieved on January 25, 2009 from

http://books.google.com/books?id=VeGLAIHujIMC&pg=PA57&dq=%22public+opinion%22+%22foreign+assistance%22#PPA57,M1

Bandow, Doug. (1999) "Foreign Aid Simply Won't Reform Dictators." Washington, DC: Cato Institute. Retrieved January 25, 2009 at

http://www.cato.org/pub_display.php?pub_id=6122

Clinton, Hillary Rodham "Senate Confirmation Hearing: Secretary of State-Designate Hillary Rodham Clinton" January 13, 2009. Center for US Global Engagement. retrieved on January 30, 2009 from http://www.usglobalengagement.org/TransitionWatch/HillaryClintonProfile/ClintonHearingQuotes/tabid/3503/Default.aspx

Craner, Lorne; Frist, Bill; Hackett, Kenneth and Patrcof, Alan. (2008) "US Aid Should be Earned" New York Times. December 20, 2008. Retrieved January 30, 2009 from

http://www.nytimes.com/2008/12/20/opinion/20patricof-frist.html?_r=3

Dugger, Celia (2007) "U.S. Agency's Slow Pace Endangers Foreign Aid" New York Times. December 7, 2007. Retrieved on January 30, 2009 from

http://www.nytimes.com/2007/12/07/world/africa/07millennium.html?pagewanted=1&_r=3

EU Business (2009) "Ukraine's pro-Western progress set back in gas crisis: analysts" 15 January 2009 retrieved January 30, 2009 from

http://www.eubusiness.com/news-eu/1231987623.42

Florini, Ann M. (1999) "Who does what? Collective Action and the Changing Nature of Authority." Chapter in Richard A. Higgott, Geoffrey R.D. Underhill, and Andreas Bieler, eds., Non-State Actors and Authority in the Global System, London: Routledge, 1999.

http://www.carnegieendowment.org/publications/index.cfm?fa=view&id=589&prog=zgp

Gootnick, David B. and Franzel, Jeanette M. (2005) "Millennium Challenge Corporation: Progress Made on Key Challenges in First Year of Operations" Washington, DC, Government Accountability Office. Retrieved January 25, 2009 from http://books.google.com/books?id=Xf9RhtZeDO0C&printsec=frontcover&source=gbs_summary_r&cad=0

Government of Ukraine (2006) "Performance Monitoring Plan. Ukraine Threshold Country Program"

Guess, George M. (1987) "The Politics of United States Foreign Aid" London & Sidney: Croom Helm. Retrieved on 25 January 2009 from http://books.google.com/books?id=DVAOAAAAQAAJ&pg=PA1&dq=american+public+development+aid#PPA1,M1

Heritier, Adrienne (2001) "New modes of governance in Europe: Policy-making without legislation?"

Herrling, Sheila and Rose, Sarah (2007) "Control of Corruption and the MCA: A Preview to the FY2008 Country Selection" Washington, DC: Center for Global Development.

Management Systems International (2007) "Ukraine – Activating Citizens to Combat Corruption" retrieved January 30, 2009 from

http://www.msiworldwide.com/index.cfm?msiweb=project&p_id=186

Management Systems International (2008) "The State of Corruption in Ukraine. Threshold Country Plan priorities"

Millennium Challenge Corporation (2008) "MCC's Role in the Fight Against Corruption" Washington, DC: MCC.

Millennium Challenge Corporation (2009a) "Making a Difference: 2008 Annual Report" retrieved January 26, 2009 from

http://www.mcc.gov/press/releases/documents/release-011609-annualreport.php

Millennium Challenge Corporation (2009b) "Selection Indicators" retrieved January 30, 2009 from http://www.mcc.gov/selection/indicators/index.php

Millennium Challenge Corporation (2009c) "Guide to the MCC Indicators and the Selection Process, Fiscal Year 2009" retrieved January 27, 2009 from http://www.mcc.gov/documents/factsheet-100908-fy09-selectionprocess.pdf

Obama Biden (2008) "Barack Obama and Joe Biden's strategy to promote global development and democracy" retrieved January 27, 2009 from http://www.barackobama.com/pdf/issues/Fact_Sheet_Foreign_Policy_Democratization_and_Development_FINAL.pdf

Rieffel, Lex, and Fox, James W. (2008) "Strengthen the Millennium Challenge Corporation: Better Results are Possible." Washington, DC: Brookings Institution.

Salaman and Anheier (1999) "The Global Revolution of Associations and Organizations"

Schuppert, Gunnar Folke (2006) The Changing Role of the State Reflected in the Growing Importance of Non-State Actors."

Stoker, Gerry (1998) "Governance as theory: Five propositions" International Social Science Journal. Volume 50, Issue 55

US Office of Management and Budget (2008) "Program Assessment: Millennium Challenge Corporation" retrieved January 27, 2009 from

http://www.whitehouse.gov/omb/expectmore/summary/10009038.2007.html

Zuercher, Christoph. (2006) "When Governance Meets troubled states"

Appendix 1: Ukraine 2009 Indicator Score Card

Ukraine FY09

Population 46,787,750
GNI/Cap: $2,550 LMIC

Ruling Justly

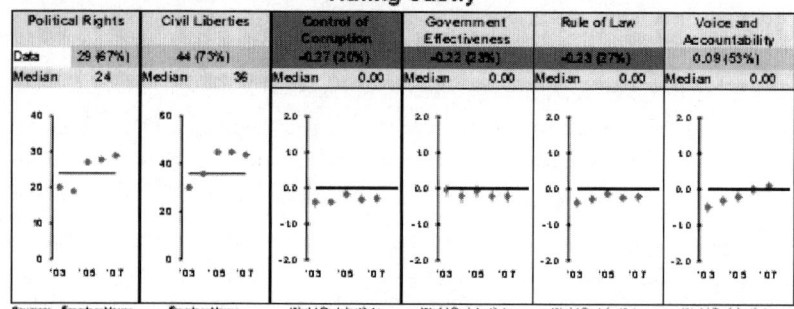

Investing In People

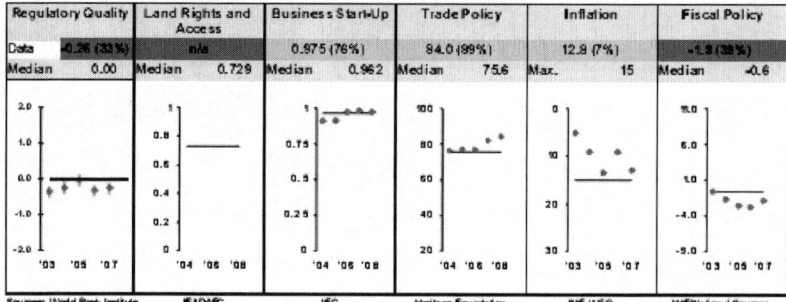

Economic Freedom

How to Read this Scorecard: Each MCC Candidate Country receives an annual scorecard assessing its performance in 3 policy categories: Ruling Justly, Investing in People, and Economic Freedom. Under the name of each indicator is the country's score and percentile ranking in its income peer group (0% is worst; 50% is the median; 100% is best). Under each country's percentile ranking is the peer group median. Country performance is evaluated relative to the peer group median. Scores above the median, represented with green, meet the performance standard. Scores at or below the median, represented with red, do not meet the performance standard. The black line that runs along the horizontal axis represents the peer group median. Each World Bank Institute indicator is accompanied by a margin of error, which is represented by the vertical blue bar.

116

Chapter 6
A Values-Based Approach to Development: Principles of Content of Development, the Right to Development, and Sustainable (Human) Development

Qerim Qerimi

Keywords: value, principles, development, social settings, environment, right of development, global interest, power, enlightenment, sustainable development, social and cultural rights

I. DELIMITATION OF PROBLEM AND CLARIFICATION OF GOALS

The magnitude of interdependency on a global scale and at all levels of formal and informal, institutionalized and non-institutionalized social settings of interaction is what has caused growing attention to human development as one of the key planetary concerns. The fate of the environment seems to be no less fortunate, at least from perspective of the frequency of its presence in national and international fora. In fact, the quality of human life is nowadays seen—and rightly so—as organically related to the notion of environment. Such a correlation between human development and the environment has given rise to what has come to be known as "sustainable development," a key concept in the field of international environmental law with growing implications in arenas of international relations, international trade, and human rights.

The precise content of sustainable development, in terms of its legal and practical implications is still open to some debate, although the concept or several of its principles have gained respectable recognition by various international instruments and institutions. It is the conceptual meaning of the notion of sustainable development, the extent and scope of its legal and policy implications that form the core object of this article. Other key notions surrounding the theme of human development, such as development itself, the right to development, and a more expansive notion of sustainable human development will also be explored.

A number of alternative solutions will be introduced at the end of this article through utilization of the value categories system, including a multi-factor practical component to be used as an instrument enhancing the process of promoting and preserving the value categories system, or a world public order creating human dignity. The method employed is integrative, in that it tends to utilize knowledge from varying fields such as legal and policy sciences.

II. BACKGROUND AND CONTEXT

The question concerning development goes far beyond the *de facto* existence of a "two-world" system, broadly categorized: the developed and the developing or underdeveloped countries (here including the least developed countries). This distinction is partially related to the artificial ideological-based views of the past that have generated, what the French jurist Karel Vasak has described as three generations human rights. According to this view, the first generation consists of civil and political rights conceived as freedom from state interference, often referred to as "negative rights."[1] The second generation consists of economic, social, and cultural rights, and requires the state action to provide such rights, widely known as "positive rights."[2] The third of these generations is the right to development—that consists of solidarity belonging to peoples and covering global concerns like development, environment, humanitarian assistance, peace, communication, and common heritage—an analogous notion to the French Revolution's concept of *fraternité*.

The right to development has been part of the international debate on human rights for over thirty years, but has not yet entered the practical realm of development planning and implementation (Marks 2003; Alston 1988; Marks 1981). From the beginning, the concept of the **right to development** has been controversial. It emerged as a result of preoccupation of newly independent countries with problems of development and the dominance of East-West issues on the agenda of the Commission on Human Rights, marginalizing the concerns of the South. Their efforts to use the United Nations to advance the idea of a New International Economic Order had emboldened Third World delegations. But the challenge to the prevailing order favoring the so-called First World countries generated reaction among Western delegations that ranged from cautious support to outright hostility for the idea of a human right to development.

The group that eventually drafted the Declaration on the Right to Development was established in 1981,[3] and key Western delegations made it clear to the other members of the drafting group that they would ensure that the Right to Development Declaration was not used as a means of resuscitating The New International Economic Order, which Keohane (1998) calls "[a] resounding failure." Nor would they allow the Declaration to create any entitlement to a transfer of resources; aid was a matter of sovereign decision of donor countries and could not be subject to binding rules under the guise of advancing every human being's right to development.. Developing countries had especially benefited from the insights of economists who occupied high positions such as international officials, Samir Amin and Raul Prebisch, who pushed the ideas that gave rise to the sense of an "unjust international economic order" that could be redressed if the "right to development" was respected (Marks 1981). Compare also (Tamene, 2006, p. 137; 2008, p.250), who confirms the argument of this article, while reflecting the failure of aid politics in Sub-Saharan Africa.

These divisions are products of the Cold War paradigm that divided the world in two parts (excluding the non-aligned nations): into (1) democratic pro-Western or pro-US world, and (2) communist pro-Eastern or pro-Soviet world. Certain sets of rights were associated with each of these parts of the world. The distinction between "negative" and "positive" rights —known as well as "justifiable" and "programmatic" rights—is a typical reflection of the Cold War paradigm. The result, as seen later, was drafted and adopted by the UN General Assembly for two different covenants: the International Covenant on Civil and Political Rights (ICCPR), and the International Covenant on Economic, Social and Cultural Rights (ICESCR).

Different theories and explanations have been advanced in order to find the reasons behind this decision, in particular with respect to the substance of guarantee and modalities of implementation of the two covenants. However, it is no longer accepted there can be clear distinction between "negative" and "positive" rights since both categories entail legal obligations on the part of States, and issues of measurability arise in relation to the obligation of both covenants. Both covenants produce legal effects upon the States's Parties and both use procedural mechanisms in order to measure the level at which obligations are implemented. Moreover, they are *recognized* as equal and interdependent. This relationship has been clearly articulated and recognized by The Vienna Declaration and Program of Action, adopted on June 25, 1993 by consensus of representatives of 171 States, at the end of the World Conference on Human Rights. Paragraph 5 of the Vienna Declaration provides:

> *"All human rights are universal, indivisible and interdependent and interrelated. The international community must treat human rights globally in a fair and equal manner, on the same footing, and with the same emphasis. While the significance of national and regional particularities and various historical, cultural and religious backgrounds must be borne in mind, it is the duty of States, regardless of their political, economic and cultural systems, to promote and protect all human rights and fundamental freedoms."*[4]

The Vienna Declaration also provides for the right to development, recognizing it as, "a universal and inalienable right and an integral part of fundamental human rights."[5] The same attitude with regard to all the rights was previously held in the Declaration on the Right to Development, adopted by the UN General Assembly in 1986:

> *"All human rights and fundamental freedoms are indivisible and interdependent; equal attention and urgent consideration should be given to the implementation, promotion and protection of civil, political, economic, social and cultural rights"*[6] (Article 6, paragraph 2).

In fact, the Declaration is the most pertinent existing instrument that would help clarify the meaning of key notions surrounding the theme of development.

III. KEY NOTIONS: DEVELOPMENT AND THE RIGHT TO DEVELOPMENT

The Declaration on the Right to Development provides some conceptual guidelines with respect to both the right to development and the process of development. Article 1 of the Declaration conceptualizes the right to development in the following way:

> *"The right to development is an inalienable human right by virtue of which every human person and all peoples are entitled to participate in, contribute to, and enjoy economic, social, cultural and political development, in which all human rights and fundamental freedoms can be fully realized."*[7]

From this statement, several components can be discerned. The first refers to the right to development as an inalienable right, something intrinsically connected to the notion of human being. The logic behind this is the natural need to development. And, a set of rights is of absolute necessity in order to make such development a realistic and possible notion. As the *ordinary meaning* of this provision suggests, this right is an entitlement to both individual human persons, and to groups of persons, or peoples. Given the collective and group-based orientation of human persons, an individual's development is naturally impacted by that of the community and vice versa; thus, there is a mutual correspondence. However, as Article 2 of the same Declarations explicitly provides, "the human person is the central subject of development," who "should be [both] the active participant and beneficiary of the right to development."[8]

As far as methods of realization of the right to development are concerned, three could be identified from the above text. First, there is a need for participation. Secondly comes contribution, which is logically conditioned by participation. The third is enjoyment. One could also speak of enjoyment only as the culmination of the other second steps (i.e., participation and contribution), however, this is a crucial, perhaps the most crucial stage of this three-steps setting, as some may indeed participate and/or contribute, but yet may not enjoy the fruits of development. This stage is what in the concept of "development," elaborated below, is recognized as "fair distribution of benefits."

As for the first two components, it could be possible to categorize them in terms of rights and duties. The first, participation, is rather to be perceived as a right, hence the right to participation, whereas the second (contribution) may be viewed in terms of an obligation in a sense of production, which is that participation has to be manifested with some practical results, in order for individuals or peoples to be able to fully realize all of their rights and fundamental freedoms, and by that, effectuate the right to development.

The third stage of the analysis of the above Article 1 is directed towards the kind of development to be enjoyed. As prescribed in the text, this development should be of economic, social, cultural and political character. This set of development settings should make it possible, and in fact, would be made possible if all human rights and fundamental freedoms can be fully realized. In this sense, there is a fixed correlation between development and human rights and fundamental freedoms.

For a better comprehension of the right to development, a more precise designation of development itself would be needed. As regards this precise conceptual meaning of *development*, the Declaration on the Right to Development is instructive, defining development as:

> "*A comprehensive economic, social, cultural and political process, which aims at the constant improvement of the well-being of the entire population and of all individuals on the basis of their active, free and meaningful participation in development and in the fair distribution of benefits resulting there from.*"[9]

Development is thus conceived in terms of a comprehensive economic, social, cultural and political process, hence the right to a process of development, which should be of an economic, social, cultural and political nature. In other words, the right to development—as put by Arjun Sengupta (2004, p. 343), a former UN Independent Expert on the Right to Development—"is the right to a process that expands the capabilities or freedom of individuals to improve their well-being and to realize what they value." Overall, "the improvement of the quality of life of human beings is the first and foremost objective of every effort towards the fulfilment of the said right" (Desai 1992, 31). The progressive realization of the right to development may be said to include not only "active, free and meaningful participation" in development, but also "fair distribution of benefits resulting" from such participation in the process of development, which entails the realization of all human rights.

As far as rights/duties equation is concerned, the same story of State-individual relationship that exists in the human rights arena applies. Article 3(1) of the Declaration provides that, "States have the primary responsibility for the creation of national and international conditions favorable to the realization of the right to development."[10] This relationship **is** in particular addressed in the case of ICCPR, whereby its treaty body is pronounced on the issue of the beneficiary of the rights protected by the Covenant. In its General Comment no. 26(61), Human Rights Committee provided that:

> "The rights enshrined in the Covenant belong to the people living in the territory of the State party. The Human Rights Committee has consistently taken the view, as evidenced by its long-standing practice, that once the people are accorded the protection of the rights under the Covenant, such protection devolves with territory and continues to belong to them, notwithstanding change in government of the State party, including dismemberment in more than one State or State succession or any subsequent action of the State party designed to divest them of the rights guaranteed by the Covenant."[11]

IV. PAST TRENDS IN DECISION: SUSTAINABLE DEVELOPMENT, INSTITUTIONAL AND LEGAL MACHINERY

A. UN Legal Structure Concerning Development

1. Charter of the United Nations

The UN Charter—as is true with a number of other issues related to international law and relations—provides a useful guideline for a wide range of questions related to economic and social development. Despite its rather general orientation on issues that may be of essential importance to development, the Charter's focus is clear in that it reaffirms, and to that end, introduces a number of provisions aiming to further the world's social progress. One such aim is stipulated in the preamble of the UN Charter, providing that the United Nations was formed to, *inter alia*, "promote social progress and better standards of life in larger freedom,"[12] as well as "to employ international machinery for the promotion of the economic and social advancement of all peoples."[13]

These aspirations are most clearly articulated in Articles 1(3), 13(1)(b), 62, and perhaps most importantly, Article 55 (a) and (b). For the sake of further elaboration and a better understanding of the Charter's provisions, Article 1(3) provides that, it is a *purpose* of the United Nations "to achieve international co-operation in solving international problems of an economic, social, cultural, or humanitarian character, and in promoting and encouraging respect for human rights and for fundamental freedoms for all without distinction as to race, sex, language, or religion."[14]

Article 13 (1) (b), prescribing the functions of UN General Assembly, requires that the Assembly initiates studies and makes recommendations for the purpose of "promoting international co-operation in the economic, social, cultural, educational, and health fields, and assisting in the realization of human rights and fundamental freedoms for all without distinction as to race, sex, language, or religion."[15] The Economic and Social Council is also assigned with the duty to make or initiate studies and reports with "respect to international economic, social, cultural, educational, health, and related matters and may make recommendations with respect to any such matters to the General Assembly, to the Members of the United Nations, and to the specialized agencies concerned."[16] The key provision of the Charter dealing with economic and social questions is Article 55, providing that:

> *"With a view to the creation of conditions of stability and well-being which are necessary for peaceful and friendly relations among nations based on respect for the principle of equal rights and self-determination of peoples, the United Nations shall promote:*
> *a. higher standards of living, full employment, and conditions of economic and social progress and development;*
> *b. solutions of international economic, social, health, and related problems; and international cultural and educational cooperation."*[17]

Article 55 should be read in conjunction with Article 1, although the former tends to be more specific in defining the scope and the range of responsibilities of the UN. To this network of provisions dealing with economic and social issues, Article 56 may be of critical value in order to strengthen the obligations of both Member States and the UN. The main contribution of Article 55 is that it adds to a culture of coherence of the purposes and goals of the UN as articulated in Article 1, making it clear that peaceful and friendly relations among nations do not require only banning the use of force, but also requires providing solutions to economic, social, health, and related problems.

Although the wording of Article 55 is framed in a very careful, legally-soft language, in that the Organization is obliged to only "promote" such "purposes" (not even principles), the connection between the promotion of economic and social development and stability, and the maintenance of international peace and security is somewhat encouraging and strengthens the legal character of the provision. Article 56 may be considered as further strengthening the obligations of Member States toward providing the economic stability and social well-being to their peoples through committing themselves to take concrete, joint and separate actions, in order to make these goals become reality.

2. *International Covenant on Economic, Social and Cultural Rights*

As now indicated, the International Covenant on Economic, Social and Cultural Rights (ICESCR) personifies what are called "positive rights" or second generation human rights. This covenant is of profound significance as it covers key components of a comprehensive and process-based right to development. Part II of ICESCR lays down State obligations concerning the implementation of the rights enunciated in the Covenant. Article 2(1) requires State Parties to "take steps, individually and through international assistance and co-operation, especially economic and technical, to the maximum of its available resources, with a view to achieving progressively the full realization of the rights recognized in the present Covenant by all appropriate means, including particularly the adoption of legislative measures."[18]

Two key references in this provision that merit further attention are the "availability of resources" and "progressive realization" of rights recognized in the Covenant. This wide and somewhat less restrictive formulation of this key ICESCR provision has led many to regard the Covenant's obligations as programmatic principles rather than genuine legal obligations. This view is mainly held by those States that do not view the ICESCR rights as legal and/or justifiable, but rather as group, programmatic principles or promotional obligations. This view has been especially shared during the period of Cold War among Western democracies.

Today, the main proponent of this view seems to have remained the United States, which has not ratified nor signed this Covenant. As quite recently reaffirmed by a US delegation at the UN Commission on Human Rights, "the realization of economic, social and cultural rights is progressive and aspirational. We do not view them as entitlements that require correlated legal duties and obligations. States therefore have no obligation to provide guarantees for implementation of any purported 'right to development'."[19]

However, the Committee on Economic, Social and Cultural Rights, which is entrusted to monitor State reports under the ICESCR, has consistently held that every single ICESCR right contains an individual rights' element.[20] It was for this reason that, in 1997 it submitted to the Commission on Human Rights a draft of an Optional Protocol to the ICESCR, which provides for an individual and group complaint mechanism alongside the existing system of State reporting.[21]

Although available economic resources may be a reason for States' failure to fully implement some of the rights, as stated by the Committee on Economic, Social and Cultural Rights, there are a number of rights that can directly be implemented without any need to allocate particular economic resources. These rights may include the following: the principle of non-discrimination in Articles 2(2) and 3; the claim for equal pay for equal work (Art.7(a)(i)); the right to form and to join a trade union (Art. 8); the protection of children from exploitation (Art. 10(3)); the right to compulsory elementary schooling free of charge (Art. 12(2)(a)), or the freedom of science and research (Art. 15(3)) (Carven 1995, p. 181-82, Tamene, 2007, p.103). In other words, the inaction or lack of implementation of the ICESCR rights on the part of States cannot be justified; in fact, the ICESCR provisions do clearly create legal duties.

3. *International Covenant on Civil and Political Rights*

Development is being recognized to include not only economic, social and cultural processes; political processes and development are another key and integrated component of the comprehensive process of development, as civil and political rights are for political development. Here lies the value of the International Covenant on Civil and Political Rights (ICCPR).[22] The ICCPR provisions also have a fundamental role in the process of effective implementation of economic, social and cultural rights. In fact, there exists a correlation of such kind that lacking one "group" of such rights would highly endanger the existence of the other "group." As perhaps most famously proclaimed in the now quoted UN Declaration on the Right to Development (article 6, para. 2), "all human rights and fundamental freedoms are indivisible and interdependent," and that "equal attention and urgent consideration should be given to the implementation, promotion and protection of civil, political, economic, social and cultural rights."[23] It is mainly in this sense of all the rights' interrelationship and interdependence that the ICCPR provisions are of critical importance to development.

B. Other Legal and Policy Development-Related Measures

1. UN Millennium Declaration

In 2000, the UN Millennium Declaration was adopted during the largest-ever gathering of heads of state and government from both rich and poor countries. World leaders committed to achieve concrete steps toward advancing human development and reducing poverty by 2015 or earlier. The Declaration recognized "a collective responsibility to uphold the principles of human dignity, equality and equity at the global level," and affirmed the determination "to establish a just and lasting peace all over the world in accordance with the purposes and principles of the Charter" of the United Nations.

The Declaration considered certain fundamental values to be essential to international relations in the twenty-first century, including: freedom, equality, solidarity, tolerance, respect for nature, and shared responsibility. According to this Declaration, success in meeting these objectives depends, *inter alia*, on good governance within each country, but "it also depends on good governance at the international level and on transparency in the financial, monetary and trading systems."

2. The *Monterrey Consensus*

The March 2002 Monterrey Consensus—reaffirmed in the September 2002 Johannesburg Declaration on Sustainable Development and the Johannesburg Plan of Implementation—provides a framework for advancing the partnership between rich and poor countries to achieve the Millennium Development Goals. The Conference was held against a background of drastic shortfalls in resources necessary to achieve the internationally agreed development goals, including those contained in the UN Millennium Declaration.[24]

The Monterrey Conference laid down basic principles for international development cooperation, embracing six areas of financing for development, aiming at the following objectives: (1) mobilizing domestic financial resources for development; (2) mobilizing international resources for development (*i.e.*, foreign direct investment and other private flows); (3) international trade as an engine for development; (4) increasing international financial and technical cooperation for development; (5) external debt; (6) addressing systemic issues, such as enhancing the coherence and consistency of the international monetary, financial and trading systems in support of development.[25]

3, The Johannesburg World Summit

The Johannesburg World Summit on Sustainable Development (26 August - 04 September 2002) reaffirmed sustainable development as a central element of the international agenda and gave new impetus to global action to fight poverty and protect the environment. Governments agreed on a set of concrete commitments and targets for action to achieve a more effective implementation of sustainable development objectives.

New Initiatives and Announcements from the Johannesburg Summit include the following:

a. Water & Sanitation (US announced $970 million in investments over the next three years on water and sanitation projects; the European Union announced the "Water for Life" initiative that seeks to engage partners to meet goals for water and sanitation, primarily in Africa and Central Asia; the Asia Development Bank provided a $5 million grant to UN Habitat and $500 million in fast-track credit for the Water for Asian Cities Program; the UN has received 21 other water and sanitation initiatives with at leas $20 million in extra resources).

b. Energy (the EU announced a $700 million partnership initiative on energy and the US announced that it would invest up to $43 million in 2003; the nine major electricity companies of the E7 signed a range of agreements with the UN to facilitate technical cooperation for sustainable energy projects in developing countries; the UN Environment Program launched a new initiative called the Global Network on Energy for Sustainable Development to promote the research, transfer and deployment of green and cleaner energy technologies to the developing world; the UN has received 32 partnership submissions for energy projects with at least $26 million in resources).

c. Health (the US announced a commitment to spend $2.3 billion through 2003 on health; the UN has received 16 partnership submission for health projects with $ 3 million in resources).

d. Agriculture (the US invested $90 million in 2003 for sustainable agriculture programs; the UN received 17 partnership submission with at least $2 million in additional resources).

e. Biodiversity and Ecosystem Management (the US announced $53 million for forests in 2002 – 2005; the U.N. received 32 partnership initiatives with $100 million in resources).

f. **Cross-Cutting Issues** (Agreement to the replenishment of the Global Environment Facility with a total of $3 billion; $2.92 billion announced pre-Summit and $ 80 million added by EU in Johannesburg; Norway pledged an additional % 50 million towards following up the Johannesburg commitments; the United Kingdom announced it was doubling its assistance to Africa to £ 1 billion a year and raising its overall assistance for all countries by 50 per cent; the EU announced that it will increase its development assistance with more than 22 billion euros in the years to 2006 and by more than 9 billion euros annually from 2006 onwards; Germany announced a contribution of 500 million euros over the next five years to promote cooperation on renewable energy; Canada announced that it will eliminate tariffs and quotas on almost all products from the least developed countries, and that by 2010, it would double development assistance; Japan announced it will provide at least 250 billion yen in education assistance over a five-year period and that it would extend emergency food aid amounting to $30 million to save children in southern Africa from famine; Ireland announced that it has allocated almost 8 million euros in emergency funding in response to the humanitarian needs of the African region).

4. The Copenhagen Consensus

Another important event in the field of development is the Copenhagen Consensus whose goal was in setting forth priorities among a series of proposals for confronting ten global challenges, as identified by the United Nations: civil conflicts, climate change, communicable diseases, education, financial stability, governance, hunger and malnutrition, migration, trade reform, and water and sanitation. A panel of some of the world's most distinguished economic experts, among which three Nobel laureates, was invited to consider these issues.

The panel assigned the highest priority to new measures to prevent the spread of HIV/AIDS. Spending assigned to this purpose would yield extraordinarily high benefits, averting nearly 30 million new infections by 2010. Costs were estimated at $ 27 billion. According to the *2004 Report on the Global AIDS Epidemic,* although international resources devoted to meeting the challenge of HIV/AIDS have increased from about $50 million in 1996 to about $2.8 billion in 2002, more than $10 billion annually is needed to stem the pandemic.[26]

Policies to attack hunger and malnutrition followed HIV/AIDS. Reducing the prevalence of iron-deficiency anaemia by means of food supplements, in particular, has an exceptionally high ratio of benefits to costs. Of the three proposals considered, this was ranked at $12 billion. The panel ranked a second proposal, to increase spending on research into new agricultural technologies appropriate for poor countries, at number five.

With regard to trade reform, the panel considered tree main proposals: (1) multilateral and unilateral reduction of tariffs and non-tariff barriers, together with the elimination of agricultural subsidies; (2) extension of regional trade agreements; (3) adoption of the "Everything but Arms (EBA)" proposal for non-reciprocal lowering of rich-country tariffs on exports from the least developed countries.

In order to give a proper answer to the problem of water and sanitation, the panel proposed, among others, small-scale water **technology for** livelihoods.

The panel also considered alternatives to improve education in developing countries. They endorsed the view that externally supervised examinations improve accountability of schools and should be promoted. Yet, some 115 million children do not attend primary school, and enrollments are woefully low in Sub-Saharan Africa (57 %) and South Asia (84 %). As put in the *Human Development Report 2003*, "lack of education robs an individual of a full life. It also robs society of a foundation for sustainable development because education is critical to improving health, nutrition, and productivity. The education Goal is thus central to meeting the other Goals."

1. The Doha Development Round

The Doha Round, named after the city of Doha, Qatar, where the trade negotiations took place in November 2001 marks a new attempt to further opening up markets, but also rectifying some of the imbalances of the past (Stiglitz 2003, p. 245). The negotiations were directing towards trade liberalization, thus lowering trade barriers between countries of varying degrees of development and prosperity.

Another meeting was held in 2003 in Cancún, intending to reach an agreement on Doha objectives. The talks failed due to disagreements on farm subsidies and access to markets. At the next meeting in Geneva in 2004, a framework agreement on opening global trade was reached, with the US, EU, Japan and Brazil agreed to end export subsidies, reduce agricultural subsidies and lower tariff barriers, and developing countries agreed to reduce tariffs on manufactured goods, but gain the right to specially protect key industries. No progress, however, was achieved in Paris talks in 2005.

During Hong Kong's 2005 WTO Ministerial Meeting, trade ministers were able to reach a deal on setting a deadline for eliminating subsidies of agricultural exports, which is the year 2013. What was seen as a step in achieving a long-pursued UN goal is the final declaration required industrialized countries to open their markets to goods from the world's poorest nations. The latest of the Doha liberalization talks were held in July

2006 in Geneva. The talks were unable to produce any agreement in matters relating to reducing farming subsidies and lowering import taxes.

The collapsed Doha trade liberalization talks will continue to have serious consequences for poor and/or undeveloped and underdeveloped or developing countries. In fact, given the state of interconnectedness between countries of the world, such an event could also have negative costs or impact rich economies in a negative way. The likely consequences of a failure to reach agreement in the Geneva talks may be translated, though not limited to the following terms:

- the failure of the international community to create an equitable and balanced multilateral trading system will create serious impediments to a sustained process of economic growth;
- there may be a considerable delay in concluding the negotiations and it seems unlikely for talks to resume in the coming months. To the skepticism of a successful outcome of the Doha Round is also the fact that broad authority granted to the United States President under the Trade Act of 2002 expired in 2007, and any trade agreement later will need to be approved by Congress;
- such a delay, in turn, will be a lost chance to further global growth and to improve the current state of poor countries;
- the suspension of this multilateral process may give rise to a shift toward bilateral, and in some cases, regional free trade agreements. Despite the advantages that such agreements create, yet they cannot substitute the effects of multilateral liberalization.

C. The Concept of Sustainable Development

1. UN Conference on the Human Environment (Stockholm Declaration)

The UN Conference on the Human Environment is famously known for bringing into life the idea and concept of "sustainable development,"[27] which it defines as "development that meets the needs of the present without compromising the ability of future generations to meet their own needs."[28]

After "having considered the need for a common outlook and for common principles to inspire and guide the peoples of the world in the preservation and enhancement of the human environment," the Commission proclaimed as the "imperative goal for mankind" the need to defend and improve the human environment for present and future generations in harmony with peace and global economic and social development.[29] Such a goal was contextualized in light of international law, thus trying to expose the legal character of it, while reminding States of their legal obligations. The Conference declared, as a matter of "common conviction," that:

*"States have in accordance with the Charter of the United Nations and the principles of international law, the sovereign **right** to exploit their own resources pursuant to their own environmental policies, and the **responsibility** to ensure that activities within their jurisdiction or control do not cause damage to the environment of other states or of areas beyond the limits of national jurisdiction".*[30] *(Emphasis added).*

The Conference, in spite of its contribution towards developing a new conceptual framework for the environment, did not prove to be a sufficient instrument for reducing environmental problems. The concept of "sustainable development" was further expanded by several other instruments.

2. UN World Charter for Nature

Due to concerns over the degradation of world's ecosystems, a decade later, the UN General Assembly adopted the World Charter for Nature, establishing the principle that all ecosystems and resources of the world "be managed to achieve and maintain optimum sustainable productivity."[31] The principle also recognized that, in exercising sovereignty over their natural resources, each State shall give effect to the provisions of the World Charter for Nature.[32] The overall effect of the World Charter may be seen more in terms of expanding upon the notion of sustainable development.

3. UN World Commission on Environment and Development (Brundtland Commission)

The UN World Commission on Environment and Development was created in 1983 to shed further light on the content, and policy and other implications of "sustainable development."[33] The Commission's mandate was to: a) re-examine the critical issues of the environment and development and formulate innovative, concrete, and realistic action proposals to deal with them; b) strengthen existing and propose new forms of international co-operation on the environment and development; and c) raise world-wide levels of understanding and commitment to action.[34] The Commission is also known as the Brundtland Commission, after its chairman Norwegian Prime Minister Gro Harlem Brundtland.

After many years of work and public consultation, the Commission issued its report entitled, *Our Common Future*.[35] The Commission conceived

131

of "sustainable development" a process of meeting "the needs of the present without compromising the ability of future generations to meet their own needs,"[36] a *notion* which is not free of limits "imposed by the present state of technology and social organization on environmental resources and by the ability of the biosphere to absorb the effects of human activities."[37] In other words, "sustainable development is a process of change in which the exploitation of resources, the direction of investments, the orientation of technological development, and institutional change are all in harmony and enhance both current and future potential to meet human needs and aspirations."[38]

4. UN Conference on Environment and Development (Rio Declaration on Environment and Development)

The UN Conference on Environment and Development was held at Rio de Janeiro in 1992. The Conference produced the Rio Declaration on Environment and Development, which contains 27 principles, covering varying aspects of the relationship between environment and development. The Declaration builds upon the U.N. Conference on the Human Environment (1972), reaffirming many of the Stockholm Declaration's principles. However, the Rio Declaration brings some new approaches and principles to environment protection and development. Of these progressive principles are the precautionary principle and polluter-pays principle (respectively principles 15 and 16). Unlike the Stockholm Declaration of 1972, the Rio Declaration makes specific reference to the right to development, which "must be fulfilled so as to equitably meet developmental and environmental needs of present and future generations" (Principle 3). This would not only mean an inter-generational equity, but also the effectuation of environmental needs in addition to developmental human needs. As Principle 4 of the Rio Declaration states, "in order to achieve sustainable development, environmental protection shall constitute an integral part of the development process and cannot be considered in isolation from it."

5. Human Development Reports and the Advancement of "Sustainable Human Development"

The United Nations Development Program (UNDP) has further developed and expanded the concept of "human development" during the 1990s. This new conception refers to a process of enlarging people's choices: human development is about people, about expanding their choices to live full, creative lives in freedom and dignity. The work of economists such as

Amartya Sen, a Noble laureate, and Mahboub El Haq have profoundly shaped the conceptual meaning of development during their work with the United Nations Development Program. Research carried out by Sen remains an integral reference of this conception, in particular his contribution in 1990 over the concept of developing human capabilities as an objective of the sustainable human development process. His basic notion of development is defined in terms of a process of expanding people's choices (Sen 1999).

Every *Human Development Report* has argued that the purpose of development is to improve people's lives by expanding their choices, freedom and dignity.[39] The Human Development Indicator (HDI) is an indicator of the degree human development enjoyed in various countries, introduced in *Human Development Report 1997*. HDI is comprised of the following measuring components:

1) Longevity (life expectancy at birth);
2) Knowledge (adult literacy rate, gross enrolment ratio);
3) Decent standard of living (GDP per capita measured in PPP$).[40]

To this list and understanding was later added several other aspects and dimensions, and the name of the concept itself was changed from "human development" to "sustainable human development" in order to highlight the importance of sustaining all forms of capital and resources—physical, human, financial, and environmental—as a precondition for meeting the needs also of future generations. By enhancing human capabilities to expand choices and opportunities for men, women and children, sustainable human development creates an environment in which human security is guaranteed and individual human beings can develop their full potential and lead a life of dignity and freedom.

The concept of "sustainable human development," thus represents an evolution of the classic concept of human development: its emphasis has moved from the material well-being of states to the well-being of people.[41] While the classical approach was based on three factors of production, namely land, capital and lobar, the new paradigm of sustainable human development places people at the center, as the principal actor and the ultimate goal of development.

By way of summary, the central subject of development and its ultimate beneficiary is, and should be, the human person who then may act either individually or in association with any group of people. As rightly provided in the Declaration on the Right to Development, the central beneficiary of the right to development is indeed the human person, and in the Rio Declaration—in the context of sustainable development—human beings are at the center of concerns for sustainable development.

D. The Status of Sustainable Development

The concept of "sustainable development" has diversified its presence in a variety of economic, legal and policy settings. It can be found in such sources as the jurisprudence of the World Court,[42] in several economic agreements, such as the WTO Agreement[43] and NAFTA.[44] Although it is recognized at a level of a "concept" (*Gabčikovo-Nagymaros*) or "objective" (WTO Agreement), and key components of it such as environment is still covered by the so-called "soft law," it is also true and should indeed be noted that sectors of environment are being translated into "hard law," by acquiring the status of custom. Yet, however, there is not single treaty codifying legal obligations concerning environment.

Those progressive principles affirmed in the Rio Declaration, *i.e.*, the precautionary and the polluter-pays principles have already acquired a stronger legal character, widely recognized as forming part of customary international law. The precautionary principle was reaffirmed by the ICJ in *Gabčikovo-Nagymaros* case. The Court held that "vigilance and prevention are required on account of the often irreparable character of damage to the environment."[45] This principle is also recognized in various international and regional instruments, including but not limited to, World Charter for Nature; United Nations Framework Convention on Climate Change; The Convention for the Protection of the Marine Environment of the North-East Atlantic (known as the "OSPAR Convention"); Cartagena Protocol on Biosafety; and African Convention on the Conservation of Nature and Natural Resources.

The same is true with regard to the polluter-pays principles, which at very least, represents a European regional custom. Most clearly, this principle is articulated in, and protected by Directive 2004/35/CE of the European Parliament and of the Council of 21 April 2004 on environmental liability with regard to the prevention and remedying of environmental damage. The purpose of the Directive is "to establish a framework of environmental liability based on the 'polluter-pays' principle, to prevent and remedy environmental damage."[46]

Other major instruments, affirming and reaffirming this principle include: OECD's (Organization for Economic Co-operation and Development) Environment and Economics Guiding Principles Concerning International Economic Aspects of Environmental Policies; EC Council Recommendation of 3 March 1975 regarding cost allocation and action by public authorities on environmental matters; OECD Council Recommendation concerning the Application of the Polluter-Pays Principle to Accidental Pollution; the OSPAR Convention; International Convention on Oil Pollution Preparedness, Response and Cooperation; and 2003 Kiev Protocol on Liability for Accidental Damage to Transboundary Waters.

The duty not to cause environmental damage, as articulated in Principle 21 of the Stockholm Declaration and Principle 2 of the Rio Declaration, is perhaps one of the most representative environmental principles that bind States through its customary character. According to Principle 2, "States have, in accordance with the Charter of the United Nations and the principles of international law ... the responsibility to ensure that activities within their jurisdiction or control do not cause damage to the environment of other States or of areas beyond the limits of national jurisdiction." The principle was also extensively dealt in the jurisprudence of the World Court and other international tribunals. In its advisory opinion on *the Legality of the Threat or Use of Nuclear Weapons*, the Court held that, "the existence of the general obligation of States to ensure that activities within their jurisdiction and control respect the environment of other States or of areas beyond national control is now part of the corpus of international law relating to the environment."[47]

The same line of reasoning was repeated by the Court in its *Gabčikovo-Nagymaros* decision of 1997. The origins of the customary character of this principle are traced to the ICJ's ruling in *Corfu Channel* case and of the Arbitral Tribunal's decision in the *Trail Smelter* arbitration. In *Corfu Channel*, the Court held that a State is under an international obligation "not to allow knowingly its territory to be used for acts contrary to the rights of other States."[48] And, in *Trail Smelter*, the Arbitral Tribunal stated that, "no State has the right to use or permit the use of its territory in such a manner as to cause injury by fumes in or to the territory of another or the properties or persons therein, when the case is of serious consequences and the injury is established by clear and convincing evidence."[49]

An effort to codify (in a non-binding instrument) the principles that constitute the body of sustainable development was made by International Law Association, leading up to New Delhi Declaration of Principles of International Law relating to Sustainable Development. The New Delhi Declaration came up with the following list of principles: (1) the duty of States to ensure sustainable use of natural resources; (2) the principle of equity and the eradication of poverty; (3) the principle of common but differentiated responsibilities; (4) the principle of the precautionary approach to human health, natural resources and ecosystems; (5) the principle of public participation and access to information and justice; (6) the principle of good governance; and (7) the principle of integration and interrelationship, in particular in relation to human rights and social, economic and environmental objectives.[50]

V. ALTERNATIVE SOLUTIONS AND RECOMMENDATIONS IN THE COMMON GLOBAL INTEREST

Going beyond the limits of normativity, this section will introduce a set of alternative solutions and recommendations built upon the global values processes (Wiessner and Willard 2004; Lasswell and McDougal 1992; Tamene, 2008, p. 92). In addition, at a more practical level, on the mode of effectuating such human dignity-based conceptual framework, this article proposes a four Is system which is meant to serve as a guide light in this process, namely: information, interaction, incentives, and institutions. These elements are critical for an adequate or better system of promoting and preserving human dignity, and help remove certain misunderstandings and obstacles that otherwise may appear in the process of reducing (as a minimum) and eliminating (as an optimum) underdevelopment, or eradicating poverty and human suffering.

A. Value Categories System

1. Power refers to the making of decisions important to the social context as a whole and enforceable against challengers when necessary by the use of severe sanctions. In order to have important decisions that could better serve human development, then good and effective governance is fundamental.

A sound system of governance is essential for creating an enabling environment in which to pursue development. The three major domains or realms of governance should be compatible and, preferably, cooperative. Governance exercises its influence, and in turn is influenced by, institutions and organizations. The institutions and organizations of governance must be designed to contribute to sustainable development by establishing the political, legal, judicial and social circumstances for poverty reduction, job creation, environmental protection and the advancement of women. Good governance[51] is now widely considered the primary means for achieving sustainable development.

For politics and political institutions to promote development and safeguard the freedom and dignity of all people, democracy must widen and deepen,[52] and this has to be done in accordance with the specifics and realities of each society.

Good governance for sustainable development requires stronger mechanisms for people to participate in politics, government, the private sector, and the organization of civil society. After what happened in many developing countries and bearing in mind their general economic, political and social situation, restoring people's confidence in the state is one of the main challenges in re-establishing sound governance. Government leaders, capable of gaining public confidence, are needed. Political parties can help develop good decision-makers. Decentralizing responsibilities and resources to local and community levels can also restore participation.

At the end, countries must build the notion of participation into education systems. In the short-term, however, teachers must be trained to instill in children the values of participation. Another means of fostering participation is through citizen charters. Other mechanisms such as local and national elections are important means of involving citizens. Developing public consciousness is also a key to ensuring that mechanisms such as decentralization result in participation, leading to stronger influence from the bottom up. Governance systems must make people feel like active citizens.

2. Enlightenment refers to the process of gathering and spreading of information, institutionalized in agencies of research and the information media. As Amartya Sen (1999) puts it, the principal idea of development is that it should be seen as a process of expanding the real freedoms that people enjoy. The best way of expanding the real freedoms is through freely accessing and spreading information.

3. Wealth is the production and distribution of goods and services, institutionalized in business corporations and partnerships, trade unions and consumers' associations. In the modern world, communications and transportation remains vital in establishing a system of wealth. Furthermore, the creation of a favorable climate to enterprise and the mobilization of local savings for investment would further help a better functioning of the system of wealth. Moreover, there is of same level of importance to foster sound financial management, including efficient tax systems and productive public expenditure.

4. Well-being is opportunity for safety, health and comfort; relevant institutions include facilities for medical care and disease prevention. Because an unhealthy population cannot be a productive labor force, because a basic standard of health should be viewed as a fundamental human right, because it is unconscionable that diseases that could be eradicated or at least controlled continue to afflict millions in the less developed world, often robbing them of any human dignity.

5. Skill is opportunity to acquire and exercise excellence in a particular operation, including schools, artistic, vocational and professional organizations concerned with maintaining and improving standards of performance and taste.

The first and the most important precondition here is the effective realization of the right to education or the growth of social opportunity in the form of widespread access to education. Education is the most important value by which human beings are able to participate and interact with society, and through which the human mind and values develop. As Justice Cardozo (1928, p. 104) once said, "[W]e are free only if we know, and so in proportion to our knowledge. There is no freedom without choice, and there is no choice without knowledge, - or none that is not illusory. Implicit, therefore, in the very notion of liberty is the liberty of the mind to absorb and to beget."

The furtherance and enjoyment by all of this value could be a decisive force in the Third World's path towards sustainable development. Thus, supporting civil education will be essential for long-term progress, and providing more information through the media will be crucial to develop public awareness and confidence in current political regimes.

6. Affection is giving and receiving intimacy, friendship and loyalty, including the institutions of family and intimate friends plus associations established to express loyalty. In this respect, certain prerequisites are necessary. First of all, man and women have the right to live their lives and raise their children in dignity, free from hunger and from fear of violence, oppression or injustice.

7. Respect is the recognition and reciprocal honoring of freedom of choice. McDougal, Lasswell and Chen suggest that using this universal principle, it is possible to cover all aspects of life requiring protection by formulations of rights (McDougal, Lasswell and Chen 1980). Distinctive institutions provide recognition of common merit as a human being and particular merit as a member of a group.

A cohesive policy, a well-defined strategy and an increased and consistent level of commitment of the world elites is the very essence of attempts to make the human values triumphant in the developing world and strengthen democratic consolidation throughout the world. Global challenges, as put in *Human Development Report 2003*, must be managed in a way that distributes the costs and burdens fairly in accordance with basic principles of equity and social justice. Those who suffer or who benefit least deserve help from those who benefit most. Furthermore, human beings must respect one another, in all their diversity of belief, culture and language. Differences within and between societies need to be understood only as a precious asset of humanity.

8. Rectitude is responsibility for conduct. Its institutions formulate and apply standards of responsibility, and justify and celebrate these norms in religious, metaphysical or ethical terms. The notions of accountability and responsibility are the key to expanding the value of rectitude. Responsibility for managing worldwide economic and social development, as well as threats to international peace and security, must be shared among the nations of the world and should be exercised multilaterally.

B. Four I's System

Shortly elaborated, the four I's system stands, contributes and operates in a rather integrated and comprehensive manner, thus covering the most-needed and critical facets of the development process. This practical operating system is necessary to promote, protect and advance the value processes.

1. Information serves the purpose of expressing the positions of the parties involved, offering clear guidelines on the process, and outlining the pathways. This element is fundamental to having informed and sustained decisions. It also encompasses the maintenance of regular channels of communication and exchange information among both institutional and non-institutional settings.

2. Interaction includes a process of genuine cooperation among parties, as well close relationship and ability to overcome obstacles and reach compromises that are in the common global interest. It does also involve meaningful participation.

3. Incentives help transform underdevelopment, create sustainability and use them in a way that best contributes to the establishment of accountable and responsible institutions and to maximizing the access of all to all the goal values. It is important to getting the incentives right and on time.

4. Institutions are broadly-defined as norms, expectations, rules, and organizations, or structures of expectations concerning who, with what qualifications and mode of selection is authorized to make which decisions by what criteria and what procedures. The ultimate concern of the institutions is and should be the individual human being who may act either alone or in association with different associations or groups. The four elements work as a system of complementary settings, so giving a due weight to this system and implementing it in the practical modes of policy interactions would considerably impact and enhance the process of reducing and eradicating the lack of human development.

VI. Concluding Remarks

In the last analysis, the future of effective realization of the right to development, and of sustainable development in general, will very much depend on the extent the above-listed values are addressed and applied at both national and international levels. As far as these values remain neglected, the success of the battle for a just and equal world would only remain a nice dream. And, this is really not the solution that reflects the global common interest. An order of human dignity asks for maximizing access of all to all the values humans desire.

The wording of the United Nations Millennium Declaration that "[i]n addition to our separate responsibilities to our individual societies, we have a collective responsibility to uphold the principles of human dignity, equality and equity at the global level" does have a perfect connotation of how this problem can be solved. However, these perfect terms seem to remain perfect only in terms of its wording and purpose. As already suggested and concluded, this is simply not enough. The most-desired human values must be widely shaped and shared by all human beings. Further, as it is seen in this discussion, there is no single solution to the problem of development.

The solution, in fact, is us; it can be found among and within all the diversity of cultures and other social associations or groups, of ideas or schools of thought, whose cooperation can bring into life a public order of human dignity through a process of rigorous implementation of justice, equality and human values at all levels and in all processes. In turn, this will be translated into living in a more secure and peaceful planet. One's freedom surely benefits from the other's freedom. The same is true with rights. Such mutual correlation is the best instrument to advance issues of the world public order of human dignity and the universe of human aspirations.

Notes

1 The so-called "negative rights" are fundamentally civil and political in nature, and are codified in Articles 3 to 21 of the 1948 Universal Declaration of Human Rights, and in the International Covenant on Civil and Political Rights of 1966. The essential aim of civil and political rights is to protect the individual from the arbitrary exercise of the State power. These rights include: freedom of speech; freedom of religion and belief; the right to a fair trial; the right to political participation; freedom of assembly and association; freedom of movement and alike.

2 The origin of the "positive rights" has mainly derived from the views of writers such as Jean-Jacques Rousseau and employed by Continental legal tradition. *The French Declaration of the Rights of Man and the Citizen* followed in 1791 by the French Constitution provides for poor relief and free public education, the first sign of what we call today: *economic and social rights*. According to this point of view, there are things to which every person is entitled and for which State is obligated. Simply, this is in line with Rousseau's argument that people agree to live in common if society protects them. Of this kind are the following: the rights to education, to legal equality, and to a livelihood. These rights fall on the second-generation human rights, and can be considered as an equivalent to equality or *égalité*. The nature of these rights is fundamentally social, economic

and cultural, which means that they are concerned with the economic, social and cultural well being of persons. These rights are codified in the International Covenant on Economic, Social and Cultural Rights of 1966, as well as in Articles 22 to 27 of the Universal Declaration of Human Rights. Among others, they include the following: the right to work and to just and favorable conditions of work; trade union freedoms; the right to education; the right to an adequate standard of living; the right to health.

3   Commission on Human Rights Resolution 36 (XXXVII) of 11 March 1981.
4   *Vienna Declaration and Programme of Action: Note By The Secretariat*, World Conference on Human Rights, Part I, U.N. Doc. A/CONF.157/23 (1993).
5   *Ibid.*
6   U.N. GAOR, 41st Sess., Supp. No. 53, at 183, U.N. Doc. A/RES/41/128 (1986).
7   *Ibid,. art. 1.*
8   *Ibid.* art. 2
9   *Ibid.* pmbl
10 *Ibid.* art. 3(1).
11 Human Rights Committee, *General Comment 26 (61)*, A/53/40, Vol. I (1998), Annex VII (p. 102); CCPR/C/21/Rev.1/Add.8/Rev.1.
12 *Charter of the United Nations*, Can. T.S. 1945 No. 76; [1976] YRBK. U.N. 1043; 59 Stat. 1031, T.S. 993 (*signed at* San Francisco on June 26, 1945; *entered into force* on October 24, 1945).
13 *Ibid.*
14 *Idid.* art. 1, 3.
15 *Ibid.* art. 13, 1 (b).
16 *Ibid.* art. 61,
17 *Ibid.* art. 55.
18 International Covenant on Economic, Social and Cultural Rights, *adopted* 16 Dec. 1966, G.A. Res. 2200, U.N. GAOR, 21st Sess., Supp. No. 16, U.N. Doc. A/6316 (1966), art. 2, 1, 999 U.N.T.S. 3 (*entered into force* Jan. 3, 1976)
19 United States Government, Statement at the U.N. Commission on Human Rights, 59th Sess., Comment on the Working Group on the Right to Development (Feb. 10, 2003).
20 CESCR General Comment No. 3, U.N. Doc. E/1991/23.
21 Draft Optional Protocol to the ICESCR, U.N. Doc. E/CN.4/1997/105.
22 International Covenant on Civil and Political Rights, *adopted* 16 Dec. 1966, G.A. Res. 2200, U.N. GAOR, 21st Sess., Supp. No. 16, U.N. Doc. A/6316 (1966), 999 U.N.T.S. 171 (*entered into force* March 23, 1976).
23 U.N. GAOR, 41st Sess., Supp. No. 53, at 183, U.N. Doc. A/RES/41/128 (1986).
24 *See* Monterrey Consensus of the International Conference on Financing for Development, *Report of the International Conference on Financing For Development*, Monterrey, Mexico, 18-22 March 2002, A/CONF.198/11, ch. 1, at 5.
25 *See ibid.*

26 UNAIDS, *2004 Report on the Global AIDS Epidemic*, 137 (2004).
27 *Report of the UN Conference on the Human Environment* ("Stockholm Declaration"), New York, 1972, UN Doc. A/Conf. 48/14 (1972).
28 *Ibid.*
29 *Ibid*
30 *Ibid.* Principle 21.
31 G.A. Res. 7, U.N. GAOR, 37th Sess., No. 51, at 239, U.N. Doc. A/Res/37/7 (1982), *reprinted in* 22 I.L.M. 455 (1983).
32 *Ibid.* 22.
33 *Of Preparation of the Environmental Perspective to the Year 2000 and Beyond*, U.N. GAOR, 38th Session., Supp. No. 47, 102nd plen. mtg., U.N. Doc. A/38/47 (1983).
34 World Commission on Environment and Development, *Our Common Future* 43 (1987).
35 *Ibid.*
36 *Ibid.*
37 *Ibid*
38 *Ibid.* at 46.
39 UNDP, *Human Development Report 2003*, 27-28 (2003).
40 UNDP, *Human Development Report 1997* (1997).
41 *Human Development Report 1994* describes "sustainable human development" as follows: "[s]ustainable human development is pro-people, pro-jobs, and pro-nature. It gives the highest priority to poverty reduction, productive employment, social integration, and environmental regeneration. It brings human numbers into balance with coping capacities of societies and the carrying capacities of nature. It accelerates economic growth and translates it into improvements in human lives, without destroying the natural capital needed to protect the opportunities of future generations. It also recognizes that not much can be achieved without a dramatic improvement in the status of women and the opening of all economic opportunities to women. And sustainable human development empowers people-enabling them to design and participate in the processes and events that shape their lives."
42 See *Gabčikovo-Nagymaros (Hungary v. Slovakia)*, Judgment of 25 September 1997, ICJ Reports (1997), and *Advisory Opinion on the Legality of the Threat or Use of Nuclear Weapons*, 8 July 1996, ICJ Reports (1996).
43 Agreement Establishing the World Trade Organization (WTO Agreement), 1994
44 North American Free Trade Agreement (NAFTA), 1993, reprinted in *International Legal Materials*, 32 (1993), at 297. *See* also North American Agreement on Environmental Cooperation, 1993, reprinted in *International Legal Materials*, 32 (1993), at 289.
45 ICJ, *Reports*, 1997, 78.

46 Directive 2004/35/CE of the European Parliament and of the Council of 21 April 2004 on Environmental Liability with regard to the Prevention and Remedying of Environmental Damage, OJ L 143 of 30.4.2004.
47 ICJ, *Reports,* 1996, 29, at 241-42.
48 ICJ, *Reports*, 1949, at 22.
49 *United Nations Reports of International Arbitral Awards*, vol. 3, at 1965.
50 ILA Resolution 3/2002. *See* also UN Doc. A/57/329.
51 The characteristics that a system of good governance must posses are as the following: participatory, sustainable, legitimate and acceptable to the people, transparent, promotes equity and equality, able to develop the resources and methods of governance, promotes gender balance, tolerates and accepts diverse perspectives, able to mobilize resources for social purposes, strengthens indigenous mechanisms, operates by rule of law, efficient and effective in use of resources, engenders and commands respect and trust, accountable, able to define and take ownership of national solutions, enabling and facilitative, regulatory rather than controlling, able to deal with temporal issues, service-oriented.
52 UNDP, *Human Development Report 2002* (2002).

References

Alston, P. (1988) 'Making Space for New Human Rights: The Case of the Right to Development', *Harvard Human Rights Yearbook*, vol. 1, pp. 3-40.
Cardozo, B. (1928) *The Paradoxes of Legal Science*, Columbia University Press, New York.
Carven, M. (1995) *The International Covenant on Economic, Social and Cultural Rights: A Perspective on Its Development,* Clarendon Press, Oxford.
Desai, P. D. (1992) *Right to Development: Improving the Quality of Life*, in *The Right to Development in International Law*, eds. Subrata Roy Chowdhury, Erik M.G. Denters, and Paul J.I.M. de Waart, Martinus Nijhoff Publishers: Dordrecht/ Boston/London.
Gay, J. (2003) 'Development as Freedom: A Virtuous Circle?', *Afrobarometer Paper*, vol. 29, pp. 1-12.
Lasswell, H. & McDougal, M. (1992) *Jurisprudence for a Free Society: Studies in Law, Science and Policy* (Vol. I), New Haven Press, New Haven.
Lasswell, H. & McDougal, M. (1992) *Jurisprudence for a Free Society:Studies in Law, Science and Policy* (Vol. II), New Haven Press, New Haven.
Marks, S. (2003) 'The Human Right to Development: Between Rhetoric and Reality', *Harvard Human Rights Journal*, vol. 17, pp. 137-168.
Marks, S. (1981) 'Emerging Human Rights: A New Generation for the 1980's?', *Rutgers Law Review*, vol. 33 (winter), pp. 435-452.
McDougal, M. Lasswell, D. & Chen, L. (1980) *Human Rights and World Public Order: The Basic Policies of an International Law of Human Dignity*, Yale University Press, New Haven and London.
Keohane, R. (1998) 'When Does International Law Come Home?' *Houston Law Review*, vol. 35, no. 3 (fall), pp. 699-713.

Sen, A. (1999) *Development as Freedom*, Oxford University Press, Oxford.
Sengupta, A. (2004) *Implementing the Right to Development*, in *International Law and Sustainable Development*, eds. Nico Schrijver and Friedl Weiss, Martinus Nijhoff Publishers, Leiden/Boston.
Stiglitz, J. (2003) *Globalization and its Discontents*, W.W. Norton & Company, New York.
Tamene, G. (2006). Problems of Development Aid in Sub-Saharan Africa, in: *Development Aid—Rozvojová pomoc*, University of Economics in Bratislava, Faculty of international relations, Ekonóm Publishers, pp.136-154.
Tamene, G. (2007). "Political Ethics and the Human polity – The African Dimension". In: Sergi, B. S. and Bagatelas, T.W. (Eds.): *Economic and Political Development Ethics: Europe and Beyond*. Bratislava, Iura Edition, pp.103-134.
Tamene, G. 'CBOs and NGOs in the Discourse of African Aid Politics'. In: *Rozvojová pomoc a spolupráca 2008*, Zborník z III. Medzinárodnej vedeckej konferencie, Ekonomická univerzita v Bratislave, Fakulta medzinárodných vzťahov, vydavateľstvo EKONÓM, Bratislava, 2008.
Tamene, G. 'World Politics and Challenges to Neoliberalism: Could the CEE-EU-US Correlation Maintain the Trend?' In: *Journal of Comparative Politics*, Brno, 2008. Pp. 86-100.
Wiessner, S. & Willard, A. (2004) *Policy-Oriented Jurisprudence*, in *International Law in Contemporary Perspective*, eds. W. Michael Resiman *et al.*, Foundations Press, New York.

Chapter 7
The Introduction to the Public Company Accounting Reform and Investor Protection Act of 2002

Branislav Bernadic

City University, Bratislava 2005

Keywords: public company, accounting reform, Investor Protection Act, Securities Exchange Act, Glass-steagall Act, Imclone system, Sarbanes-Oxley Act, corporate responsibility.

Abstract

The purpose of this paper is to introduce fundamental provisions of the Public Company Accounting Reform and Investor Protection Act of 2002 (the Sarbanes-Oxley Act) to students of the Management Accounting course. Implications of the Act as well as circumstances that preceded and influenced its creation are also discussed, with a few words on problems of today's financial reporting at the end.

The Sarbanes-Oxley Act in the Context of Financial and Corporate Regulation

The first main regulation of American financial markets came after the Wall Street crash in 1929. Similarly as nowadays, a crucial problem had been accuracy of information offered to investors and the weakened integrity of financial markets. The response consisted of two acts, the 1933 Securities Act and the 1934 Securities Exchange Act, which set up the Securities and Exchange Commission and obliged corporations to disclose selected financial information verified by independent auditors.

In order to prevent the use of depositors' funds for extremely risky and speculative projects, the Glass-Steagall Act was adopted in 1933, which formally separated investment and purely commercial banking activities of American banks. However, the financial strength, economic importance, as well as lobbying ability of the main corporations had gradually grown over time and policies for easing some of the norms adopted in the 1930s became politically possible, especially in the context of economic problems experienced during the 1970s.

The 1980s and 1990s had seen strong deregulation, which was believed to be a necessary step towards greater economic growth, which in the end was the case. These deregulation tendencies of the two decades culminated in the revocation of the Glass-Steagall Act in 1999. Adoption of the Sarbanes-Oxley Act in 2002 has been the most important and most complex reform of the corporate sector since the 1930s.

Situation before Sarbanes-Oxley

The Sarbanes-Oxley Act came into existence during difficult times, in which the American economy and entire society had to face several extraordinary challenges, which in the end substantially influenced the strength and width of the new legislation. The massive economic growth of the 1990s ended with a rapid decline in stock markets, mainly influenced by the burst of the dot-com bubble, and the transition into an economic slowdown. The September 11, 2001 terrorist attacks in New York City and Washington D.C., as well as subsequent security uncertainty and the prospects of war in Afghanistan and Iraq contributed the slowdown. However, the series of corporate scandals had the most devastating impact on the American and global economy, and soon after the first corporate scandals erupted, it became clear the recovery would be difficult.

These tremendous corporate frauds not only significantly harmed the American and global stock markets, and destroyed the investments and pension savings of thousands of employees and investors, but essentially attacked the fundamentals of corporate capitalism. Everything began with the fall of energy giant Enron in December 2001, followed by telecommunications leader WorldCom in 2002 and other corporations. This included one of the „Big Five" global accounting firms Arthur Andersen, Adelphia Communications, ImClone Systems and some others.

In the majority of cases, the executives of the mentioned companies heavily engaged in restatements of financial records, covering up losses and expenses, insider trading and destruction of evidence. These corporate scandals, particularly the Enron collapse, were the immediate impulse for the legislative response.

The Sarbanes-Oxley Act of 2002[1]

The Sarbanes-Oxley Act, officially entitled the "Public Company Accounting Reform and Investor Protection Act of 2002" was adopted in order to strengthen the reliability of financial statements issued by public companies as well as shareholders' protection and the accountability of corporate executives. The bill was sponsored by Senator Paul Sarbanes and Congressman Mike Oxley and signed into law by President George W. Bush on July 30, 2002.

The law consists of 11 titles:

I - PUBLIC COMPANY ACCOUNTING OVERSIGHT BOARD
II – AUDITOR INDEPENDENCE
III – CORPORATE RESPONSIBILITY
IV- ENHANCED FINANCIAL DISCLOSURES
V – ANALYST CONFLICTS OF INTEREST
VI – COMMISSION RESOURCES AND AUTHORITY
VII – STUDIES AND REPORTS
VIII – CORPORATE AND CRIMINAL FRAUD ACCOUNTABILITY
IX – WHITE-COLLAR CRIME PENALTY ENHANCEMENTS
X – CORPORATE TAX RETURNS
XI – CORPORATE FRAUD ACCOUNTABILITY

TITLE I - PUBLIC COMPANY ACCOUNTING OVERSIGHT BOARD

Sections under this title establish the Public Company Accounting Oversight Board (PCAOB), as an independent non-profit corporation in order to oversee the audit of public companies that are subject to the securities laws. The main duties of the board are to register public accounting firms preparing audit reports for public corporations, establish auditing, quality control and other standards related to the preparation of audit reports, conduct inspections of registered accounting firms, enforce compliance with the Sarbanes-Oxley Act, rules of the PCAOB and the securities laws governing preparation and issuance of audit reports.

Section 102 specifies registration of the accounting firms with the PCAOB; the accounting firms are supposed to submit the names of all relevant subjects for which they prepared or issued audit reports during the immediately preceding year or for which expect to do so during the current year, list the annual fees received for audit services, other accounting services and non-audit services, respectively; they should submit a statement of the quality control policies for their auditing and accounting practices as well as a list of all accountants associated with the firm who are involved in the preparation of audit reports and any information relating to criminal, civil, or disciplinary actions pending against the auditing firm or any firm's person in connection with any audit report.

Section 103 further specifies quality control, independent standards and rules that should be established by the PCAOB and defines cooperation with designated professional groups of accountants and advisory groups. Sections 104 and 105 define inspections of registered accounting firms as well as investigations and disciplinary proceedings conducted by the PCAOB. Section 106 addresses foreign public accounting firms operating in the U.S.

In general, all foreign public accounting firms that prepare or furnish valid audit reports in the U.S. are subject to the Act and additional rules issued by the PCAOB, in the same manner any public accounting company organized and operating under U.S. laws does. However, the Act allows certain exceptions in special cases. Section 107 subordinates proceedings of the PCAOB to the oversight of the Securities and Exchange Commission. Section 108 contains amendment to the Securities Act of 1934 regarding accounting standards and defines when the Securities and Exchange Commission may recognize accounting principles as generally accepted.

TITLE II - AUDITOR INDEPENDENCE

Section 201 amends the Securities Act of 1934 and lists non-audit services that are considered unlawful for registered public accounting firms and any associated person of that firm to perform for the same company for which they prepare an audit report. These activities include bookkeeping or other performance related to the accounting records or financial statements, designing and implementation of financial information systems, internal audit outsourcing services, management or human resources functions, investment advising or investment banking services as well as all legal and expert services unrelated to the audit. Section 203 amends the Securities Act of 1934 and makes it unlawful for public accounting firms to provide audit services for any subject for more then 5 consecutive fiscal years. Section 204 amends the Securities Act of 1934 and requires all registered public accounting firms to report all critical accounting practices and policies used as well as all alternative treatments of financial information within GAAP that have been discussed with officials of audited company and other documents regarding written communication between the auditor and management of the audited company. Section 206 amends the Securities Act of 1934 and covers conflicts of interest.

According to this section, the CEO, CFO, controller, chief accounting officer or any person in an equivalent position in an audited company cannot have been employed by the accounting firm conducting audit services in this company and participated in the audit during the 1-year period preceding the initiation of the audit.

III – CORPORATE RESPONSIBILITY

Section 301 amends the Securities Act of 1934. According to this section, the Securities and Exchange Commission must direct the national securities exchanges and national securities associations to stop the listing of any security of a corporation not in compliance with provisions of this title. One of these provisions is defined in Section 302, which obliges CEOs and CFOs of audited public companies to personally certify each annual or quarterly report and review these reports. The signing officers are also responsible for establishing and maintaining internal controls. If a signing officer certifies a financial statement and s/he knows the statement does not comply with requirements of this law, then s/he is subject to criminal penalties under Section 906. Other sections of this title prohibit insider trading during pension fund blackout periods and provide rules of professional responsibility for attorneys.

IV- ENHANCED FINANCIAL DISCLOSURES

Section 402 enhances conflict of interest provisions and, in general, makes it unlawful for any public corporation directly or indirectly to extend or maintain credit to any director or executive officer of the particular corporation. Section 404 addressing management assessment of internal controls is expressly the most discussed and criticized part of the bill. The section requires every public corporation to add an internal control report to its annual report, which should state the responsibility of management for establishing and maintaining an adequate internal control structure and procedures for financial reporting as well as effectiveness of the internal control and reporting procedures. Additionally, the assessment made by the management of a company should be attested by the company's auditors. Other sections under this title address code of ethics for senior financial officers and enhance review of periodic disclosures.

TITLE V - ANALYST CONFLICTS OF INTEREST

Section 501 addresses the treatment of securities analysts by securities exchanges and registered securities associations. The main provision is that the Securities and Exchange Commission, or upon its authorization, securities exchanges or registered securities associations, in order to improve the objectivity of research and provide investors with more reliable information, are supposed to adopt rules designed to address conflicts of interest that can arise when the analysts recommend securities in research reports and public appearances.

TITLE VIII – CORPORATE AND CRIMINAL FRAUD ACCOUNTABILITY

This title is also cited as the "Corporate and Criminal Fraud Accountability Act of 2002" and amends the United States Code. The main provision addresses destruction, alteration or falsification of records in a bankruptcy or Federal investigation. Auditors of public corporations are required to maintain, all audit or review work papers for a period of five years. Section 806 enhances whistle-blower protection for employees of public corporations who provide evidence of fraud.

TITLE IX - WHITE-COLLAR CRIME PENALTY ENHANCEMENTS

This title, also cited as the "White-Collar Crime Penalty Enhancement Act of 2002" amends the United States Code and significantly increases the white-collar crime penalties. For example, maximal penalties for mail and wire frauds have been increased from 5 to 20 years. Section 906 addresses the failure of corporate executives to certify financial reports and defines penalties for such failures, as well as penalties for knowingly certifying a non-compliant financial statement.

TITLE XI - CORPORATE FRAUD ACCOUNTABILITY

The title, also cited as the "Corporate Fraud Accountability Act of 2002", establishes a sentence in prison up to 20 years for whoever in a corrupt manner alters, destroys, or conceals a record, document or other object or attempts to do so with intention to impair an official proceeding; or otherwise obstructs, influences or impedes any official proceeding or attempts to do so. The title also increases criminal penalties under the Securities and Exchange

Act of 1934 and authorizes the Securities and Exchange Commission to prohibit persons from serving as officers or directors of public corporations in particular cases cited in the bill.

Implications of the Sarbanes-Oxley Act

Cost of Implementation

In 2004, which was the first year of reporting under the Act, surveyed companies spent an average of $7.8 million on compliance, about 10 percent of their revenues (the survey included 90 clients of large accounting firms - Deloitte Touche Tohmatsu, Ernst & Young, KPMG, and Pricewaterhouse Coopers) (Swartz, 2005). Another survey of 217 companies conducted by Financial Executives International states the average cost of Section 404 compliance was $4.4 million. (Swartz, 2005)

The costs vary, depending mainly on the size of the particular company and its revenues. The major part of the costs are generated by additional audit hours that need to be spent in the auditing process, so it basically holds that the higher the revenues, the higher the implementation costs. Even though some insiders say that costs will rise, more probably they will gradually decrease, thanks mainly to the learning curve effect, as less audit hours will be needed to get the same work done, as well as a new guidance issued by the PCAOB last May, which allows higher flexibility in applying the rules.

Whatever the case may be, it is already obvious expenses have been much higher than the Securities and Exchange Commission's initially estimates. One of the reasons may be the fact that motivated by Sarbanes-Oxley Act compliance, companies often spend money on unnecessary things. The Act has in many cases been used in the marketing of such products as CRM systems, or other analytical tools.

Direct Improvements versus Unreasonable Overload

Supporters of the law maintain the Act addresses the issue and has achieved results. According to Donaldson of the SEC, about 200 companies out of 2,500 that filed reports with the Securities and Exchange Commission found weaknesses in controls and some of them discovered errors in their financial statements. McDonough of the PCAOB states that 79 percent of 222 financial executives surveyed by Oversight Systems reported Section 404 strengthened their internal controls (Swartz, 2005). Other sources declare that thanks to the Sarbanes-Oxley Act, 49 percent of surveyed companies have more efficient financial operations and 31 percent reduced error rates. (Corporate Board, July-August 2005)

J. Carcello of the Corporate Governance Center says stronger controls lead to real benefits in the form of eliminating waste and better information for improved decision-making (Corporate Board, July-August 2005). On the other hand, critics of the law say the Act is too complicated and its implementation too expensive. The main reservation is the law can make executives too busy with its implementation and make them too anxious and excessively risk averse. As Michael Moran of Goldman Sachs puts it, "the biggest cost is the business activity that didn't occur," (Smith, 2005).

According to a Foley & Lardner LLP survey, in 2004 21 percent of companies were considering going private as a result of the regulations (Bronstad, 2005). Probably the most significant representatives of U.S. public companies, the US Chamber of Commerce, the Business Roundtable and the Financial Services Roundtable say, „compliance with the Sarbanes-Oxley Act is too expensive and time-consuming" (Francis, 2005). After all, one of the sponsors, congressman Oxley, admitted that "after WorldCom happened it was difficult to legislate responsibly in that type of hot-house atmosphere......some of the reforms were excessive and could have been introduced more responsibly" (Parker, Tucker, 2005).

Impact of the Act on Securities Exchanges

American securities exchanges are also affected by the Sarbanes-Oxley Act and other related legislation as some companies, especially European ones are delisting from American exchanges or are considering doing so. And there is also lost business when new listings, many from emerging markets, do not occur in America, but go to Europe or elsewhere. According to Dealogic, the number of American Depository Receipts has fallen from 38 billion to 40 million (Baird, 2005). Last December, Air China listed at the London Stock Exchange instead at NYSE to raise $604 million in a dual listing with Hong Kong. (Baird, 2005)

The trend seems to be obvious also in the case of smaller, growing companies. In 1994 London's AIM, which is an exchange for middle-sized companies had 61 international listings compared to 16 in 2003, and in the first five months of the last year there were 33 new international listings (O'Connor, 2005). Steven Gartner of Willkie Farr & Gallagher admits, "there are fewer foreign companies showing up for US listings" (Baird, 2005). One of the reasons for this move seems to be higher costs and regulations, which come with listing at American Exchanges. Philippe de Buck of UNICE says that the burden on European firms listing in the U.S. goes beyond what is needed to achieve the results sought and European firms must win an exemption from controversial parts of the regulation instead of complying with another layer of burdensome and unnecessary legislation which would hinder their functioning and competitiveness. (Economist Intelligence Unit, 2002)

European companies, especially German ones, raising capital in the U.S. financial markets point out the incompatibility of the regulation with their national rules on corporate governance. However, here we need to mention that besides new U.S. regulations there are also other factors causing this move, particularly significant changes in financial markets, which have taken place in the last decade. These are primarily globalization and liberalization, and also the fact there is much more money available in Europe markets than before. Public companies and securities exchanges are also not the only ones affected by the new regulation. Section 201 has brought new business opportunities for small accounting and consulting firms across the U.S., as under the new regulation big accounting and consulting firms providing multiple services found themselves in conflicts of interest.

Regulation of Credit Rating Agencies

Section 702 of the Sarbanes-Oxley Act, requires the Securities and Exchange Commission to study and report concerning the role and function of credit rating agencies in the securities markets, analyze any conflicts of interest they face as well as barriers to entry they may encounter into the rating industry. Such a report was published by the Commission in January 2003 with a promise of further work on the issues that later became a regulation initiative proposing new legislation. These require rating agencies to disclose their books to inspection and addresses conflicts of interest, misuse of internal information and other concerns.

Even though there were in fact some efforts to regulate the industry, since 1975 when five main agencies were labeled by the Securities and Exchange Commission as Nationally Recognized Statistical Rating Organizations, considered the US government's approval of quality, nothing else much has happened since them. The industry has developed in such a way that even though 130 ratings agencies exist in the U.S., Moody's Investors Service and Standard & Poor's currently hold 80 per cent market share. Similarly as in the case of the Sarbanes-Oxley Act, the initiative evokes intense discussions and strong opposition from the major players in the industry. Furthermore, representatives of Standard & Poor's have argued with the First Amendment, reasoning that they perform journalistic functions and thus enjoy the same freedom and protections as journalists. Charlie

Brown of Fitch Ratings worries that because of the bill „some rating agencies will be forced to drop out of the rating business and some may be deterred from entering it." (Hume, 2005)

Challenges of Today's Financial Reporting

The current economic environment, essentially determined by rapid technological and financial innovation, creates new challenges for management and accountants. The constantly growing numbers of trades in capital markets, wide availability of instant business and economic information as well as difficult economic times, increase sensitivity in capital markets and pressures on economic performance, particularly on short-term performance, which greatly effects the extremely rapid nature of current capital flows. Thus besides other reaities in general, accounting practices and business structure strategies are increasingly employed in management's efforts to create value and support their short-term indicators.

I must also mention that creation of special purpose entities and transactions with related parties involving off-balance sheet transactions, and aggressive mergers and acquisitions, are examples of techniques often employed in ratios enhancement. These practices together with continual innovation in capital markets make business structures and transactions highly complex and sophisticated, thus making their accounting and audit coverage as well as internal control effectivity more and more challenging. Financial globalization and liberalization as was stated before, naturally contribute to problems overall, as firms operating globally must often deal with different accounting and auditing standards, which in the end further complicate an already intricate situation.

Notes

1   For the purpose of this paper, which is to introduce the Sarbanes-Oxley Act to the Management Accounting course students, we have covered just basic and most important provisions of the law and in some cases we have simplified some of the provisions as a more detailed explanation would go beyond the scope of the course and actual needs of the students

References

Baird, Roger. *Nyse pays the price for regulatory overload.* (New York Stock Exchange Inc.) Finance Week, June 29, 2005

Bronstad, Amanda. Corporate reform. *Los Angeles Business Journal*, July 4, 2005

Employee morale is one factor driving SOX compliance automation. *Corporate Board.* July-August, 2005 v26 p27.

EU finances: Businesses attack US listing requirements. *Economist Intelligence Unit: Country ViewsWire*, Sept 16, 2002

Francis, R. David. The corporations strike back. *Christian Science Monitor.* Boston, Mass.: Jun 6, 2005

Hume, Lynn. SEC Lays Out Possible Regulatory Regime for Rating Agencies. *Bond Buyer.* New York, N.Y.: Jun 24, 2005

O'Connor, M. Colleen. Sarbanes-Oxley: Frying the Small Fry As third anniversary looms, many small caps are turning private or going overseas. *The Investment Dealers' Digest.* New York: Jun 27, 2005

Parker, Andrew and Tucker, Sundeep. Sarbanes-Oxley reforms 'go too far', says author. *The Financial Times*, July 8, 2005

Smith, K. Anne. Business gets put on Hold. *Kiplinger's Personal Finance Magazine.* July 2005

Swartz, Nikki. Executives praise SOX but seek changes; it's not quite a backlash, but after the first full year of reporting under the Sarbanes-Oxley Act, many business leaders are seeking changes. *Information Management Journal.* July-August 2005

Chapter 8
Free Trade but not yet a Two-Way Street

Zoltan Boka

Keywords: free trade, Western imperialism, globalization, NAFTA, European Union

Abstract

There are, to be sure, populations segments all over the world who fear intrusion from the outside world and the changes such interaction bring. Free trade, in its present form, is also vulnerable to charges of Western imperialism.

This paper is concerned with the economics and politics of globalization and the effect it has on poor communities in its present form as well as with offering certain pragmatic suggestion, which are sound both morally and economically, in order to help make free trade more of a two way street.

For the sake of clarity and convenience, I have divided this chapter into three parts- an economic and political primer on free trade as it stands today-in the late 20th and early 21st Centuries- and studying the specific effects of globalization on poor communities as well as offering suggestions on how to make free trade more fair and palatable to those, primarily in the third world, who are resistant to the idea (Tamene, G. 2008, p. 260).

Because globalization is a Western-initiated proposition, it is inevitable that Western perspectives dominate the ensuing discussion. This, in itself, is often a problem, as we shall see.

An Economic and Political Overview

The number of people world-wide, who are unemployed, is 195.2 million, according to the statistics of the United Nations (AP, 2007). This figure represents 6.3 percent of the world's able-bodied workforce and almost half of these people are under the age of twenty-five. Not in school and not working, 13.7 percent of these young people are watching their lives go by, through idle survival. It was not supposed to be this way.

When former U.S. President Clinton signed the North American Free Trade Agreement on September 14 1993, thereby kicking off the fight for its passage in the U.S. Congress, he remarked that NAFTA would "create 200,000 American jobs in the first two years' of its effect" (White House, 1993). Similarly, Canadian and Mexican leaders assured their constituents that the free flow of goods would mean a flow of new opportunities. Like Clinton, they contrasted isolationism and globalization and came to the same conclusion as the first President Bush, that "democracy will be given a setback" if the trade agreement faltered. (*id.*)

These two Presidents framed the argument as a choice between engagement and isolation, between helping our fellow men and shunning them, between economically open democracies and closed autocratic hegemonies. The Dartmouth Review, a Massachusetts college student newspaper went further recently, claiming that former Senator and presidential candidate John Edwards pitches his anti-free trade rhetoric at "the worst combination of the American voting bloc: the poor and the stupid." In addition, Dartmouth referred to Edwards' populist platform as "the scum of American politics" (Silvaraman, 2007).

This heated rhetoric obscures facts and stifles a discussion well worth having. The fundamental arguments of free traders are logical ones- the world is getting smaller, and isolation is no longer possible, or even desirable. I write this from Trencin, a central Slovakian city of 70,000 which is home to at least three families of Turkish immigrants, a Nigerian family, a Japanese professor of business and economics and the Hungarian-born, U.S.-raised author. Mobility is irreversible at this point. While the EU dithers about whether or not to accept Turkey into the European Union, motivated, one suspects, by fears of Islam and memories of the Ottoman Empire, many Turkish immigrants are settling in locations as diverse as Slovakia and Germany. They do not simply move for the sake of economics- all of the aforementioned Turkish families involve Slovak partners and bi-national children. One of them has mentioned that having successfully gained asylum in Sweden, over twenty years ago, he had no particular need to come to Slovakia.

Furthermore, if wealth is created in poor nations, it will allow individuals to access a greater level of education. Thusly empowered, these educated people would become more independent and independent-minded (Griswold, 2001). Framed in such terms, with free trade bringing about wealth, knowledge and liberty, a counterargument would be destined to sound foolish, bigoted or uncaring and uninformed. When contrasting Griswold's words with the commentary of Silvaraman and the Dartmouth Tribune regarding Edwards, a clear winner emerges and it surely isn't Edwards, with his appeal to and exploitation of "the poor and the stupid." Of

157

course, only politicians imagine that life is that simple (Tamene, G., 2004, p. 389).

The International Monetary Fund, which tracks economic progress world-wide, calculated Niger's GDP (Gross Domestic Product) at 708.87 U.S. Dollars in 1990. In 2000, the IMF pegged Niger's GDP at 743.42 U.S. Dollars. While Niger was 109 million Dollars in debt back in 1990, by 2000 Niger was indebted to the tune of 186 million. These figures seem to suggest that Niger's prosperity and indebtedness go hand in hand. Hence, those opposed to free trade, may well point to the Niger figures to make the claim that free trade does not, no matter what Mrs. Bush and Clinton say, lift all boats. When looking at the above figures, we see that Niger's debt increased fifty-nine percent while its GDP growth, during this same period, was a sluggish five percent- a nearly twelve-fold discrepancy which does no favors to those who claim that free trade and open markets will improve poor economies.

Of course, some may say that it is unfair to make an argument with statistics from what the IMF has termed the world's poorest nation. However, shifting our attention to Mexico, which was played up as a major beneficiary of NAFTA, does little to improve the fiscal picture. Mexico's GDP was 3139.08 billion in 1990 and has skyrocketed to 5935.00. With increased wages, however, came increased debt, and Mexico's debt, which stood at 7.45 billion in 1990, nearly tripled in a decade to 18.62 billion in 2000. A cursory look at these numbers reveals that in the ten years between 1990 and 2000, Mexico's debt increased by a greater percentage point than its GDP- in other words, Mexico's increase in debt is outpacing its increase in funds, which places it in the same category as Niger- and it further serves to underscore the argument of those against free trade that it does more harm than good.

The contrast between Niger and Mexico regarding their GDP is noteworthy. Perhaps most tellingly, while Niger's GDP only increased by five percent; Mexico's increase was posted at fifty-two percent- more than twice Niger's gain. This figure again tends to lend credence to Clinton, Grisworld and other free traders who believe that a rising tide of economic activity lifts all boats. This is so since Mexico is in close proximity to major trading partners and has been invited to a number of trade agreements and treaties by economically powerful allies while Niger, an impoverished desert nation, has not been so courted. Hence, in raw economic terms, one can safely conclude that Mexico's increasing wealth, which outpaces the increase in Niger, is at least partially due NAFTA, free trade, and its proximity to a wealthy, industrialized country. Still, as the above paragraph delineated, opposing views abound.

We could easily conclude at this point, and use the foregoing economic evidence to buttress the claims of Bush, Clinton, Silva Raman and

Griswold and proclaim free trade a sound economic policy. However, our mission goes deeper than that surface analysis. We wish to explore the specific impact of globalization on poor countries and communities, using the foregoing arguments regarding free trade and the corresponding economic data presented as our framework.

Globalisation's Specific Impact on Poor Communities

According to current and former Indian finance minister, Palaniappan Chidambaram, "Growth is the best antidote to poverty. Growth gives incomes to people who are employed, throws up jobs for those who are not employed. Therefore growth is imperative. But growth obviously is not sufficient in a country that you introduced a minute ago as a country where a significant proportion lives in poverty the growth must be inclusive growth. So the task of the government - the task of the finance minister - is to ensure not only growth but that this growth is inclusive growth" (Williams, 2007).

Minister Chidambaram's statement is perhaps the most logical starting point for this prong of our discussion, for two reasons: First, Mr. Chidambaram's qualifications in the realm of finance are impeccable. A graduate of Harvard Business School, Chidambaram served as India's Finance Minister under Rajiv Gandhi and has been selected for this position a second time by current President Manmohan Singh. Secondly, Mr. Chidambaram's personal experiences contrasted the two major streams of economic thought of his student years- communism and capitalism Having experienced both the Western business model and India's Soviet-inspired system, he came to embrace the former, partly because the latter was shown to be a failure.

As the Soviet Union collapsed in 1991, India was busy implementing reforms-spurred not by the collapse of the former empire but rather by economic troubles on the home front, such as declining reserves, an increased pace of borrowing and the eventual necessity of mortgaging India's reserves of gold. Additionally, Chidambaram took note of the success of expatriated Indians in Britain. It seemed to him that these expatriates were far more successful in capitalism systems than on their native soil. Hence, he concluded, along with like-minded Indians such as Yashwant Sinha, India's current finance minister, that a capitalist democracy with a globalist world-view was the only feasible choice for a country of India's size and social and economic needs (WGHB and PBS 2007). This attitude and accompanying new openness of the Indian economy had notable effects and continue to do so.

Industrial production, an Indian mainstay, went up by about eleven percent in December 2006, following a gain of over fifteen percent the previous month. Much of this production is consumed domestically- as

Indians become wealthier, they take out more loans and mortgages and purchase more and more of the products they once produced almost exclusively for export. As Indian companies grow and seek to acquire foreign-owned businesses overseas, the Indian economy is expected to surpass that of China.

India's stock market has gained about forty percent in value over the past year. Additionally, Vodafone plans to spend over eleven billion U.S. Dollars on improving mobile phone service and access all over India. The current government is actively seeking $320 billion by 2012 in order to improve India's infrastructure- roads, ports, mass transit and so on- so that they may achieve and maintain an annual growth rate of nine percent over the coming decade. However, in spite of these numbers and the championing of free trade and globalization as the causes of this economic surge, we would be remiss not to note, as the Bloomberg article itself did, that more than six hundred million people in India live on less than $2 per day (Thomas and Goyal, 2007). In addition, let us not forget the U.N.'s figure of 195.2 million jobless people world-wide.

What has globalization done to or for them? In Globalization and Its Discontents, author Joseph Stiglitz makes the argument that despite Western moral outrage at Eastern sweatshops and slave labor-like conditions, a sense of perspective is required: A dollar a day may be a pittance to us, but to many who work for this wage, it is a considerable and valuable asset. In addition, goods produced cheaply are also sold cheaply in those very same nations, enabling the most impoverished to have access to material goods and comforts.

Despite the title of the book, Stiglitz is not against the notion of globalization. Rather, he writes about being repelled by the way globalization has been interpreted and implemented, chiefly by the International Monetary Fund and large businesses which see globalization as a one-way street, with large companies flooding emerging markets with their goods while advanced nations erect trade barriers against the inflow of exports from the very same emerging markets (Stiglitz, 5). Indeed, globalization has not met its lofty goals, due at least in part because of the greed of established markets- such as medicine manufacturers who have frozen out generic drugs and insist that only name-brand ones be sold to developing nations which can scarcely afford them, leaving many destitute and ill- as well as dying- due to a stop in the flow of medications (Stiglitz, 8).

Here is the crux of the problem with globalization as it is currently practiced: it is a one way street with the flow of traffic directed by the International Monetary Fund and wealthy corporations, which often place onerous burdens on poor countries in desperate need of aid. This outside interference has palpable effects. Both Russia and China began the move towards market economies in 1990- Russia spurred on by the collapse of the

Berlin Wall, and China rocked by the protests at Tienanmen. Russia was guided by a plethora of international organizations, many of which promised Eastern Europeans during the Cold War that a new economic system would lead to vast riches. By contrast, China, remained politically isolated and untouched by the IMF and corporations- and their promises. Somewhat unsurprisingly, in Stiglitz's view (as well as the authors'), China, who's GDP was only 60% that of Russia in 1990 surged ahead and by 2000 it was Russia whose GDP declined to only 60% of China- in other words, a perfectly inverted result (Stiglitz, 6).

Why would this be so? For all the positives of free trade, it is axiomatic that one must have something of value to trade, be it minerals, food or government officials. The International Monetary Fund (IMF), while seemingly outwardly committed to free-trade values and open governance has been upholding a system which one commentator called "a game of one-way strip poker" where the IMF insists that developing nations abandon trade barriers while not mentioning the barriers erected by Western nations in an attempt to slow the flow of cheap consumer goods (Klein, 2007).

Given the preceding data, from Niger's dismal performance to Mexico's decidedly mixed economic record and their contrast with the economic strength displayed by China and India, it is not a matter of simply being pro or anti-globalization. Globalization is here to stay- NAFTA and the IMF's policies; encouraging Western involvement in poorer nations assures that. In fact, many of the organizations which helped Eastern Europe transfer from communism to capitalism- popularly called NGOs or Non-Governmental Organizations- are still in place. Rather, the question becomes whether globalization, *as it is currently practiced by Western corporations and nations* is a feasible and moral long-term strategy.

As an example of these globalization practices, when a project in development or agriculture, one that is advocated by Western forces, fails in a developing country, that nation still has to bear the burden of repaying the loans it took out to fund the project unless it is granted debt forgiveness (Stiglitz, 8). Compare also (Tamene, 2008, p. 89), who confirms the line of argument of the foregoing, while explaining the roles of nongovernmental organizations (NGOs) and community based organizations (CBOs), emphasizes the skepticism that surrounded NGOs in causing development in less developed countries such as Sub-Saharan Africa, these days. In relation with human security, the case of Africa is much worse (Tamene, G., 2005, p. 472).

Understandably, this practice enrages the people of the effected societies. A recent example of this is the so-called Left Bank Outfall Drain (LBOD) project. LBOD was a part of the Pakistani National Drainage Program, designed to alleviate flooding issues in the country. Funded by a $285 million loan from the World Bank, it was designed to advance irrigation and drainage technologies in the country, and, in the elusive words of the Word Bank "support the implementation of major policy and institutional reforms in the water sector, finance urgently-needed investments in irrigation and drainage, and promote research to strengthen Pakistan's technical knowledge based on irrigation and drainage" (Bureau, 1997). However, the project had to be abandoned due to safety concerns- hence, Pakistan was stuck with a loan for a project it could only partially complete and benefit from. While this may be just the cost of doing business, it is time to ask whether that cost is too great for the world's poor to bear- and whether such acts, too numerous to mention, help or hinder the notion of free trade.

References

Associated Press. "Equal Lack of Opportunity: Global Job Market Squeezes Out the Old and Young," 8 February 2007, The International Herald Tribune, retrieved from http://www.iht.com/articles/2007/02/08/business/jobs.php on 12 February 2007.
Bureau Report. "WB Okays $285m Loan for Drainage Scheme," 6 November 1997 Dawn- the Leading English Newspaper of Pakistan, retrieved From http://library.wustl.edu/~listmgr/devel-l/Nov1997/0017.html on 13 February 2007.
Griswold, Daniel. Seven Moral Arguments for Free Trade, the Cato Institute, 2001.
International Monetary Fund. Report for Selected Countries, retrieved from http://tinyurl.com/2fskng and http://tinyurl.com/yqp5no (Original URL's reduced via http://www.tinyurl.com) on 12 February 2007.
Klein, Naomi. "Sacrificial Wolfie," 1 May 2007, The Nation, retrieved from: http://news.yahoo.com/s/thenation/20070501/cm_thenation/20070514klein_1 on 3 May 2007.
Office of the Press Secretary. "Remarks by President Clinton, President Bush, President Carter, President Ford and Vice President Gore in Signing of NAFTA Side Agreements," 14 September 1993, The White House, retrieved from http://www.multied.com/Documents/Clinton/SigningNaFTA.html on 12 February 2007.
Silvaraman, Aditya A. "Ravenous Radical in Sheep's Clothing", 11 February 2007, The Dartmouth Review, retrieved from:
http://www.dartreview.com/archives/2007/02/11/ravenous_radical_in_sheeps_ clothing.php on 12 February 2007.
Stiglitz, Joseph E. Globalization and Its Discontents, W.W. Norton & Company, 2002.
Tamene, G. 'CBOs and NGOs in the Discourse of African Aid Politics', in.:

Development Aid -- ROZVOJOVÁ *POMOC A SPOLUPRÁCA. Vol. III.*
International Scientific Conference, University of Economics in Bratislava, Faculty of international relations, Ekonóm Publishers, 2008. Pp. 248-266.
Tamene, G. 'World Politics and Challenges to Neoliberalism: Could the CEE-EU-US Correlation Maintain the Trend?' In: *Journal of Comparative Politics*, Brno, 2008. Pp.86-100.
Tamene, G. 'Globalization and Progress. The Impact on Central European Regions'. In: B.S.Sergi and W.Bagatelas (eds), *Ethical Implications of Post-Communist Transition Economics and Politics in Europe*, Iura Edition, Bratislava, 2004, pp. 381-396. ISBN 80-8078-045-5.
Tamene, G. 'On Resolving the Growing Security Problems in Sub-Saharan Africa'. In: Ľubomír Lupták *et al* (eds.), *Panorama of Global Security Environment 2005-2006*, Ministry of Defense of the Slovak Republic, Department of Security and Defense Policy, Bratislava 2005, pp 471-83.
Thomas, Cherian and Goyal, Kartik. "India Industrial Production Surged 11.1% in December (Update 3)", 12 February 2007, Bloomberg TM, retrieved at http://quote.bloomberg.com/apps/news?pid=20601087&sid=a2hBboXe35V4 on 13 February 2007.
WGBH and PBS. "Commanding Heights: The Battle for the World Economy", 2002, retrieved from http://www.pbs.org/wgbh/commandingheights/shared/pdf/int_palaniappanchidambaram.pdf on 13 February 2007.
Williams, Mike. "The Interview: Indian Finance Minister," 3-4 February 2007, BBC News International, retrieved from http://news.bbc.co.uk/2/hi/business/6330691.stm on 12 February 2007.

Chapter 9
Why People Break the Law and Get Rich

Jana Straňáková[1]

Keywords: consumers, misleading adverts, consumer protection, respondents, deception, complaint, municipalities, stricter control, ethics

The author of this chapter thinks that one of the strongest desires of human beings is to own something or to control others. There are various ways to gain power; however, money certainly plays an important role in many cases. Getting wealth through fair practice has never been always the case for all people. Therefore, it does not surprise us to see some individuals or several people taking the opportunity of making a huge amount of money, even at the expense of other people.[2] Unfortunately, this unpleasant behavior of mankind has evolved to be not only the practice of a few individuals but the whole society (Tamene, G., 2005, p. 385; 2007, p. 130). Nowadays, we witness how large companies publically cheat on consumers and do all they can, fair or unfair, to sell their products to many people, and it seems that even legal norms[3] can not prevent them from so doing. Consumers are more often victims of misleading adverts, they buy products in the faith that they get good deals; however, the opposite is true.[4] Similar practices are quite typical in the developing parts of the world.[5]

To be concrete, let's take the particular example of misleading advertising of "Phone calling program ST Pohoda" of the *Slovak Telecom* (a joint-stock company operating in the field of mobile communications), see picture 1.

Picture 1: **Adverts of "Phone calling program of Slovak Telecom Pohoda"**

Source: Photo archive of the author. (Bratislava Ruzinov, August 2004)

The advert stretching over the majority of the surface on the billboard states that the user of the new phone program "ST Pohoda" will pay one Slovak koruna "for each call". The word "each" is a general quantifier that expresses aggregate without limitation. However, small letters, located on the left side (see picture 2), annul the condition of being unlimited and provide further information about the conditions under which consumers should pay 1 Slovak koruna for each call.

Picture 2: **Additional information to the advert "Phone program ST Pohoda" located on the left side of the billboard.**

Source: Photo archive of the author (Bratislava Ruzinov 2004)

Additional information which is written in small letters warn the users that the advert informs about the price 1 Slovak koruna per each call, nevertheless it excludes value added tax (VAT), thus eventually increases the total price (after adding VAT). Accuracy of the information is limited also in time – it applies only to calls in off-peak hours, Saturdays and to local and long-distance calls, and only up to 30 minutes. The small letters explaining the conditions of the new phone program can be read only from nearest distance. Also, small letters providing additional info regarding the advert are difficult to read because they are in vertical position. A user who sees the advert from the bus, car, etc. can therefore read only misleading, inaccurate and incomplete information, the explanation of which actually exists, but is not visible at the first sight.

Let's focus on the legal standards of the Slovak Republic, which deal with the issue of misleading advertisements. Legal document of the Slovak Republic contains Act No. 634/1992 Coll. on Consumer Protection, whose § 8 stipulates that no person is allowed to cheat on a consumer, especially by providing false, inaccurate, unjustified, incomplete, unclear, double-sensed or exaggerated information, or withhold information about real features of a products, services, or purchase conditions.

General requirements for advertisements and protection of consumers from the effects of misleading advertisements, and the measures to be taken by State administration in the supervision of the advertisements are governed by Act no. 147/2001 on Advertisement and on Amendment to Certain Acts. Under the § 3 of this Act, an advertisement must not be misleading, or hidden, and must not abuse the confidence of the consumer, his insufficient experience or lack of knowledge.

This issue is also dealt with in Act. no. 513/1991 Coll. (Business Code), whose § 45 stipulates that circulation of data, which might provoke a misleading vision, thus making financial profit for one's own enterprise or an enterprise of someone else in competition at the expense of other competitors or consumers, is considered to be misleading advertising. An accurate datum is also considered inaccurate if circumstances or the context in which such datum has been provided might lead to misunderstanding.

The notion of "misleading advertising" is also defined in the European Commission Directive 84/450/EEC relating to the approximation of laws, regulations and administrative provisions of the Member States concerning misleading advertising. According to which 'misleading advertising' means any advertising which in any way, including its presentation, deceives or is likely to deceive the persons to whom it is addressed or whom it reaches and which, by reason of its deceptive nature, is likely to affect their economic behavior or which, for those reasons, injures or is likely to injure a competitor.

How are the effects of misleading advertisements seen by Slovak consumers? This question was posed in shopping malls to 200 random respondents in two Slovak cities: Bratislava (BA) and Žilina (ZA) (200 respondents in each city). The survey was carried out as a part of the research for a diploma thesis in October 2004. In the questionnaire, respondents could present their views on accuracy of information contained in Picture 1, page 1. Subsequently, they had opportunity to think over as to whether they would buy the program based on information provided in the advert. Respondents were then asked whether they would or would not feel misled, if after some time they found out the company, which published the advert, had not kept the advertised price. We also wanted to know whether consumers generally decided to buy based on adverts when buying goods or services. Those who answered positively (buying because of ads), were further asked as to whether they felt misled after they had bought the advertised product or service. In the next question these respondents were to answer as to what measure, if any, they undertook to sanction the company which published the advert. Below are the results:

Table 1 contains answers of the respondents to the question whether the adverts on picture 1, page 1 is accurate or not.

Table 1: **Assessment of accuracy of the adverts on picture 1**

	Bratislava		Žilina	
	number of respondents	%	Number of respondents	%
Yes (accurate)	20	10	12	6
No (misleading)	180	90	184	92
Not able to answer	0	0	4	2
Total	**200**	**100**	**200**	**100**

Source: processed by the author, 2004

As we can see from the data above only 10% of the Bratislava respondents trust this advert. Slovak telecom (a joint-stock company) failed to convince up to 90% of respondents of the advantages of the new phone program ST Pohoda. Respondents in Žilina responded similarly. Only 6% of all respondents think data of the adverts are accurate, while 92% do not see the advert as accurate and 4% was not able to answer. Picture 1 relates to the next question, which examines whether consumers would buy the new program based on the advert. Results can be found in Table 2, page 5. Results indicate that no Bratislava respondent would buy the dial program "ST Pohoda" offered by Slovak Telecom based on the text on the billboard. Fifty six percent (56%) of all respondents in Bratislava would verify the accuracy of the advertisement first, and 44 % of respondents would decide not to buy the product. Respondents in Zilina answered similarly: the same number, i.e. 2% of them think accuracy of the advert is OK; four respondents out of 200 would buy the product. Fifty six percent (56%) of Zilina´s respondents would be cautious in buying this new dial program, while 42% respondents, compared to 44% in Bratislava, would not buy the product.

Table 2: **Decision to buy the phone program based on the advertisement on Picture 1**

	Bratislava		Žilina	
	Number of respondents	%	number of respondents	%
Yes (I would buy)	0	0	4	2
I would check the accuracy of the data first	112	56	112	56
No (I wouldn't buy)	88	44	84	42
Total	**200**	**100**	**200**	**100**

Source: processed by the author, 2004

In the next question, we asked whether respondents would feel cheated or misled if they bought the program or service based on the presented dial program and, after some time, they found out they are to pay higher telephone bills than the advert promised. Answers to this question can be found in Table 3, below. Analyzing this, we came to the conclusion that 86% of respondents would feel misled if they, following receipt of the phone bill, found they have to pay much more than the promised 1 Slovak koruna for each call the advert has promised. Respondents in Zilina would feel similarly, almost 92% of them would feel misled and cheated on.

Table 3: **Feeling of deception by the adverts in Picture 1**

	Bratislava		Žilina	
	number of respondents	%	number of respondents	%
Yes (I would feel cheated on)	172	86	184	92
No (I would not feel cheated on)	28	14	16	8
Total	**200**	**100**	**200**	**100**

Source: processed by the author, 2004

The data above show that a large majority of respondents considered the advert as not correct, that they would feel cheated and would check out the data first or would not buy the product at all. Based on these results, one might think consumers are careful, and therefore the company, despite the published, misleading advert, does not have to make a profit necessarily. However, let's look at the answers to the questions, regarding whether the advert is generally a decisive factor in buying the product or a service. Results can be found in Graph 1, below:

Graph 1: **Decision to buy the product or service based on the advert**

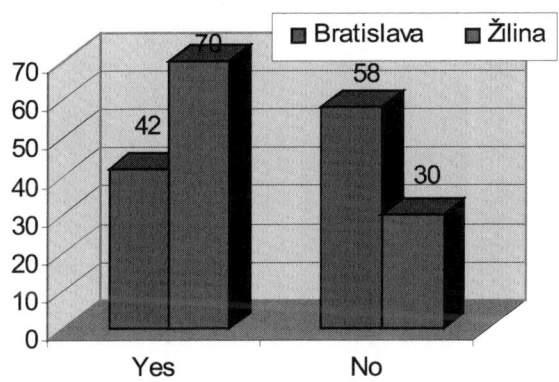

Source: processed by the author, 2004

When analyzing answers to this question we found out, that in BA 42% respondents would decide based on the advert, while in ZA it was 70%. Comparing these results with Table 2 on page 5, we can see interesting facts. If the respondents are to consider purchase of the product based on a particular advert, which might seem related to misleading information, the majority of consumers would try to verify such information or would not buy the product at all. However, when asked if they usually decide about purchase of product or service on a commercial basis, 42% of respondents in BA and up to 70% in ZA replied positively.

We may therefore conclude that if adverts contain information, which clearly seems inaccurate or misleading, consumers will be careful. However, if the advert appears to be trustworthy at first sight, almost half of respondents in BA and 70% in ZA would decide to buy advertised products or services. How much of a percentage from the advertised products or services really fulfill the data presented in the advert, is still questionable.

Let's analyze whether people who decide to buy goods based on the advert, would feel cheated on. Table 4 shows (blow) the data of those users, who answered positively to the previous question. In BA it was 84 respondents, in ZA 140 respondents.

Table 4: **Feeling of deception by the advert after the purchase of a product or service.**

	Bratislava		Žilina	
	number of respondents	%	number of respondents	%
Yes, (I feel being cheated on)	32	38	104	71
No, (I didn't feel being cheated on)	52	62	36	29
Total	**84**	**100**	**140**	**100**

Source: processed by the author

As we can see from the table, 38% of Bratislava's respondents felt being cheated after buying this product, while 62% respondents were satisfied with the product or service. This issue is perceived completely differently in ZA. While 71% of the addressed respondents felt deceived, only 29% of randomly chosen respondents expressed satisfaction with the product or service, for which they decided to buy based on the advert. This might be related to the fact that Bratislava's consumers are more careful in buying products or service (compared to Zilina's consumers), which is also reflected in the graph on page 6. We can notice the percentage of consumers who felt cheated in both cities is significant enough to be taken into consideration however in smaller cities the percentage is more alarming.

Our survey continued yet further and we asked respondents with damaged products the following: based on the advert, did they take any measure to protect their consumer rights and take such steps, which would result in sanctions imposed on the company publishing the misleading advert. Results can be found in graph 2 on page 8. Again, we only show answers for 32 respondents from BA and 104 from ZA who stated after buying the product based on the advert, they felt cheated. Graph 2 shows that in BA, all 32 respondents remained rather passive.

The answers differed in ZA, where 21 respondents (20%) declared they undertook measures leading to sanctions imposed on the company, whose products caused injury to them. These consumers were further asked which measures they took against such companies. Twelve respondents lodged a complaint to the Slovak Commercial Inspection Office (Slovenská obchodná inšpekcia, SOI), and nine respondents took indirect measures to sanction the company, which includes informing their friends and family relatives on the unreliability of the advert.

Graph 2: **Measures to sanction companies that circulate misleading adverts**

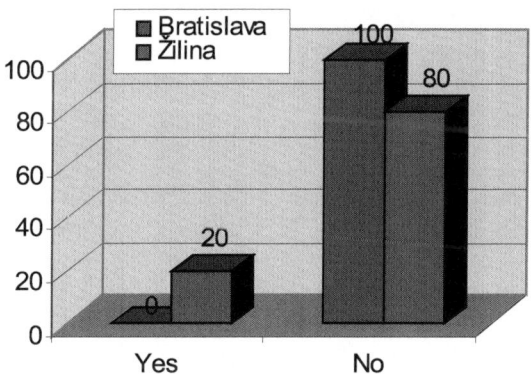

Source: processed by the author, 2004

Based on the results of this survey, we may conclude peoples' responses to misleading advertising are rather sensitive in nature. When we assess examples of misleading advertising, people were even willing to take radical approaches to remedy their anger. On the other hand, however, when it comes to undertaking measures that lead to sanctions against the company causing injury to them, they did almost nothing, or measures were undertaken only by a small percentage of respondents (21 respondents out of 136, i.e. 15%). According to these results we may say consumers, by their passivity, actually enable companies to continue publishing such misleading advertisement. In addition to consumers, this process also involves institutions whose role is controlling whether laws concerning protection of consumers are complied with.

In the legal system[6] of the Slovak republic, the Slovak Commercial Inspection Office is appointed to be a surveillance body in charge of compliance with the Act on Advertisement. This authority is in charge of all commodities except for drugs, (food) products and supplements for babies, veterinary drugs and products, which fall under the competence of the Slovak Veterinary and Food Administration. Also, Slovak Commercial Inspection consists of the Bratislava-based Central Inspectorate and eight regional inspectorates (by territorial division of Slovakia). This body is therefore addressed by both consumers and organizations, should they experience violation of consumer rights. What has been the experience of the SOI with issues concerning misleading information? The data below was provided by the Press Department of the Central Inspection Office of the SOI.

In 2004, the Slovak Commercial Inspection Office received 4.500 complaints concerning violation of consumer rights, in which 163 persons (i.e. 3, 62%) complained about misleading information concerning prices on the advert and advertising leaflets. Complaints concerned deceptive and misleading information for prices of products on leaflets; circulating the adverts electronically without prior consent of the user; misleading and inaccurate advertisement in ordering products advertised in the press; misleading offers by travel agencies, erotic, or other unethical forms of advertising.[7]

Is the above number of complaints on misleading advertisements high or low? Can the issue of misleading information be solved solely by complaints of consumers with reference to effective legislation? Can society rely on the vigilance of consumers and should the control and supervisory bodies be more effective? It will help if we once again look at results of the survey carried out in Bratislava and Žilina, and view how the work of control authorities is perceived by consumers.

In the survey, consumers had an opportunity to suggest what measures would ensure better protection of consumers against misleading advertising. One of the suggestions was more frequent control of producers and sellers by state authorities. We therefore consulted experts from the Section of Protection of Consumers of the Slovak Ministry of Economy, under the competence of which SOI falls, whether they consider the work of control authorities sufficient, and how they see the situation themselves.

Based on their responses, it may be concluded that control authorities fulfill their duties sufficiently however, the issues are also investigated with insufficient numbers of employees in competent bodies. Included with this problem is the high number of administrative procedures necessary for such work requires. The abolishn of district inspectorates of the SOI might also influence the situation, according to experts. Controls and supervision are carried out only by Regional inspectorates of the SOI. Increasing numbers of employees for control authorities might lead to improvement of protection for consumers. Experts also mentioned municipalities could contribute to improvement of consumer protection, since it is within their competence to carry out controls on open markets and other local commercial centers.

Activity of the municipalities is, however, currently insufficient, caused most probably by lack of experts in the field. Compare also (Tamene, G., 2006, p. 144; 2008, p. 111), who confirms findings of the author of this chapter. He states this unethical trend remains even more endemic at global levels because societies have been left to market alone in the absence of any strong norms able to regulate such global behavior. On the other hand, the global economy is very much seen as a source of progress and innovation.[8] In the end, what else can we add to all this? It is questionable whether Slovak society will be able to enrich individuals and companies at the expense of consumers through misleading advertising. Or, perhaps Slovaks will continue supporting them indirectly without protesting. This article also suggests ways for consumers to protect themselves. However, attention and vigilance of consumer in the purchase of goods or services based on an advert remains the essential requirement for consumer safety. If a consumer allows himself/herself to be misled or notices unethical behavior of companies towards consumers, they should be aware of their rights and react in timely ways in certain situations. They should subsequently inform control and supervisory bodies regarding the less serious activity of the given companies. Last but not least, the role of the State is essential in preventing unethical exploitation of consumers. The State should, through its experts and competent bodies, consider whether steps leading to stricter controls are necessary, which might contribute to solving of these extremely important ethical issues for society.

Notes

1 Jana Straňáková is an employee at the Economics University of Bratislava, in Bratislava, Slovak Republic.
2 See also, Klamlivé konania a klamlivé opomenutia, at:

   http://www.betterregulation.sk/archive/file/Monitoring/Monitoring_45_priloha.pdf
3 Tamene, G. (2005). 'Globalization and Progress: The impact on Central European Regions', in: *Ethical Implications of Post-Communist Transition Economics and Politics in Europe* (eds.) Bruno S. Sergi and William T. Bagatelas, Iura Edition, pp.381-396. ISBN 80-8078-045-5
4 See Slovenská obchodná inšpekcia upozorňuje na nekalé obchodné praktiky holandskej spoločnosti at: http://www.edb.sk/sk/spravy/soi-upozornuje-na-nekale-obchodne-praktiky-holandskej-firmy-a285.html

5 Tamene, G. (2006). 'Problems of Development Aid in Sub-Saharan Africa.' In: *Rozvojová pomoc*, vydavateľstvo EKONÓM, Bratislava.
6 Zákon č. 250/2007 Zb., § 7; Zákon č. 250/2007 Zb., § 8; Zákon č. 250/2007 Zb., § 9
7 See Agresívna obchodná praktika, and Sankcie at: http://openiazoch.zoznam.sk/info/zpravy/zprava.asp?NewsID=56806#
8 Tamene Getnet – Martin Matušovič: Globalna ekonomika ako zdroj pokroku a inovácií. In: *Nová teorie ekonomiky a management organizací*, sborník z medzinárodní vědecké conference. Nakladatelství Oeconomica— 2008, Praze, 2008. ISSN 978-80-2451403-1

References

Business Code of the Slovak Republic, No. 250/2007 Zb., § 7; No. 250/2007 Zb., § 8; No. 250/2007 Zb., § 9
Tamene, G. (2005). Globalization and Progress:The impact on Central European Regions, in: *Ethical Implications of Post-Communist Transition Economics and Politics in Europe* (eds.) Bruno S.Sergi and William T. Bagatelas, Iura Edition, pp.381-396. ISBN 80-8078-045-5
Tamene, G. (2006). Problems of Development Aid in Sub-Saharan Africa. In: *Rozvojová pomoc*, vydavateľstvo EKONÓM, Bratislava. s. 136-154.
Tamene, G. (2007). "Political Ethics and the Human polity – The African Dimension". In: Sergi, B. S. and Bagatelas, T.W. (Eds.): *Economic and Political Development Ethics: Europe and Beyond.* Bratislava, Iura Edition, pp.103-134.
Tamene Getnet- Matušovič Martin (2008). 'Globalna ekonomika ako zdroj pokroku a inovácií.' In: *Nová teorie ekonomiky a management organiyací*, sborník z medzinárodní vědecké conference. Nakladatelství Oeconomica— 2008, Prague, 2008. ISSN 978-80-2451403-1
See also, Klamlivé konania a klamlivé opomenutia, at: http://www.betterregula tion.sk/archive/file/Monitoring/Monitoring_45_prilo ha.pdf
See Slovenská obchodná inšpekcia upozorňuje na nekalé obchodné praktiky holand skej spoločnosti at:- http://www.edb.sk/sk/spravy/soi-upo zornuje-na-nekale-obchodne-praktiky-holandskej-firmy-a285.html
See Agresívna obchodná praktika, and Sankcie at: http://openiazoch.zoznam.sk/info/zpravy/zprava.asp?NewsID=56806#

Chapter 10
Increasing democratization in local governance to improve regional competitiveness using the constructed regional advantage (CRA) concept

Danes Brzica

Institute of Economic Research, Slovak Academy of Sciences
danes.brzica@savba.sk

Keywords: increasing democratization, local governance, regional competitiveness, CRA, participative governance, political regime, knowledge accumulation, stakeholder, regional partnership, institutional quality, social capital, innovative regions, corruption

Introduction

Democratic countries enhance the capacities of citizens to work together in their common interests as they try to solve public issues. Participation in public life, open discussion, the rule of law, pluralistic party systems and responsible public administration form the core of democracy. A new policy design, constructed regional advantage (CRA), represents a step to improve regional action, governance, regional policy and also, indirectly, political responsibility. A region's competitiveness depends on changes of actors and "learning spillover" generated in modern sectors, and highlights the role played by CRA in regional development. Governments should not view seeking higher regional competitiveness as a way to increase technical and knowledge capabilities only, but also social capital.

Since the early 1990s, Slovakia has attracted growing attention to its reforms, peacefully acquired independence and reportedly dynamic economic development. In the 1990s, Central European regions had to combine democratic principles of the new society with old institutions of command economy characterized by lack of democratic mechanisms. Nowadays, global pressures force the regions to further increase their competitiveness and cohesion. The competition-cohesion balance is important as it enhances the shift to a knowledge-based economy, social stability and prosperity. Various authors focus on different levels related to CRA regarding socio-spatial and economic dimensions of regional and urban development. Gertler (2004) studies local social knowledge management from the point of view of community actors, institutions and multilevel governance. Keane (1997) analyzes the problems and possibilities of employment in local/community economic development, Malecki (2007) looks at cities' and regions' knowledge and local development policies, and Salet (2006) studies rescaling territorial governance and the responsiveness of spatial and institutional strategies to changing socio-economic interactions.

Historically, links exist between growth and democratic values. This chapter tries to identify the interdependence between democracy and regional competitiveness. It focuses on relations between regional competitiveness and the need to use participative and networking approaches, which recent research on knowledge economy stresses. The chapter focuses on how increasing democratization in governance and the application of new regional policy concepts can improve regional competitiveness. Regions become more autonomous and base their development on the broad cooperation of regional actors. The chapter identifies the role of knowledge production through dynamic regional networks as a step to legitimizing regional action and improving democratic mechanisms. By using the CRA concept, stressing the local dimension in designing policies and measures for increasing regional competitiveness, competitiveness and cohesion balance within regional innovation systems is further fostered. The chapter works with the idea that regional development and participative governance are among the main factors enhancing regional economic development. It tries to increase understanding of how democratic processes contribute to regional development.

The Constructed regional advantage concept and contextual democratization

Democratization, as the transition to a more democratic political regime of governance structures, can increase the potential of a region to involve a whole set of regional stakeholders (local government and self-government representatives, local businesses etc.) in designing its future by better understanding the needs of all important stakeholders and by more open resolution of often conflicting goals. It can be accomplished by organizing community consultation through a committee or by jointly developing an action plan with local/regional stakeholders and holding workshops to find or develop solutions. This process is in line with the CRA concept developed in

Asheim et al. (2006). The concept may explain the formation of regional capacities/capabilities for the implementation of local projects.

The study explains the policy associated with a region's changes in innovation patterns. The constructed regional advantage concept provides key recommendations – among them: the importance of territorial competence bases (including people and business climates as well as regional knowledge infrastructures); small and medium-sized enterprise policy and entrepreneurial policies (especially technology-based entrepreneurship) and governance dimensions of upgrading and building regional innovation systems, such as creative knowledge environments. CRA requires an identification of the basic building blocks for developing this approach by using several dimensions: (1) related variety[1]; (2) differentiated knowledge bases[2] and (3) distributed knowledge networks.[3] These elements provide the foundation for formulating trans-sectoral platform policies[4] for potential applications across a wide range of industries (Asheim et al., 2006). The core of change is the elements of the regional advantage for each region. Cooke (2006) provides an overview of this regional development approach based on the idea that any region can become innovative and specialized.

The dynamics of structural transformation then depends on how dense the institutional environment is (e.g., how governance at local levels is a result of the interplay between formal state and other institutions such as NGOs, firms, and traditional institutions) and how networking functions in a region (e.g., how business and community leaders have been building their own networks and links to state authorities). Picture 1 below shows the CRA concept with its main element. The theory of constructed advantage allows for more attention to the role and impact of the public sector in the economy. It also highlights policy support, preferably in public-private partnerships, by acknowledging to a greater extent the importance of institutional and economic complementarities in knowledge economies than do theories of comparative and competitive advantage (Asheim et al., 2006).

Picture 1: **Concept of constructed regional advantage**

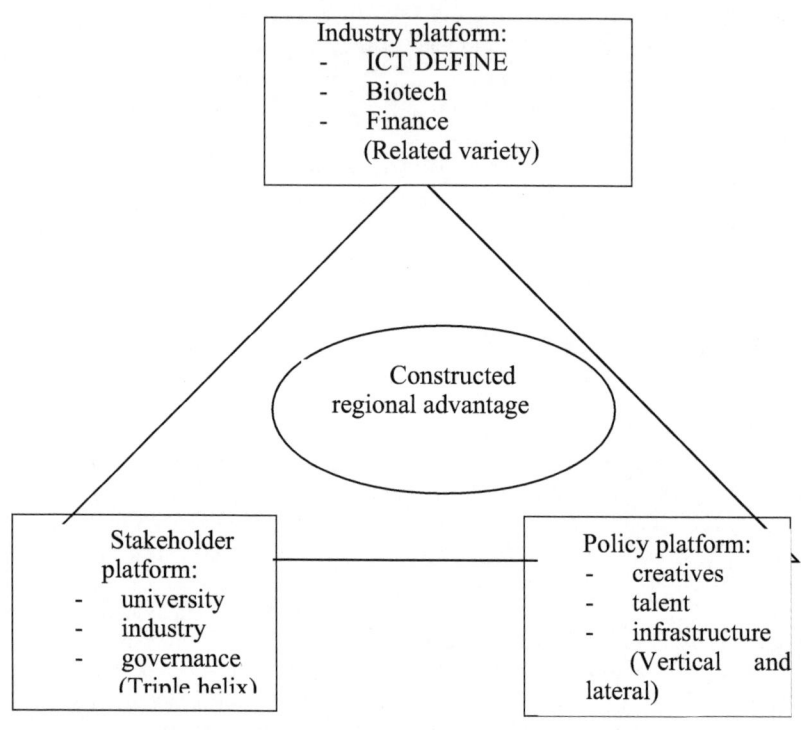

Source: Adopted from Cooke (no date)

Asheim *et al.* (2006) shows that the value of the CRA approach is in that it changes the region's existing policy and product mix. Such changes are made due to more efficient identification of the basic building blocks by using the above-mentioned dimensions - related variety, differentiated knowledge bases, and distributed knowledge networks. Successful regions are also able to establish strategies that deeply change the reality. The variety of available CRA policies determines how rapidly the country's regional advantage emerges. It means that following the CRA approach helps because it widens the scope of public participation in searching high-productivity activities, eases the mutual strengthening of different kinds of relevant knowledge, and makes structural changes easier (i.e., the changes reflecting better production potential of a region). It is thus a proper tool of building/increasing regional competitiveness, which reflects dynamic interactions of state and civil society.[5]

The CRA approach allows for more attention to be given to the role of the public sector and policy support, preferably in public-private partnerships, by largely acknowledging the importance of institutional and economic complementarities in knowledge economies[6] than theories of comparative and competitive advantage do. Institutional specificities form the context within which different organizational forms and mechanisms for learning, knowledge accumulation and use evolve. Instead of market failure, the rationale for policy intervention is the reduction of interaction or connectivity deficits, which lies at the core of a networked regional innovation systems approach (Asheim *et al.*, 2006).

The idea behind CRA is that regional effects arise from individual regional strategies and specialization. According to this concept, the region's success is reached by focusing on strategies specific to the region. This CRA policy platform represents the interaction of (1) stakeholders, (2) technologies, and (3) support instruments. The combination of democratic processes and corporate activities – together forming regional partnerships - can balance better the existing competition-cohesion trade-off. This approach takes the state, firms and civil society actors (triple-helix actors) as the actors exerting certain control over the region. Using the concept, regional strategies are designed and applied to improve regional capabilities and competition-cohesion balance. Although specifics apply to the regions, certain practices are common to successful regions and make them different from the less successful ones.

The government can stimulate political and social organization, whereas the market requires bargaining over various issues that promote development. Recent development shows the dynamic trends in the innovative activities in European countries. As the regions gradually become more diversified in terms of their production, they promote regional development. Their innovation activity serves as a driver of regional growth. Compared with richer regions, poor regions produce a much-narrowed range of goods and often fail to stimulate regional development based on a shared vision. Ongoing, there must be not only regional transformation, but also the process of diversification of regional activities.

Enhancing regional productive capabilities is thus an integral part of economic development. The broader the knowledge base that the regions are able to build and maintain, the higher their innovative capacity. This idea is explained in Asheim *et al.* (2006), where the authors state that innovative capabilities in different regions can change substantially. This performance relates to underlying regional assets and a weak policy regime. Asheim *et al.* (2006) also focus on both successful and unsuccessful cases of regional development. These cases allow asking whether networking plays a role in shaping regional performance. Brzica (2008, forthcoming) examined the cases of regional cohesion and found that, at least for Slovakia, this is an important issue in its regional development.

Regional capabilities depend on the quality of regional assets and social capital. Both social capital and regional policy play a positive role in shaping regional production structures. Poor policy can weaken an emerging knowledge base, but the question is whether regional policy can play a substantial role if regional assets are weak. Successful innovative regions have always tried to increase their regional advantages and diversify into new activities. If regions have done it well, it is because their regional advantages allow them to compete in modern activities. They can also diversify into innovative activities that stimulate regional growth. High-performing regions have gradually changed their profiles that are now oriented towards highly innovative products.

While the quality of a region's changes is given by its overall productive capacity, social capital, policy and institutions also matter. In particular, the link between social capital and institutional quality is evident. While specialization patterns are substantially determined by a region's factor endowments (e.g., by specific configuration of local knowledge assets or by context specific advantages) that does not mean that regional advantage strategies are not important. European regions are able, if supported by the CRA concept and given their skills and capital endowments, to make substantial progress. Regional assets are similar among regions, but weaker regions have capabilities that are lower than developed ones. In addition, the regional effort to acquire technology from abroad and diversify is also contributing to higher competitiveness.

Democratic governance, institutional density and regional development

Democratic societies have respect for the rule of law, transparency in government activities, responsible public administration and social rights. Democracy works if stakeholders believe that democratic institutions reflect their interests. Democratic countries are diverse as their development reflects national specifics, but in all of them citizens participate in politics based on tolerance, cooperation and compromise (Department of State, 2008). Democratic principles motivate central governments to decentralize decision-making to regional levels, because regional and local governments must be accessible and responsive to the people. The rate at which innovative activity develops increases with the level of a region's networking activity. The resulting effects provide benefits for the region. A large innovative sector increases productivity.

What matters for regional competitiveness is the competition-cohesion balance in the region[7] regardless of what kind of assets are used. Networking of local firms generates learning spillovers and consequent changes may improve productivity in the region. Networking among firms and other actors also requires a democratic environment, where different views are considered. Democratic regional governance structures provide new opportunities for the regional economy and help to reinforce societal knowledge and skills by better reflecting local capacities, capabilities and interest.

Strengthening cohesion among various actors helps to clarify and balance/harmonize the stakeholders' interests and this may further foster regional cooperation. Ineffective policy coordination, also due to democratic deficiencies, seems to be the main obstacle for growth of less-developed regions. An example can be lack of democratic control over decisions of local authorities, which sometime result in 'short-termism,' i.e., preference for decisions of local authorities that prefer solutions that seem to be good from a short-term perspective but are not that suitable from a medium-term perspective. Some local politicians try to gain votes and be re-election by using this approach.

Democratization of governance structures increases the potential of a region to involve regional actors in designing its future. In particular, CRA can enhance formation of regional competitiveness that reflects the dynamic interactions of different actors. The mix of (a) democratic processes, involving civil society and state, and (b) corporate actions can improve the competition-cohesion balance. This means a broad-based democratic exerting of politico-economic control over the region. Governments at all levels prepare and coordinate policies formulated to meet regional needs. In doing this, they cooperate with other actors and together solve problems.

Participation enhances the government's accountability to the citizens and encourages citizens' responsibility by allowing regional governments to initiate changes. Whereas regional governments should satisfy local needs efficiently, central government does some things better. Hence, broad cooperation across all levels of government exists when the problems require a joint approach in addressing issues. The state has the authority to mediate disputes among regions, and through policies that redistribute tax revenues it can also solve disparities among regions. By allowing citizens to run for governmental positions at all levels, the state provides them the opportunity to change their regional communities (Department of State, 2008).

Interest groups form partnerships to promote their own interests. Political parties, representing various interests, form coalition governments and there exists the potential for conflicts. In democracies, not all interest groups support policy decisions. Therefore, both central and regional governments have to identify potential problems and assist actors to resolve conflicts. Coalitions for regional development are formed when stakeholders agree on issues of common interest. In reality, government and other actors cooperate as partners. The region's capability to agree upon the new - socially acceptable and economically viable – model of regional development assures coherence and compromise on important decisions. It allows regional governments to function efficiently. Democratic procedures used in the process make consensus possible.

In democratic societies, education also helps to develop governance. Educated citizens have more opportunities to join political life and thus improve their situation. This is important as effective governance helps to enhance regional development and increase the initiative of citizens. Positive changes depend on the activity and interests of individual actors. Discussions continue on the role of the region in creating regional innovation systems. By guaranteeing individual freedom, democracy increases people's capacity to govern socio-economic development in their localities (Department of State, 2008). By reducing poverty and improving living standards, regional growth helps reduce social and political tensions. In democracies, citizens establish organizations that serve the needs of their community. For example, non-governmental organizations help to improve society by initiating activities focusing on public issues.

The region's innovative capabilities are determined by many factors – e.g., by the level of productivity in the region. Each region has a different socio-economic structure, which modifies the way in which policy and globalization affects it. In most regions, regional governments have seen their capacity of action reduced through the engagements implied by the central government, which have limited their scope of operation. A coalition of dynamic actors usually promotes the effort to introduce changes, but groups profiting from the status quo can hamper this process. Any economic change has social impacts, both in terms of costs and effects. Reform success thus depends on the ability of the actors to promote changes, balance their interests and eliminate possible negative impacts. Democratic governments are more capable of reforming regions. If the state cooperates with civil society, regional governments have higher capacities to carry out their decisions.

It is because civil society organizations and initiatives help to identify broader sets of priorities and interests as well as to settle potential conflicts, which might have disturbed the effects of common efforts. All regions are competing globally and their success depends on their policies.

Using CRA-related policies can enhance regional progress and resource transfers and building knowledge capital can reduce inter-regional differences. By improving regional institutions, higher regional competitiveness can be reached. External factors determine local democratic institutions and shape the regional patterns.

One example is the impact of European legislation, which serves as an institutional anchor. Especially during the pre-accession period, the "acquis communautaire" had helped substantially to improve national legal frameworks. However, sometimes such external factors can also negatively affect the local environment and institutions. The core of regional competitiveness is the regions' learning capacity. Without policy intervention, regional competitiveness would be low. As mentioned above, weak democracy also affects negatively the region's capabilities. The best option is thus to promote regional competitiveness and cohesion combined with support for democratic principles.

The prosperity of regions depends on the state's ability to form stable political and business environments. The efficient institutions allow building a credible intra-regional coalition, which is a prerequisite for regional development. Broad consensus and cooperation of regional actors make regions economically more efficient than are those that lack such cooperation. The higher the social instability, due to a lack of consensus, the higher the costs needed to solve the problems. Regions that lack the cooperation of actors and democratic rules that govern their behavior have poor prospects and risk conflicts and economic decline.

To increase competitiveness, regions need to be capable of forming a broad variety of institutions assuring that people can act freely. It is important to maintain democratic rights, because a "knowledge society" requires the creation of political consensus. A certain degree of participation in a region is thus crucial, as economic changes applied by autonomous regional bodies reflect the networking dynamics of regional actors. A region can perform well only if it is embedded in an integrated society and then its regional policy is likely to lay the foundations for viable changes.

Developing activities for which the region has no local conditions is not efficient. For example, trying to focus on products requiring a wide web of local research firms is not suitable for a region, where such a cluster of firms does not exist. Another example can be an effort to build a hub for certain international service activities in a city, where inadequate airport capacities exist. Even regions with similar policies have often ended up with different effects. Constructed regional advantage thus becomes a driver of economic performance only in some cases. Besides, there is expected a positive relationship between the initial level of a region's institutional density (including social capital) and subsequent regional growth and increasing regional competitiveness. It is expected that regions effectively applying the CRA concept could grow dynamically (see Asheim et al., 2006).

Focus on innovative products promotes, in general, technological catch-up. Economic convergence with richer regions becomes a goal mobilizing innovative forces to focus on growth. Poorer regions try to catch-up with rich countries through a process of social capital accumulation. The dynamics with which a region starts to follow its strategy depends on broader social consensus. Regions need to have a complex policy with high participation of various actors, to improve it permanently and to catch-up to the most developed regions.

The absence of a competitiveness-cohesion balance at the regional level must be due to the structural features of weaker regions. Less-developed regions remain poor because they are not producing the kind of goods the richer ones produce. The convergence at the regional level is promoted by innovation activities. Constructed regional advantage should be designed by stressing the specifics each region possesses. Even in the same country, the specifics of regions can differ in terms of cohesion, institutional density and social capital.

For example, in certain regions, regional assets and institutional density are developed more than in others. In Europe the differences in regional advantage are substantial. The CRA approach thus can offer regions a way to design policies at different levels of complexity. Changes continue only when actors decide to undertake the investments needed. Various learning externalities stimulate entrepreneurship and investment into new activities. Another reason for growing regional competitiveness is that specialization patterns, based on existing regional assets, present a better platform for shifts towards new and more productive activities. Innovative regions are more likely to take advantage of new opportunities than those focused on traditional industries.

Modern approaches to regional development, like CRA, allow regions to expand the range of innovation activities and products that they can produce, but will not help other regions with different institutional environments. Certain business activities require different institutional densities (e.g., highly sophisticated financial services require many formal and informal institutions to be in place – among them trust, advanced state legislation, high ethical and self-regulation standards of financial organizations), features that are not relevant for all regions. Regions having modern knowledge bases are better off, because such bases serve the production of a wide range of goods. This facilitates structural transformation and diversification.

The CRA concept uses the idea that regional development is driven by learning and enhanced capabilities accumulated within the regions. While many factors can contribute to regional competitiveness, social capital[8] is one of the main sources of knowledge spillover. Using the CRA concept allows clarifying policy issues. Simultaneously, there exist regional activities and policies that can enhance regional competitiveness and regions can acquire regional advantage. In addition, changes – based on social capital - generating competition-cohesion balances are needed. The problem is that, whereas all regions operate in highly competitive global areas, democratic governments function predominantly within a national state.

Nevertheless, the problem is how these different structural features of the region mutually interact. Consider social capital. One of its advantages is that it stimulates regional development. That happen in regions, where broad democratic participation stimulates learning and productivity spillovers and where the regions have thus new sources of growth. If production of innovative goods generates productivity spillovers, then the new environment stimulates learning. As only a democratic environment and trust generates learning spillovers, the new governance becomes a dynamic tool for producing desirable changes.

Democratic processes eliminate the threats of resource misuse and corruption. However, less is known about the competition-cohesion balance with respect to democratic components in regional governance. Success depends on the wide participation of regional actors in local changes; if they stimulate such changes, the results are positive. Often the problem is not growth, but little social cohesion limiting movement to a knowledge-based economy. The participation in regional development becomes an urgent need. A more participative governance system increases democratic principles in the regions while stimulating innovative changes.

The regional structural changes are complemented by innovative policies that help the region to become competitive. Improving democratic processes and participation enhance this process. Older types of policies with rather poor results, weakened the regional knowledge base and reduced regional dynamism. The result was a decline of regional competitiveness. EU countries then reformed their regional policies by focusing on more advanced approaches with different governance scope, participation intensity and applied at the different territorial levels (an example is platform approach or regions of knowledge).

As networking increases, regional growth is higher. In fact, in all regions, significant changes were undertaken. In the context of Slovakia and the Slovak economy, regional strategy has taken the form of wide-scale policy changes. Nevertheless, there is an asymmetry between governance-stimulating policies and policies focused on improving technological capabilities. The knowledge base, generating regional growth, requires strategic policies directed at new activities. Better governance cannot produce the intended effects automatically.

As demonstrated by the CRA concept, it has direct effects on the level of democracy in the regional economy. Democratic participation is usually associated with a better expression of stakeholders' interests. Modern governance, implied by regional governments, hardly hampers the expansion of new activities. In promoting regional development, gradual regional changes are often more efficient than state-level intervention.

While governments can often control only large-scale national-level programs, what really matters is regional governance, as the government's decisions shape regional competitiveness. Democratic participation and open discussion over regional issues by stakeholders can lead to better governance and regions that are more competitive. Moreover, regions that focused on competitiveness in their policies have managed to maintain sufficient levels of social capital. Better governance has become a policy objective and has played a key role in fostering a diversified knowledge base.

One implication of this is that regional strategies previously used by regions were not always suited to their needs (an example was the top-down approach leading to inadequate reflection of local potential and capacities). A consequence has been the need to shift to a higher participation in regional development processes.

Dynamic regional changes in democratic context - Slovak reforms since 1989

In most of the post-transition countries, bold political changes preceded economic ones. Since 1989, governments have reduced dependence of firms on the state and guaranteed the irreversibility of these changes. Intense democratic debate on the form of reform models helped support reform changes in the 1990s. The changes resulted from the problems caused by a poor mix of centrally planned economies and one-party political systems. These changes reduced political instability, eliminating the leading role of the communist parties and formed new business and political elites. States supported decentralization, which gave rise to market-based systems.

In Slovakia, the new policies helped to create new social actors and institutions and this allowed the Slovak government to be more autonomous in applying structural policies. Government had the capacity to follow reform policies because the institutions allowed it. The Czechoslovak federal government centralized and coordinated the whole reform process. Because that government largely controlled the reform process in Slovakia (until the dissolution of the federation) and because it had broad public support (except for voucher privatization and military conversion), it could complete its reforms. Since then, a shift towards an open economic model (from the previous inward-looking) one has further increased competitiveness. The opening of the Slovak economy has been quick, as the government has had no interest in protecting some areas of the economy. Reforms in Slovakia indicate only minor difficulties newly democratic governments have in implementing measures to liberalize their economies.

Due to democratic elections, the new regime had a high level of legitimacy, which helped to continue the reform process. This eliminated protests of potential opponents, e.g., trade unions, and imposed the reform model without substantial resistance of the public. This reform has made the new system more dynamic, competitive and flexible and allowed regions to decide their local priorities and strategies. The result has been stimulation of the growth of innovative firms and the creation of a democratic society. Success in implementing the new economic model has helped to integrate the country into the EU. The Slovak reform model, based on the federal Czechoslovak reform concept of complex socio-economic changes, has fostered a complex set of reform policies including macro-economic stabilization, micro-economic reform based on privatization and restructuring, as well as the opening and reorientation of trade and investment.

Privatization has helped to change the state-firm relationships. The government allowed actors to cooperate and the regional policy has been transformed. Emerging democratic mechanisms allowed more power to be given to regional governments. The state promoted public participation in regional issues through consultations of stakeholders and by consensus building on important issues.[9] It also focused its regional policy on programs providing higher participation to citizens in regional changes. Since 1989, Slovakia has developed a policy that has intended to stress the structural transformation of the economy. The new reform model used reflected the consensus made upon what kind of economic system would be desirable.

The reforms and new policy model in Slovakia have stabilized the country and improved its economic performance (e.g., GDP growth - average annual percentage volume change – for 1996-2006 was 4.1, but for the period 2005-2006 8.3; the unemployment rate in 2001 was 19.3%, in 2006 13.3% and in January 2008 only 8%); (OECD, 2007 and SITA, 2008). These changes have transformed the economy, which is now characterized by high openness, and - in the automotive sector - Slovakia has become an important car exporting country. The transformation has also had important regional effects.

Whereas the ongoing FDI (foreign direct investment)-led processes concentrated mainly on the automobile sector in three cities: Bratislava, Trnava and Zilina (Brzica, 2007), the tendency has been to narrow regional disparities by designing incentives for investors to invest in less-developed regions (Act, 2007). This has changed the regional industrial structure, but center-periphery differences, like employment, investment activity and productivity disparities have remained.

The central government has changed the existing regional governance system that constituted one of the pillars of the reform process. The new model offers regulatory mechanisms increasing social cohesion and coherence among the economic, social and political issues. Since 1993, the institutional framework of the Slovak Republic has been developing dynamically.

The new territorial reform started only in January 2002 and, compared to Austria, the transfer of responsibilities and financial power from state to local and regional governments has continued unabated. According to Act No. 221/1996 Coll., the new territorial structure, i.e. the new administrative units of Slovakia, is formed today by eight regions that are further divided into districts. Municipalities and regions are the local governmental units in Slovakia. Regarding territorial governance, the decentralization process has led to the empowerment of these units that are now autonomous from the central government and have their own competences and responsibilities. The transfer of responsibilities covers diverse policy areas, such as education, health care, social welfare, territorial planning, and transport (Brzica, 2008).

The focus on low-cost production in some regions implies weak human capital, low profits and a low level of productivity growth. Although the focus on low-cost production was an option for transition countries, Slovakia has started to change its economy towards a knowledge-based one characterized by high value added as well as by developed human and social capital. The increase in human capital and technology has had a positive impact on productivity. Increasing the economy's competitiveness by improving the educational level of citizens, firms started to be more open to networking. An institutional path has partly determined the way in which regions apply the new economic model. Further improvement requires more investment in social capital. Democratization has also improved economic conditions in the country and the institutional quality of political representative bodies.

In the future, the Slovak regions must modernize their institutions to better serve the needs of their citizens and to improve confidence in regional government. Various programs are trying to increase the efficiency and transparency of regional institutions as well as to encourage citizen participation. By promoting regional policies that ensure citizen engagement, regions contribute to preserving their (in) formal institutions and to strengthening the role of their regions. Structural transformation relates to regional development policies and plays an important role in this development. The shift from traditional industrial activities to modern sectors raises regional competitiveness and fosters growth. Rapid growth is associated with the expansion of regional activities.

Conclusion

This chapter stressed the role of democracy and citizens' participation in support of regional development. What is needed is a new regional strategy focused on higher competitiveness and supportive institutional changes that promotes networking and participative democracy. Without targeted regional policies, governance structures alone cannot be an efficient tool for promoting competitiveness. An innovative activity based on the CRA concept, stressing more the role and impact of the public sector in the economy, helps both traditional regions and modern ones. It highlights policy support, (preferably in public-private partnerships) by acknowledging to a greater extent the importance of institutional and economic complementarities in knowledge economies more than do theories of comparative and competitive advantage. The success of innovative regions lies in a mix of regionally-tailored policies, because central governments do not have adequate knowledge to select the best strategies. As discussed in (Asheim et al., 2006), regional policy is more conceived as a process whereby the state and the private sector jointly find solutions to emerging problems. Regional policy requires the government to assess carefully the activities to be promoted and the measures to be used. The role of social capital and institutional density are among the driving forces behind regional competitiveness and specialization patterns.

Democracy enhances regional development as the region's attractiveness increases and thus stimulates FDI and growth. Dynamic regions change production and investment strategies and reduce threats of global competition through dynamic innovation. What may prove important is regional development based on broad cooperation of regional actors centered on modern CRA-types of concept strategies. Despite this, recent economic policies pay attention mostly to nationally-coordinated structural changes and regional development of technical infrastructures.

Moreover, current top-down regional policy has been rather reluctant to prefer some economic activities to others. Especially some political parties do not accept the targeted economic policies promoting regional development. However, as long as a region is open to innovative changes and foreign investment and uses regionally-embedded development strategies, the regional system then orients resources to the areas with the highest potential for regional growth. In reality, externalities and spillovers follow the expansion of knowledge-based activities also in low-income regions. Firms investing in knowledge-based activities cooperate through networks, generate technological spill-overs and learning and provide supply and demand for the production of other firms.

Notes

1. Innovation is favoured by the presence of a diversity of sectors that complement each other, and, thus, produce knowledge spillovers. Related variety is defined in Boschma and Iammarino (2007) as industrial sectors that are related in terms of shared or complementary competences. In other words, there is some degree of cognitive proximity required to ensure that effective communication and interactive learning take place, though not too extreme, in order to avoid cognitive lock-in. Thus, it is neither regional diversity nor regional specialization per se that stimulate innovation, but rather local specialization in related variety that is more likely to induce effective interactive learning and innovation. Related variety accounts for spill-over effects, combining the strength of the specialization of localization economies and the diversity of urbanization economies.
2. Differentiated knowledge bases (synthetic, analytical, symbolic), refer to different mixes of tacit and codified knowledge, codification possibilities and limits, qualifications and skills, as well as specific innovation challenges and pressures (Asheim *et al.,* 2006). Innovation is shaped by the interplay of different mixes of tacit and codified knowledge, codification possibilities and limits, qualifications and skills. A key policy issue is hen*ce* connectivity, i.e. what kind of policies and measures can be adopted to favor the mutual strengthening of different kinds of relevant knowledge.
3. Local knowledge bases are increasingly shaped and influenced by increasingly interconnected networks that transcend regional and national borders.
4. The three above-mentioned dimensions (related variety, differentiated knowledge bases and distributed knowledge networks) provide the base for formulating sectoral transcending platform-oriented policies.
5. Civil society refers to the arena of uncoerced collective action around shared interests, purposes and values (LSE, 2004).
6. The knowledge economy differs from the traditional economy in several key respects. The economics is not of scarcity, but rather of abundance.

Unlike most resources that deplete when used, information and knowledge can be shared, and actually grow through application. The effect of location is either (a) diminished, in some economic activities: using appropriate technology and methods, virtual marketplaces and virtual organizations that offer benefits of speed or, (b) on the contrary, reinforced in some other economic fields, by the creation of business clusters around centres of knowledge, such as universities and research centres having reached world-wide excellence (Wikipedia, 2008). Institutional and economic complementarities play a more important role in this (CRA) approach than in more traditional approaches, where the stress is given to classical production factors rather than institutional density, complementary assets etc. Hence, the approach can more actively and complexely stimulate and motivate regional actors to find optimal local solutions for increasing their local and regional competitiveness.

7 For attracting talents from abroad.
8 The term social capital is used to refer to the outcomes from the network of relationships among people in a community that help that community to operate effectively (Robinson 1997).
9 Examples are regional development agencies (RDAs), which are non-profit institutions, which stimulate economic and social development of a region by institutional linking of public administration, private sector and third sector. These are independent interest associations of legal persons established based on Act No. 40/1964 Coll. RDAs serve the role of organizations helping the Ministry of Building and Regional Development of the Slovak Republic (MVRR SR) for promotion of development especially of less developed regions. They are carriers of institutional coordination based on the principle of partnership in the regions. An integrated network of RDAs (IN RDAs) was established based on the resolution of the government of the Slovak Republic No. 738/2000. IN RDAs consist of RDAs that meet certain conditions and MVRR SR passed their request to be included into the IN RDAs. The mission of IN RDAa is the support of regional development as specified in Act No. 503/2001 Coll. (The Act on support of regional development), which defines regional development as the sustainable growth of the economic and social potential of a region, which implies increasing its productivity, competitiveness and the living standard of its population (MVRR SR, 2008).

References

Act (2007): Zakon o investicnej pomoci a o zmene a doplneni niektorych zakonov. (The Act on investment assistance and on changes and complements to certain laws), Zbierka zakonov No. 561/2007 Coll. Part 235 (in Slovak language).

Asheim, B. (2001): "Learning regions as development coalitions: partnership as governance in European welfare states? Concepts and transformation" International Journal of Action Research and Organisational Renewal, 6, (1) pp. 73 – 101.

Asheim, B. T. - Cooke, P. - Annerstedt, J. - Blažek, J. - Boschma, R. – Brzica, D. - Dahlstrand Lindholm, A. – Del Castillo Hermosa, J. - Laredo, P. - Moula, M. - Piccaluga, A. (2006): "Constructing Regional Advantage: Principles - Perspectives – Politics": DG Research Expert Group on 'Constructing Regional Advantage'. Brussels, DG Research, 2006.

Boschma, R. - Iammarino, S. (2007): Related variety and regional growth in Italy. The Freeman Centre, University of Sussex. September 2007 SPRU Electronic Working Paper Series, Paper No. 162.
www.sussex.ac.uk/spru/documents/sewp162.pdf

Brzica, D. (2008, forthcoming): "Positioning Bratislava in an emerging cross-border metropolitan area." In: Ache, P., Andersen, H. T., Raco, M., Maloutas, T., Tasan-Kok, T. (Eds.), *Cities Between Competitiveness and Cohesion: Discourses, Realities and Implementation.* 2008, Kluwer Academic Publishers.

Brzica, D. (2007): "Automobile sector in the Slovak republic : current situation and future prospects." In: Heijman, W. (Ed.), *Regional externalities.* Berlin: Springer, 2007, pp. 131-147.

Cooke, P. (no date): "Entrepreneurs, Innovation systems and policy platforms." Presentation, Centre for Advanced Studies Cardiff University.
http://www.primenoe.org/Local/prime/dir/General%20Presentation/2006%20Annual%20Conference/Presentations/Stakeholder%20Day/Stakeholder%20day%20-%20Presentation%20Cooke.pdf (accessed February 27, 2008)

Gertler, M. S. (2004): "Local social knowledge management: community actors, institutions and multilevel governance in regional foresight exercises" Futures, 36, pp. 45 – 65.

Department of State (no date): "Principles of Democracy."
http://usinfo.state.gov/products/pubs/principles/what.htm(accessed February 27, 2008)

Keane, M. J. (1997): "New fields of employment: problems and possibilities in local and community economic development." Working paper No. 18, National University of Ireland, Galway.

LSE(2004):What is civil society?
http://www.lse.ac.uk/collections/CCS/what_is_civil_society.htm (Accessed April 21, 2008)

Malecki, E. J. (2007): "Cities and regions competing in the global economy: k nowledge and local development policies" Environment and Planning C: Government and Policy, 25, pp. 638-654.
MVRR SR (2008): Koncepcia rozvoja Integrovanej siete regionálnych rozvojových agentúr.
http://www.build.gov.sk/mvrrsr/source/document/001394.doc(Accessed April 23, 2008)
OECD (2007): OECD in Figures. 2007 Edition. OECD, Paris.
Robinson, D. (1997) Social Capital and Policy Development, Institute of Policy Studies, Victoria University of Wellington.
Salet, W. (2006): "Rescaling Territorial Governance: The Responsiveness of Spatial and Institutional Strategies to Changing Socio-economic Interactions." European Planning Studies, Vol. 14, No. 7, August. 959-978.
SITA (2008): Miera nezamestnanosti koncom januára vzrástla na 8,06 %. SITA, 18. 02. 2008 http://www.e-katalog.sk/spravodajstvo/4894/
Wikipedia (2008): Knowledge economy.
http://en.wikipedia.org/wiki/Knowledge_economy.(Accessed April 21, 2008)

Chapter 11
SUPPLY-SIDE ECONOMICS: KEYNES AND BATRA'S CRITICISM APPEARS STRONGER WITH TIME

William T. Bagatelas

Abstract:

The following article assesses an understanding of the economic causes and specific forces, which help determine economic reality. I have primarily assessed the current assessment ideas of economist Ravi Batra. Professor Batra's assessment methods are offered in the context of their continuing support for more traditional economic assessments offered by John Maynard Keynes. The purpose of the paper is to strengthen the primary conclusions made by Keynes and later Batra, regarding the primary causes of economic depressions.

Keywords: supply-side, demand, supply, tax cuts, government, wealth, debt, Einstein, depressions

Introduction

Regarding the overall credibility of Keyne's analysis, though it has been questioned by some and even more lately, his solution to economic depression is now questioned by yet more. It is the continuing and growing credibility of Keynes analysis concerning causes of the Great 1929 crash that concern us here. Keyne's analysis of the catastrophe permanently weakened the credibility of supply-side theory as a rational way to run society or the planet. Strangely, however, beginning in 1981, the election of supply-sider Ronald Reagan to the US presidency, allowed supply-side policies to return, seemingly spreading the world over. To some like myself it did appear as if there was a repeat of US economic policy during the 1920's. It is as if the field of economic history and realities of The Great Depression and WWII did not exist or had never occurred.

Further confirmation of Keyne's permanent and everlasting contribution to understanding causes and cures for depressions comes through no less an authority then 2001 Economics Nobel Prize winner, Joseph Stiglitz. He is one of today's most influential economists. He is the only man in history to serve as Senior Economist with the World Bank and Chairman of the Council of US Economic Advisors (under former US President Bill Clinton during the 1990's). His support regarding credibility of Keynes carries great weight through economics and political communities worldwide.

According to Stiglitz: "Keynes would be rolling over in his grave were, he to see what has happened to his child." (Stiglitz, 2002, p. 13) In other words, Keynes would be deeply distressed if he were alive today and witnessed global business, economic, and government policy repeating supply-side errors of the 1920's. These errors began in 1981, continue to the present, and no doubt are continuing. Or, put another way by Stiglitz regarding Keynes and his great contributions: "The fact of the matter is that before government intervention to regulate the overall macroeconomy – (systematic efforts under the influence of Keyne's ideas began after World War II) – economic fluctuations were far worse than they are today [post-WWII to 1981]. Downturns were longer and booms were shorter" (Stiglitz, 2003, p. 284).

Put differently, Keyne's greatness was due to his ability to prove the necessity of government intervention in any economy at any time to bring about balance after business and economic collapse. This would help maintain demand-supply balance at all times as well so collapse is not a reality. Therefore, Keynes, as we have seen and the world should already know, effectively began the systematic destruction of supply-side policy as a theory and rational course for business and economy as a whole (Stiglitz, 2003). It was effectively left to current economist Ravi Batra, to specifically analyze for all-time the larger question concerning why entire economies collapse sooner or later, when following supply-side practice.

Batra's equivalent to relativity theory in the economics and business fields is showing why supply-side practice creates a dramatic increase followed by dramatic collapse in a stock market's value. In other words, there is dramatic imbalance during certain periods, which then must lead to business, economic, wage and employment collapse. In short, it was left to Batra to prove what Keynes had already observed: natural Demand (using cash, not debt) must always keep up with Supply in any market and region. Also, government must always undertake specific measures to ensure this happens.

Supply-side Policy: Problems Identified by Batra

Ravi Batra is currently at a similar stage in his career that Einstein was in around 1902. That was three years before Einstein's now well-known relativity theory was announced. After that, Einstein was a household name. Batra has already earned respect privately from the economics profession, but not yet in public. That will probably come soon as in the next decade. The growing imbalance between rich and poor in all countries globally continues to explode. This appears to be the reality in nearly every society and market on the planet. The timeless universal validity concerning the laws of Demand and Supply, are already showing unmistakable trends (Batra, 1990). This would be the following.

If nothing changes, we will have a planet in no more than fifteen years, where the middle class has nearly ceased to exist. This permanent destruction of the middle class must eventually violate Demand and Supply greatly in each society. Because of supply-side policy in practice globally since 1981, social chaos may be a likely outcome (Batra, 1988). What is currently happening in Greece may be next for many other nations. According to Batra, the following is why, which represents the missing Demand problem.

Batra states as long as wages for employees in any society always rise as their productivity increases for any business large or small, then natural Demand (cash not debt) will always equal natural Supply. In other words, all employees as consumers will then have enough money to purchase all Supply being produced inside a nation. The key is allowing official wage rates to rise equally with increased productivity. Thus everyone in society will benefit (Batra, 1985). Employees benefit as consumers because their increased wages naturally increase their Demand for higher living standards. Business owners earn higher profits at the same time, which would increase because local Demand would naturally keep increasing if wages keep increasing with rising productivity. Growing high wage employment must result as growing Demand everywhere would create greater need for higher paid employees.

As simple as this concept is, we must realize supply-side theory and practice does not accept this. Because of narrow and selfish reasons, major corporate leaders and politicians refuse to speak openly against supply-side realities. Supply-side policy requires government to immediately reduce taxes dramatically on the wealthiest 20% of any society, while increasing the tax burden on the non-wealthy 80%. This effectively makes the wealthiest 20% of any society much wealthier and more quickly. All this is accomplished without selling another single product. Politicians primarily do this so big business will support their careers financially and in other ways.

This is how too many in politics ignore the costs to society as a whole (Batra, 1996). Batra has observed this for over three decades.

This has been economic reality for the world since 1981, when US President Reagan reintroduced supply-side policies of the 1920's into US tax structures. Europe, Asia and the rest-of-the-world had no choice but to follow, or else much wealth would gravitate towards much lower US tax rates. This created a financial Tsunami of global wealth racing for the US since the 1980's. Batra believes this has been a contributing factor to current global economic instability as well. Even with lower tax rates, the rest-of-the-world has still witnessed dramatic outflows of capital from poor to rich nations. To appreciate what is happening globally, Batra asks us to understand the following.

Because President Reagan gave US high income tax payers, or the wealthiest 20% of US society, the then largest tax reductions in US economic history (since the fateful supply-side experiments of the 1920's), the top US tax rate dropped from 70% in 1981 to 28% by 1986. This led to a large drop in tax revenues for government. This is why US government debt began to explode in 1981. This debt continues to dramatically increase to the present (Batra, 1996). Equally important, and worth repeating, once US taxes on highest incomes went from 70% to 28%, the world's wealthiest 20% in all societies sent their wealth in great amounts to the US. This was a natural response unless top income tax rates were dramatically lowered in those societies as well. Thus globally starting in 1981, the world basically had no choice but to follow the US lead. This is where major problems begin for the post-World War II business, economic and political communities worldwide (Batra, 1993).

Why Large Tax Reductions for the Wealthiest Create Economic Instability

Ravi Batra argues strongly that huge tax cuts on the wealthiest of any society create immediate incentives for global business leaders to greatly increase production/supply. This occurs because of the major tax cut global businesses have just been given. The major tax cuts are on business profits and capital gains. This ensures business productivity or supply will now grow very quickly. At this point, Batra states the major problems with Supply and Demand begin and grow worse. Government, by giving big business the major tax break, must now increase taxes on the non-wealthy 80% of society to regain lost tax revenue. The middle class is where most Demand has always come from in any society and always will. Batra argues that, by raising taxes on the middle class to regenerate lost tax revenue, one cannot increase non-wealthy living standards.

The major problem with Batra being the first in current times to expound on this is the following. The non-wealthy 80% of society must now use large amounts of debt to maintain their living standards. Classical, supply-side, and Keynesian economists have never produced an answer to this. In other words, the wealthy are now wealthier because their taxes go down. The non-wealthy 80% see their taxes increase without a wage increase. The gap between wealth and the middle class has now grown because middle-class wages have not increased. The major tax cuts for the wealthiest 20% all went into increasing their Supply, not increasing wages for employees.

After the major regressive government tax benefit for the wealthiest 20%, there is now a major shift in wealth disparity between rich and everyone else. The wealthiest 20% now own more total wealth in society. The non-wealthy 80% own less total wealth. For Demand and Supply to remain in balance, the non-wealthy 80% must see their incomes or wages increase as well, not decrease relative to the wealthiest 20%. Batra very clearly, like Keynes before him, shows us how Demand must always come from the majority, 80% of the non-wealthy population.

According to Batra, extrapolating beyond Keynes, refrigerators, clothing, food, cars, fuel, housing, etc. (the living standard), depend on every family in the nation having enough money to buy what is needed. If they don't, the wealthiest 20% will not suddenly use their extra wealth to make for lost middle class demand. The wealthy would have to buy millions of new cars, homes, refrigerators, clothing, food, etc. Batra believes this is the only way to make up for falling Demand by the non-wealthy 80%. Obviously the wealthy will not do this, nor should they be expected to. The wealthiest 20% of any society already have what they need. Who could ever believe argues Batra, the wealthiest 20% would deliberately increase their Demand to maintain national or international demand-supply balance. This is a fatal supply-side assumption with no provable support behind it. Common sense just as easily provides our answer. This would never happen.

Slovakia has 5 million people. Would the richest 1 million if they were given new huge income tax reductions, suddenly buy an extra four million of everything? Of course not. Demand nationwide has fallen because the non-wealthy 80% have less money to spend. Their taxes went up. Wealthy families in the meantime, continue to buy one of each when they need it. If the public can be made aware of such a fallacy, then such an illusion cannot possibly be believed by non-wealthy public in any country. Once the populations are given the facts, this will help rectify current economic problems facing the world today.

Supportive Evidence against Supply-side Policy

The following graphs, tables, and statistics tell a powerful story. Specifically, they show us through a wide variety of means the following: How major lowering of income tax rates on highest incomes/major corporate profits weakens overall economic performance throughout society. I use graphs from economist Ravi Batra because of their accuracy. When we think of the current economic crisis and its worsening performance in nations like Greece, Batra's credibility is strong. He is the only forecaster to predict decades in advance the current crisis and its causes. As you will see in the graphs below, when the world's economists and other experts were confidently stating the 1990's represented the greatest economic decade in history, Batra said just the opposite. Only Batra said this

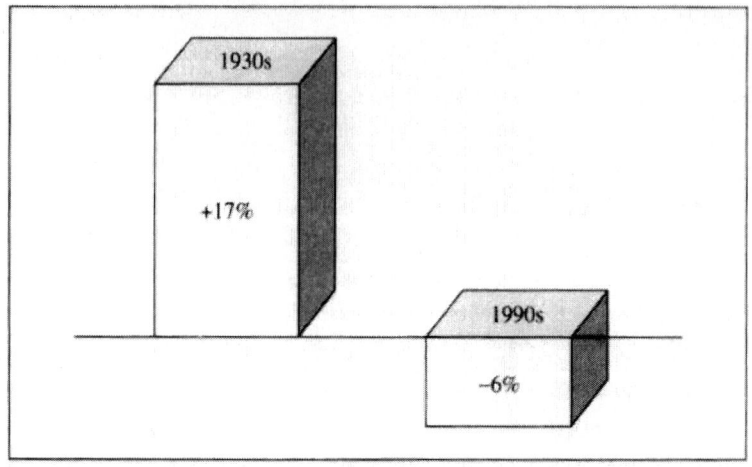

FIGURE 1.2 Real family income or wages in America, 1930s vs. 1990s. In some respects the quiet American crisis of the 1990s has been worse than that of the Great Depression in the 1930s. At the end of that decade, real wages had jumped 17 percent. In the 1990s (1990–1995), however, real family income has dropped in five out of six years by a total of 6 percent. (*Source:* Tables 10.2 and 10.3 in Chapter 10.)

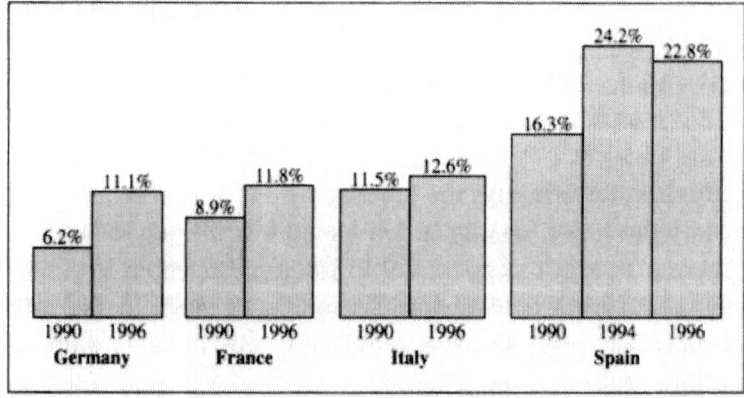

FIGURE 1.3 Unemployment rates in the 1990s in Europe. In terms of unemployment, America and Europe have switched places

202

The Batra graphs above for the US and Europe compare the first half of the 1990's with the decade of The Great Depression. Though US and world stock markets went up until 2000 (not shown), one can clearly see real wages for most families in the US dropped considerably. Incredibly, by the end of The Great Depression, real wages for most US families increased by 17%.

These powerful realities of the 1990's allow us to currently realize the current economic problems in the US and globally should not have come as a surprise. The Batra graphs above clearly show as well that unemployment rates in major European economies from 1990-1996 greatly increased at the same time real US family wages were falling dramatically. The US was then and still is Europe's major source of demand. It would be wise to assume large, falling US wages for at least two decades have greatly led to today's global economic difficulties for Europe and much of the world. hese first Batra graphs regarding the US and Europe going back two decades, effectively allow one to see to see this long-term and historic pattern.

TABLE 2.1 Average hourly and weekly earnings of nonsupervisory workers in 1982 dollars: 1972-1995 (selected years).

Year	Hourly Earnings	Weekly Earnings
1972	$8.53	$315.44
1975	8.12	293.06
1980	7.78	274.65
1985	7.77	271.16
1990	7.52	259.47
1995	7.42	255.90

Source: Economic Report of the President, 1996, The Council of Economic Advisers, Washington, DC, p. 330.

Interestingly, one can clearly see from the Batra graph above how hourly earnings have not increased over nearly a quarter of a century for nonsupervisory US employees. That trend continued right up to the current crisis. The statistics above are shocking when one realizes that nonsupervisory working people in the US, who are the world's biggest consumers, have seen there real wage drop since 1972. Surely this is a major cause of the current global economic down-turn.

Since I don't want to include so many graphs allowing the reader to lose interest, I must repeat what I said before the graphing begins. Batra made accurate predictions regarding the current global crisis at least three decades before the current events. Therefore, I deliberately use his graphing from the 1990's to show the trends he identified then leading/contributing today's problems globally.

TABLE 2.2 Median family income (in 1994 dollars) and poverty rate: 1972–1994 (selected years).

Year	Family Income	Poverty Rate
1972	$37,959	9.3%
1976	37,319	9.4
1980	37,857	10.3
1985	38,200	11.4
1990	40,087	10.7
1994	38,782	11.6

Source: *Economic Report of the President*, 1983 and 1996, The Council of Economic Advisers, Washington DC.

This next Batra graph clearly shows average US family income remaining the same from 1972 – 1994. As the first graph indicated as well, this is even worse then US families did during The Great Depression of the 1930's. If the US has been the world's biggest source of demand since the end of World War II, we can probably conclude the following from above. From 1972 all the way to 2010, falling US demand for global products has been the result (Tamene, 2010, p. 210). Falling real US family and hourly wages have consistently caused US consumption of foreign products to fall for decades as well.

TABLE 2.3   Per-capita GDP (in 1987 dollars) and output per hour: 1972–1994 (selected years).

Year	Per-Capita GDP	Output per Hour
1972	$14,801	75.2
1975	14,917	79.0
1980	16,584	84.1
1985	17,944	91.9
1990	19,593	96.2
1994	20,476	101.0

Source: *Economic Report of the President*, 1996, The Council of Economic Advisers, Washington, DC, p. 332; *Statistical Abstract of the United States*, 1995, U.S. Department of Commerce, Washington, DC, p. 456.

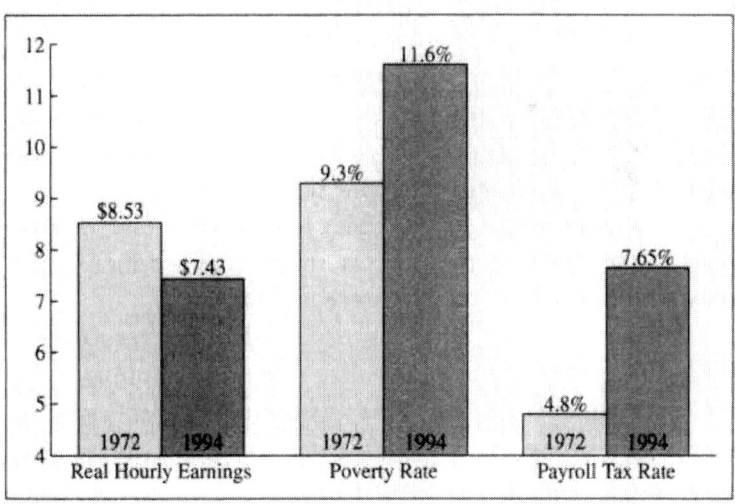

FIGURE 2.1   U.S. economic conditions in 1972 and 1994. In 1972, real wages were higher, and the poverty rate lower than in

205

The Batra graphs above show US per capita GDP per person rising only about $6,000 US dollars from 1972, leading to lower living standards by 1994 in the second graph. This small wage increase over twenty two years could not possibly keep up with rapidly increasing costs of living. At the same time, worker productivity per hour over the same time period increased 25%. We can see US employees were working harder and harder while making less and less. Stated differently, worker productivity in the US was increasing faster then wages and demand over time. This is consistent with Batra's conclusion that supply-side economic policies always increase worker supply/productivity long-term while wages/demand fall farther and farther behind. This seems a logical primary reason for the current economic problems facing the world. For decades until 2007, supply-side policy, first in the US beginning in 1981 then around the world, allowed supply/productivity to race farther ahead of overall wages/demand. Supply racing ahead of demand cannot happen without negative consequences for the non-wealthy.

TABLE 2.4 Announced corporate layoffs and after-tax profits: 1990–1995.

Year	Layoffs	After-Tax Profits (Billions)
1990	300,000	$229.0
1991	550,000	249.1
1992	400,000	258.4
1993	600,000	300.7
1994	516,000	331.2
1995	600,000	390.0
Total	2,966,000	

Source: Economic Report of the President, 1996, The Council of Economic Advisers, Washington, DC, p. 379; Lester Thurow, *The Future of Capitalism: How Today's Economic Forces Shape Tomorrow's World,* William Morrow, New York, 1996, p. 26.

The next Batra graph above clearly shows the ever-increasing, even overwhelming number of job layoffs in the US for first half of the 1990's. These numbers are almost unbelievable. Clearly notice after-tax profits for each year following the layoffs. This overall trend continued all the way to the present global downturn. The record after-tax profits recorded above are what fueled the exploding stock market upward. Most US working people could not benefit overall during this time frame.

Previous graphs showed real hourly wages and salaries falling for decades. Therefore, the primary beneficiaries of the record profits above were major corporate CEO's and the wealthiest 20% in the US overall. They were the ones who could afford to heavily invest in a rapidly increasing stock market. The same thing happened around the world. For decades until 2007, supply-side policy, first in the US beginning in 1981 then around the world, allowed supply/productivity to race farther ahead of overall wages/demand. By 2007, supply had been so far ahead of demand for decades that massive layoffs had to occur over these decades. The current economic downturn surely had to result from this as well.

TABLE 3.1 Workers' willingness to make concessions to their employers, 1996.

Questions Asked	"Yes" Replies among Respondents Who Are Working	"Yes" Replies among Respondents Hard-hit by a Layoff
Will you:		
1. Get more training?	93%	95%
2. Work longer hours?	82	87
3. Accept smaller benefits?	53	69
4. Challenge the boss less often?	49	66
5. Accept a smaller wage?	44	59

Source: New York Times, March 4, 1996, p. A9.

One of the many false rumors spread by Wall Street and global executives, politicians, and other irresponsible elites was that working people always refuse to accept wage freezes, wage cuts, and reduced overall benefits. This was supposed to justify mass layoffs year-after-year just witnessed in the previous graph. As the reader by now should be aware, this is nonsense. Just the opposite occurred for decades.

Previous graphs already indicate dramatic reductions in working wages for individuals and families. Only a heartless person could possibly believe working people never received wage cuts since the 1980's in the US. The evidence is overwhelming that working US citizens for decades have seen their wages and hourly pay fall farther and farther behind the wealthiest. This trend also spread to other nations worldwide. It is worth repeating: this trend began in the US and spread around the world.

The graph above shows US working people and families clearly willing to work more hours (for same pay), receive more training, accept smaller wages and benefits, question boss less etc. since the mid-1990's. In other words, working people for decades have been willing to more than compromise with major corporate leaders on many key issues in the workplace to keep their jobs. This trend also spread around the world. Those with economic and political power who falsely accused working people of being selfish are guilty of gross ethical negligence.

TABLE 4.1 Top-bracket income tax rate and personal rate of saving: 1980–1995 (selected years).

Year	Top-Bracket Income Tax Rate	Personal Rate of Saving
1980	70%	8.2%
1985	50	6.9
1988	28	5.2
1990	31	5.0
1993	39.6	4.5
1995	39.6	4.3

Source: *Economic Report of the President*, 1996, The Council of Economic Advisers, Washington, DC, p. 310; Robert Hall and A. Rabushka, *The Flat Tax*, Hoover Institution Press, Stanford, CA, 1995.

TABLE 4.2 Top-bracket income tax rate and personal rate of saving: 1960–1980 (selected years).

Year(s)	Top-Bracket Income Tax Rate	Personal Rate of Saving
1960–1963	91%	7.0%
1965	70	7.6
1970	70	8.4
1975	70	9.0
1980	70	8.2

Source: *Historical Statistics of the United States: Colonial Times to 1970, Part 2*, U.S. Department of Commerce, 1975, p. 1095; *Economic Report of the President*, 1996, The Council of Economic Advisers, Washington, DC, p. 310.

Another supply-side myth or falsehood states that savings rates for the wealthiest in society increase when their income tax greatly falls. This is clearly false as the above two graphs easily indicate. The two Batra graphs clearly show the personal rate of saving does not increase when the wealthiest in society see their tax rates drop dramatically. One can easily see by comparing the lower graph, 1960-1980 (when tax rates on wealth were much higher) with the upper graph showing much lower tax rates after 1980, the savings rate drops dramatically when income tax rates on the wealthiest fall considerably.

This is another supply-side myth consistently retold over and over in new clothing. The graphs clearly show however, the same result always occurs. Therefore if the wealthiest in the US or any society have much lower tax rates, their rate of savings fall. It absolutely does not increase. Very low savings rates are also assumed to be a key reason for very poor US economic performance and the current economic downturn everywhere.

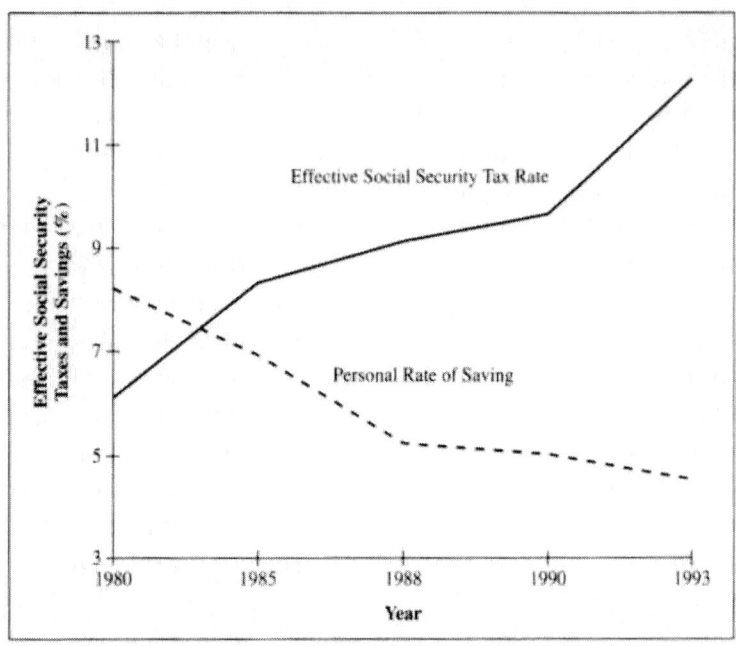

FIGURE 4.1 The effective social security tax rate and the personal rate of saving: 1980–1993. As the Social Security tax soared after 1980, the rate of saving collapsed. (*Source:* Appendix Tables A.1 and A.2.)

Yet another supply-side economic myth also states the following. Social security taxes can increase on everyone in the US, meaning the non-wealthy 80% of US society will pay most of such an increase. Former US Federal Reserve Chairman, Alan Greenspan, during the early 1980's, led a US government commission that required the US middle class to pay higher amounts of social security taxation. For the most part, this effectively allowed the wealthy in the US not to pay social security taxation. The graph above indicates dramatically falling savings rates after 1980 when social security taxes dramatically increased on the non-wealthy 80% of US society. Shorty after this, much of Europe, Asia, and the world followed suite.

To truly appreciate the impact of rising middle class social security taxes on the personal rate of saving, first in the US then around the world, consider this. During the mid-1980's, the world was experiencing very low oil prices. Not even this however, was able to prevent the US rate of saving from collapsing throughout the entire decade of the 1980's and beyond. Clearly, moving the main tax burden for paying social security onto the backs of the middle class was a disaster for overall US savings. Since other nations in Europe did similar things, it seems likely this contributed to current economic problems world-wide. The trend continued right up to the current US and global economic downturn. This supply-side myth like most others, seem to never die.

Supply-side Myths Continued: Why Falling Demand is the fatal Achilles Heel in Supply-side Theory

The public has never been told the whole story as to what happens when business and government promote huge tax reductions for extreme wealth. The public has only been told that business leaders, if given the largest tax cuts, now have more money to invest/increase their supply (supply-side). Somehow, this is supposed to naturally create more demand for jobs. That is the total explanation offered by politicians. This implicit but mistaken supply-side assumption assumes the non-wealthy 80% will always have enough money (cash) to buy major increases in supply/production caused by huge tax cuts for highest incomes. That was the message to the public in the 1920's, and has been from 1981 to the present. Demand and supply's universal validity simply destroy such wishful and arrogant thinking. Batra has shown this and continues to do so (Batra, 2005).

As I stated earlier, major global newspapers as well as certain journals and magazines have publicly accepted falling Demand as the primary cause of the current economic downturn. Beginning in the US in 2007 under former President George W. Bush, falling demand more and more appears to be the primary problem. Further observation supports this. I have discussed the observational ability of economist Ravi Batra in connecting the problems currently witnessed to the following.

The largest wealth gap globally in history, both in the US and many parts of the world, existed at the time the crisis began three years ago. This historically high wealth gap still exists. The smallest legal percentage of taxes required on highest incomes, starting in the US and then around the world, contributed greatly to the record wealth gaps in the current crisis. Stated differently, regressive tax policy is the primary culprit or cause for the current economic crisis. I believe this is the greatest economic transformation since the Great Depression leading to World War II. Batra predicted this over thirty years ago.

Batra has shown the validity of demand and supply easily supporting the decades-long trend leading to current problems globally. This is the destructive nature of supply-side policy globally. Batra shows that the non-wealthy 80% of any society, if not receiving wage increases as their productivity/supply increases, will maintain or increase demand needs through borrowing or debt. This has been achieved in the US and to some extent in Europe through large borrowing against their homes and mortgages, etc. Whatever the public can borrow against, they have done so.

For a while, the non-wealthy 80%'s use of debt allows increasing demand needs to occur. There must come a time, however, like the current world situation (which Batra predicted, and is the fundamental point of his overall analysis), where greatly increasing debt will cause explosive growth. At some point the banking sector of the country is less willing to lend to the non-wealthy. At this point, mortgages, credit cards and whatever to finance living standards are difficult to use. We are at this point in the US and globally. Living standards are difficult to maintain in such a setting. This is the point at which The Great Depression was triggered 1929 (Batra, 1985).

The world is close to this point because global debt is now experienced by banking, government, etc. in all sectors of many, many societies. Such debt exposure or debt growth caused through huge borrowing by governments, banks, corporations, families, communities worldwide etc., is currently the largest in history. Continuing to lend to the public to use more such debt to finance or pay existing debt is self-defeating. The dramatic growth in every kind of debt worldwide is weakening currencies of these nations and markets. Global investors become frightened when they see an entire country's total debt levels explode in growth and size, in all areas of society.

Global investor demand for the dollar thus falls. It has been falling for years not because investors become frightened to own dollars. This lowers living standards as the dollar's value falls, not just in the US but worldwide. Banks try and continue offering more debt to the public, to meet the public's ever increasing need to maintain and improve their living standards. Only the opposite can now happen, however. Continuation of bank lending creates more debt, and smaller global demand for dollars, thus lowering/destabilizing the dollar's value or any currency's value faster. This is also why the Euro is so unstable. In reality, this has always been the reality of the dollar/Euro relationship. Batra states the world is now at the point where continued use of debt by the public will only weaken a country's currency. The dollar and most major global currencies are now weak and unstable, even collapsing.

Stated differently, global demand for the dollar is falling for non-US investors. Who would want to own collapsing dollars or Euros, which buy less and less. It takes more of the same dollars to pay back the original debt or purchase stronger currencies. This is the same with the Euro. This lowers demand even more, though too much supply still exists, three years after the current problems globally began (Tamene, 2004, p. 383). This is a losing proposition on all sides. This is common sense, but supply-side support, based on half-truths, still survives. Hopefully, the global public everywhere is starting to see through the unsupported substantiations by supply-side theory and practice. Perhaps further strong examples against supply-side are the following. Perhaps governments and leaders world-wide, who offered, unconditional/unquestioned support for supply-side theory and practice, are rethinking this as well.

Specifically, those government leaders in the US, Britain, France, Germany, Slovakia, Italy, Spain, Russia (before Putin), and elsewhere globally who decisively supported supply-side polices (Tamene, 2008, p. 97). In these nations and regions, such leaders today usually, not always, have been defeated democratically by the same public who first voted for them. After experiencing the drop in living standards that accompanies long-term support for supply-side policy, leaders like former US President George W. Bush, are now very unpopular. We should consider as well that presidential candidates from Bush's own political party who ran for president in 2008, refused to endorse Mr. Bush or his supply-side performance over the last six plus years of his presidency.

Conclusion

In its simplest form then, Batra is writing, talking, discussing and attempting to prove roughly the economic equivalent to Einstein's relativity theory. The economics field, unfortunately, has lost credibility through supporting reintroduction of a discredited economic theory and practice. Beginning again in 1981, when theory and practice from the 1920's, commonly referred to today as "supply-side economics", was thought to be dead, buried and forgotten because of its poor previous record. It is perceived by many to be the cause of The Great Depression followed by World War II.

These events were simply the most graphic examples of economic, political and military forms of human destruction witnessed historically. Concerning the current economic problems globally, global debt for every consumer and society was growing until the current crisis hit in 2008. Business leaders until 2008 produced more and more supply because historically large tax reductions on highest incomes stimulated their vast expansion in global supply. This was also followed by the explosion in global debt, as major corporate leaders simply assumed there will always be buyers for their products.

Demand has now slowed globally because of the previous explosion in debt. Greece is now experiencing the perils of too much debt and too little investment throughout its economy. Chaos and violence in Greece may soon be followed by chaos and violence elsewhere globally. Weakening currencies and overall demand for products and currencies are rapidly falling globally. Supply is now racing ahead of demand everywhere, which Batra believes explains why unemployment must increase. If demand is falling for your product everywhere, eventually extra supply never sold sits forever on shelves and warehouses worldwide. This is when major recessions and depressions happen.

The massive amount of unsold supply in all areas of global productivity has forced big business leaders to lay off employees everywhere. This is happening as I offer these words. The larger the amount of unsold supply, the longer business and economic depressions will last. The Great Depression lasted ten years, followed by World War II. Let us work towards the universal goal that another depression does not occur from current problems. If it does then history has repeated itself and no lessons were learned from the fateful supply-side era of the 1920's.

References

Batra, Ravi. *Regular Economic Cycles: Money, Inflation, Regulation and Depressions.* St.Martin's Press, Inc., New York. NY 1985.
Batra, Ravi. *The Downfall of Capitalism and Communism: Can Capitalism be Saved?* Venus Books, Dallas, 1990.
Batra, Ravi. *The Myth of Free Trade: A Plan for America's Economic Revival.* Macmillan Publishing Company. New York. NY, 1993.
Batra, Ravi *Greenspan's Fraud: How Two Decades of His Policies Have Undermined the Global Economy*, Palgrave/MacMillan, New York, NY, 2005.
Batra, Ravi *The Great American Deception: What Politicians Won't Tell You About Our Economy and Your Future*, John Wiley & Sons, New York, NY, 1996.
Stiglitz, Joseph *Globalization and Its Discontents*, W.W. Norton & Company, Inc. New York, NY, 2002.
Stiglitz, Joseph *The Roaring Nineties: Why We're Paying The Price For The Greediest Decade in History*, Penguin Books Ltd., London, England, 2003.
Tamene, G. (2004). 'Globalization and Progress. The Impact on Central European Regions'. In: Sergi B.S.; Bagatelas, W. T. (Eds.). *Ethical Implications of Post-Communist Transition Economics and Politics in Europe.* Bratislava, Iura Edition, 2004, pp. 381-396. ISBN 80-8078-045-5.
Tamene, G. World Politics and Challenges to Neo-liberalism: Could the CEE-EU-US Correlation Maintain the Trend? In: *Journal of Comparative Politics*, Brno, 2008. Pp. 86-100.
Tamene, G.: Required Managerial Capacities in the Face of 21st Century Global Expectations, in: *Management Challenges in the 21st Century*: How to Tackle the Crisis: Theory and Practical Experience. Vysoká škola manažmentu/City University of Seattle: Bratislave 2010, pp. 208-224. ISBN: 978-80-89306-08-4

Conclusion for the Book

The chapters you have just read cover a broader range of economic interpretation then current economic literature. This is significant, especially when we realize these chapters are offered during the on-going and worsening economic difficulties facing the world today.

This is the greatest economic downturn since The Great Depression of the 1930's. Therefore, the confidence we display in publishing our book at this time is testament to our conviction of the following. The methodology we offer in these chapters clearly takes economic interpretation to a new level. Everyone would agree this is obviously needed during these times. Why would we bother risking our good names to publish such sensitive analysis if we doubted the sincerity of our conviction? There is no more important time then now to establish a new economic consensus regarding causes and cures of economic downturn.

Recent events in Greece offer a glimpse of what other nations face should they not confront primary economic issues causing the crisis. Stated differently, the cause of the current crisis we address throughout this book, directly and indirectly. By making ethical and other non-traditional considerations priorities in our overall analysis, we achieve the following. We offer policy-makers, media, the public, and institutions globally the larger reasoning to understand the current crisis.

We also offer readers specific ethical interpretations regarding why the crisis occurred from several perspectives. Other chapters allowed one to see ethical use of information technology and economic analysis achieve better ethical outcomes. This included how economics and information technology as fields of study must change. In other words, we offer the public the strongest analysis yet concerning why ethical considerations must be a priority in all economic decision making. Whether such decision-making is made by policy-makers globally or people locally, ethics matters more than any other consideration when the use of money is involved.

At the policy level certain chapters in our book clearly diagnosed the current crisis by looking back twenty or more years. This kind of historical use of specific economic forecasting was used by only one forecaster to accurately predict today's crisis. At least two of our chapters offered all readers the means by which this accurate forecasting occurred as well. The economist's tools allowing these predictions to be made are exhaustively examined to see why he was the only person for over three decades to make these accurate predictions.

Finally, we must realize that today's economic transformation and challenges are similar to causes of The Great Depression of the 1930's. Then and now, record levels of wealth concentration or the gap between rich and poor were occurring globally especially in the US by 1929. Today worldwide, there is even greater wealth concentration. Simply stated, we mean the gap between rich and poor worldwide is now greater then any era previously in world history. This is quite something. Clearly, we believe ethical considerations must be the most important determinant used to lower these record gaps between rich and poor everywhere.

We strongly believe ethical policy making regarding all fields related to economics in any capacity, which would be almost any field today, has no choice now but to accept the following reality. If capitalism is to survive, economic policy-making must promote increasing living standards for all and not just the few. As current events regionally and globally now attest and continue moving in the wrong direction, survival with economic dignity requires moving far beyond the simple and crass individualism the world has today. This is the way it must be for all and not the few. It is the only ethical and rational choice left when thinking and acting economically at levels of society. Our book understands and explains this.

William T. Bagatelas
Getnet Tamene,
David Reichardt
Bruno Sergi

INDEX

A
accounting reform 15, 145, 147
artificial intelligence 39, 48, 50-52, 66, 68, 70

C
civil society 9, 14-16, 92, 102, 104, 106, 109-113, 137, 181, 183, 184, 193, 195
classic economics 77
Complaint 125, 164, 172, 174
consumer protection 164, 166, 174
Consumers 19, 57, 78, 137, 164, 165, 167, 168, 170-175, 198, 203
corporate responsibility 145, 147, 149
corruption 12, 63, 106-111, 113, 115, 164,177, 187
corruption control 102
CRA 9, 11, 16, 37, 43, 44, 56, 63-65, 111-115, 119, 137, 139, 145, 157, 159, 177-187, 191, 193, 196, 213, 217

D
debt 17-19, 127, 158, 161, 196- 200, 212, 213
deception 37, 57, 164, 170, 172, 214
demand 17, 18, 22, 26, 27, 29, 33-36, 44, 53, 78, 86, 87, 192, 196, 199-207, 211-214
demand and supply 17, 18, 22, 35, 198, 200, 211
development 9-11, 14-16, 38, 42, 43, 45, 50, 53, 61, 102, 103, 106-108, 111, 112, 114, 115, 117-140, 142-144, 161, 163, 176, 178, 179, 181, 182, 184-188, 191, 193, 194, 195
development assistance 9, 14, 15, 102, 103, 108, 128
development strategy 91, 92-94, 97

E
economic models 77, 80, 81, 86, 88, 92
economic policy 12, 13, 17, 19, 158, 197, 217
Einstein, depressions 196
eligibility 102, 106, 108, 112
enlightenment .117, 137
environment 15, 39, 40, 41, 43, 47, 49, 51-57, 61, 62, 65, 67, 70, 80, 94, 100, 111, 117, 118, 127, 128, 130, 131-136, 142, 143, 154, 163, 179, 183, 185-187, 195
ethics 9, 41, 43, 56, 57, 58, 66, 77, 78, 88, 101, 144, 149, 164, 176, 216

European Union 40, 127, 156

F
fairness, economic agents 77
falling demand 17, 26, 27, 33-35,
free trade 156

G
Glass-steagall Act 145, 146
global debt 17, 212, 213
global interest, power 117
globalization 15, 37, 39, 40, 41-47, 61, 66, 67, 91-93, 98-101, 144, 153-157, 159, 160, 161, 163, 175, 176, 184, 214
globalization and regionalization 91, 93, 98
government 13, 16-19, 35, 36, 42-44, 46, 53, 93, 97, 102-104, 107, 109-113, 122, 126, 127, 137, 142, 159-161, 177, 181-184, 187, 187-200, 211-213

I
Imclone system 145, 146
increasing democratization 177
innovative regions 177-181, 183-194
institutional quality 177, 182, 190
institutions 39, 41-43, 46, 47, 49, 50, 55, 58, 59, 61-67, 93-97, 103, 117, 136-139, 173, 177-179, 182, 185, 186, 188, 190, 193, 194, 216
international actors 39
international environment 15, 39, 47, 62, 67, 117
international relations 9-15, 38, 39, 41, 43, 44, 69, 101, 117, 126, 144, 163
Investor Protection Act 9, 15, 45, 147

K
knowledge accumulation 45, 177, 181
knowledge management 9, 13, 14, 39-42, 45-51, 61, 62, 64, 66-70, 76, 178, 194
knowledge mobilization 14, 39, 49, 61-63

L
Leadership 35, 55, 56, 61, 63, 69
Legitimity 102
local governance 9, 193, 195, 197

M
managerial behavior 39
managerial requirements 39
MCC, non-state actors 102
misleading adverts 164, 173
modus operandi 102, 104
municipalities 164, 174, 190

N
NAFTA 156, 157-159, 161

P
participative approach 91
participative governance 177, 178, 181
political regime 138, 177, 178
principles 6, 69, 117, 124, 126, 131, 132, 134-136, 138, 140, 148, 177, 182, 185, 187, 194, 195
public company 145

Q
qualitative methods 14, 91, 92, 94-97, 99, 100
quantitative methods 91-94, 95, 99

R
regional competitiveness 9, 16, 177, 178, 181, 183, 185-188, 191, 193
regional partnership 177, 181
respondents 45, 59, 61, 146, 167-173,
right of development 117

S
Sarbanes-Oxley Act 15, 145-147, 151- 154
Scenarios 14, 91, 92, 94, 96, 99,
Securities Exchange Act 145
self-interest 14, 77, 79, 83, 86, 89
social and cultural rights 117, 119, 120, 124-126, 141
social capital 16, 177, 182, 186-196
social settings 117
stakeholder 177, 178, 180-184, 188, 189, 194
stricter control 164, 175
supply 9, 13, 16-22, 26, 35, 36, 46, 192, 196-201, 206, 215
supply side policy 17
supply-side 16, 17
supply-side economics 9, 17, 19, 196

sustainable development 15, 93, 117, 122, 126, 127, 129-132, 134-140, 144
systematic approach 8, 9, 91

T
tax cuts 196, 199, 200, 211

U
utility theory 14, 77

V
value 9, 21, 45, 50, 56, 59, 66, 67, 70, 88, 92, 93-95, 98, 117, 118, 122, 124-126, 136-140, 154, 160, 161, 166, 178, 180, 190, 193, 197, 212

W
wealth 17, 18, 20, 22-25, 27, 29, 35, 36, 43, 44, 95, 137, 138, 158, 159, 164, 196, 199-200, 206-217
wealth gap 17, 22, 25, 211
Western imperialism 156